To: Deird...
daug

Fre... ...olston
August 3, 2003

DR. BENJAMIN E. MAYS SPEAKS

Representative Speeches of a Great American Orator

EDITED BY

FREDDIE C. COLSTON

University Press of America, Inc.
Lanham • New York • Oxford

Copyright © 2002 by
University Press of America,® Inc.
4720 Boston Way
Lanham, Maryland 20706
UPA Acquisitions Department (301) 459-3366

12 Hid's Copse Rd.
Cumnor Hill, Oxford OX2 9JJ

ISBN 0-7618-2343-3 (paperback : alk. ppr.)

This book is dedicated to my wife, Doris M. Colston, my daughter, Deirdre Colston Graddick, and to the memory of my grandparents, Clinton Taylor and Katie Mae Taylor.

Dr. Benjamin E. Mays speaking at Michigan State University, 1968.
(Courtesy of Moorland-Spingarn Research Center, Howard University,
Washington, D.C.)

Contents

Foreword

Benjamin E. Mays: An African American Spokesperson as an Agent of Political Socialization

HANES WALTON, JR.
UNIVERSITY OF MICHIGAN

B enjamin E. Mays was, from his inception, a warrior against the secular religion in America known as segregation.[1] In this titanic struggle, he never hesitated, never wavered, never backtracked, and most importantly, he never retreated. Mays was ever confrontational, ever continuous and ever vigilant. Mays was ever on track, always carrying the battle to the prophets, disciples, proponents, propagators, and defenders of this secular religion. Thus, this secular religion of segregation never found comfort, peace, rest, and/or tranquility as long as Mays stood his ground on the battlefront. In this fight, Mays was relentless and because of his ceaseless fighting he would ultimately see the dismantling of this secular religion's legal foundations and structures, such as the "For Colored Only" signs, and formal and informal habits, customs and traditions. Mays would also see the near disappearance of the prophets of white supremacy. When this educational warrior left the battlefield, segregation had literally "Gone with the Wind." The African American educator, Mays, had slain the Goliath of American Democracy.

The South as the Land of the
Secular Religion: Segregation

Shortly after the Era of Reconstruction ended, the South fastened upon African Americans and the region a social system of second class citizenship for people of color grounded in an unscientific belief in biological inferiority. Once this belief pervaded the South, leaders in the region tried mightily to force acceptance of this belief upon the nation-state itself. Therefore, one might ask, how did a committed educational warrior like Mays undo a secular religion that was more than a century old and one that had the genius of southern political leadership thoroughly committed to its doctrines, dogmas, and designs of white supremacy? In addition to these leaders, there were the legion of followers and the enduring values of the southern culture that continued to reproduce in each and every generation a flock of true believers in the tenets and cardinal principles of segregation. But beyond the political elites, the leaders and the endless flow of followers, there were the institutions.[2]

Mays had to not only confront the political elites, the leaders, the followers, and the southern culture, he had to resist the institutions of this secular religion known as segregation. There were the white churches, the white educational institutions, the white scholars, the white businesses, and the white public symbols such as the confederate flags, commemorative statues, parks, icons, posters, and the white confederate societies and their shadow institutions like the Ku Klux Klan. The institutional base of this religion was omnipresent. These, however, were not the only institutions, that Mays had to confront and survive. There was the institution of Southern Politics, the dominant one in the region and the nation-state.

Southern leaders, political elites, followers, and institutions captured the organs of democratic politics in the region and turned them into an oligarchy and thrust them down an anti-democratic path. Once this was done, the nature, scope, essence, and significance of Southern Politics was to protect, enrich, and enhance the secular religion of the region by using the awesome powers of the state and national government to maintain and sustain it. Southern Politics used the constitutional power and authority of the national government, as well as the political, economic, and social powers of the national government to achieve its ends and goals. Thus, the central objective of the national government when it was under the domination and sway of the South was the perpetuation of the South's secular religion. And with the national government's help and assistance—even if it occurred only on a spotty bases—the South had a new ally and alliance for its religion. Segregation had a new backer and sponsor. Democracy itself, at least, at the level of praxis, embraced this secular religion with the precepts of white supremacy. This made Mays's task a formidable one. The institutions of the region and most notable, Southern Politics, stood against Mays. This indeed required a different kind of battlefield warrior and few like Mays have been able to arise and stand the storm. He did.

The Scholarship of Professor Freddie Colston

To understand how Mays conquered this secular religion with all of its armor and power and obtained the impossible dream, it is both necessary and essential to read, reflect, and think upon what Professor Freddie Colston has brought together in this pioneering and brilliant collection of speeches, sermons, commencement addresses, and eulogies. Moreover, it is not just the riches of the collection but the organization and structure of the volume as well. Professor Colston has so composed this collection that it will give the reader its maximum impact and influence. Hence, this is one rare collection of documents that is so carefully organized around thematic issues and themes that it will impart the absolute best in African American oration to its readers. Clearly, Professor Colston in crafting this volume has not only wonderful research skills and talents but perceptive listening skills as well. The reader cannot help but to be moved.

Given these realities, there is the need to commend Professor Colston for the many years that he spent gathering the materials to create this representative collection of Mays's speeches. The thirty-one speeches contained in this book of documents literally came from numerous and diverse sources that took great patience to track down and secure for this volume. Obviously, Professor Colston's hard work, diligence, and per-severance clearly paid-off. Here are the moving words, word images, and thoughts of one of the greatest African American and American orators of this or any century. These speeches, even in written form, will not fail to move the reader. In fact, I heard several of these speeches while I was a student at Morehouse College (1959-1963) during Mays's presidency. Now, more than thirty years later, I am still moved to excitement, tears, and intellectual joy. In addition, these speeches have not failed to motivate. Professor Colston has made some outstanding and exceptional choices. The reader will be greatly rewarded.

Thus, Professor Colston's previous scholarly work, which became a signal contribution to the literature on African American politics, is now joined by this new work which will add immeasurably to the thin and small literature on African American oratory.[3] This work will demonstrate the wide range and great versatility of this American orator. Secondly, it will indicate to the reader that the words, word images, and word pictures of Mays speak across time, place, and space. Mays's speeches are as relevant now as they were when he initially made them. They speak to current events in an everlasting and ever powerful way because Mays was concerned with the enduring issues and problems of humankind. Thirdly, Mays's speeches addressed some of the enduring personalities and historical figures of our time like his former student, Martin Luther King, Jr., and Senator Robert Kennedy. His speeches also took unique political stands like the one that endorsed President Jimmy Carter for reelection in 1980.

Finally, embedded in Mays's speeches is his dynamic point that a social conscience and a set of spiritual values are essential in this human journey given humankind's capacity for sin and evil. As Mays saw it, one's moral courage and will can serve one well throughout one's life and career. These are timeless matters that transcend generations, institutions, leaders, secular religions, time, and space. We owe Professor Colston a great debt for his unmatched scholarship that retrieved these wonderful and thoughtful documents. They are a gift to the scholarly and intellectual community of great magnitude.

Professor Colston's stellar scholarship gives us one more area of richness!

Benjamin E. Mays as an Agent
of Political Socialization

This excellent collection of representative speeches is not just a window on an African American and American orator and the types of issues and concerns that he addressed through time. Perhaps the most profound and singular contribution inherent in this volume of documents is the insights, reflections and revelations that it provides about the types of agents of political socialization within the African American community and how they resocialize that community.

In an enslaved population as well as in a segregated population of people like African Americans, the normal and main agents of political socialization—i.e., the family, schools, peer groups and the media— have been using the ideas and tenets of their secular religion to get the members of the African American community to accept their plight and oppression and reduce their resistance. Oppositional socialization agents in the oppressed community are usually limited, small, circumscribed, and sporadic.[4] Few avenues are open and even fewer resources are available with which the community can resocialize itself, political leaders and community and political activists. Hence, individual scholarly presidents like Mays who acquired a sense of mission, and purpose early, can and did, serve as an agent of political socialization. Mays trained both Dr. King and Dr. Samuel DuBois Cook as well as thousand of others who attacked the secular religion of segregation in numerous and successful ways. When seen in this context, Mays was a dominant figure in political socialization and through his speeches had significant influence and import.[5]

Usually, political scientists overlook such individuals like Mays because they are beyond the dominant and acceptable categories of agents based on mainstream conceptualizations. But racial and ethnic communities have developed agents of socialization that are outside of the mainstream categories. Hence, individuals like Mays[6] would be seen as no more than an orator. But Mays clearly transcended this role and trained several generations of men to play a role in diminishing, if not outright destroying, the idols, percepts, and institutions of America's secular religion. When seen in this context, i.e., the area of socialization, the speeches in this volume become even more invaluable because they were the tools, if not the weapons, with which Mays as an intellectual and educational warrior reshaped this democratic society. Therefore, when Mays left the battlefield, he left this society in much better shape than when he found it at his birth. And the changes he wrought served not only the African American community but also the nation-state and the international community as well.

Professor Colston is to be saluted for giving us this volume of great and harrowing words. They changed America and through it the world. This is scholarship at its very best. This is a book that I highly recommend to political scientists, students of public speaking, and students of social movements, students of political socialization, and historians. It will be highly rewarding and a terrific intellectual treat.

Notes

1. See his autobiography, Benjamin E. Mays, *Born to Rebel* (New York: Charles Scribner, 1971).

2. Hanes Walton, Jr., "Moral Man and a Moral Journey," in F. Thomas Trotter, ed., *Politics, Morality and Higher Education: Essays in Honor of Samuel DuBois Cook* (Tennessee: Providence House, 1997), pp. 1-9. See also Numan Bartley, ed., *The Evolution of Southern Culture* (Athens: University of Georgia Press, 1988), pp.1-13.

3. For a review of Professor Colston's earlier scholarship in political science see Hanes Walton, Jr., *Invisible Politics: Black Political Behavior* (Albany: SUNY Press, 1985), pp. 170-171.

4. Hanes Walton, Jr., "Introduction: Compromising Morality: The Creation of the Political Leadership of Malcolm X" in Robert Jenkins and Mfanya Donald Tryman, eds., *The Malcolm X Encyclopedia* (Westport, Connecticut: Greenwood, 2002), pp. 1-12.

5. For another unique way to see and understand the different agents of political socialization beyond the mainstream ones see Hanes Walton, Jr., Oliver Jones, Jr., and Pearl K. Ford, "African American Political Socialization: The Protest Resignations of Councilpersons Jerome Woody and Renee Baker," in Hanes Walton, Jr., *African American Power and Politics: The Political Context Variable* (New York: Columbia University Press, 1997), pp. 113-128.

6. Trotter, pp. 1-9. See also James C. Scott, *Domination and the Arts of Resistance* (New Haven: Yale University Press, 1990).

Preface

My research on the speeches of Dr. Mays began shortly after his death in March 1984, but my interest in the great educator, orator, teacher, role model, and humanitarian goes back to my student days at Morehouse College, 1955-1959. I can still remember the first time I saw Dr. Mays when he addressed my freshman class on a mild September afternoon during Orientation Week in 1955. He mesmerized and challenged the group of approximately 211 men, when he remarked:

> Education is like a voice calling from a high hill. The voice calls out, Come up here! Come up here! One moves up to the point where he heard the voice call out only to find out that the voice has moved to an even higher peak, and beckons, Come up here! Come up here! And the process continues as the voice moves to higher and higher altitudes and calls out, Come up here! Come up here!

Mays's remarks clearly indicated to the neophytes, soon to embrace the mystique of the "Morehouse Man," that education is a continuous process; that one is never completely educated, but is always engaged in the process of becoming. As one reaches a certain level of academic achievement, one must reach further and further to grasp ever higher possibilities, promises, goals, and challenges. His classic admonition was that one's reach should exceed one's grasp, and that the sky, not just the ceiling, is the goal for which one should aim. Thousands of his former students, as well as the audiences to whom he spoke, were moved by his words of wisdom and advice, and their accomplishments and contributions to society serve as vivid testimony to his monumental legacy to American society and to the international community.

My research over the past years embraced hundreds of sources, places, and people. Thanking all of those who so unselfishly and graciously contributed to the essential research efforts is impossible, but a few who rendered significant service or made important contributions to the project's success are listed below.

Jean Bolduc assisted me in developing a special data base containing several speeches of Dr. Mays. For her expertise and compassion, I am highly grateful. I would also like to thank Mrs. Anita E. Osborne-Lee, who provided valuable assistance in formatting this document. Mrs. Esme Bhan, Manuscript Research Associate at Moorland-Spingarn Research Center, assisted me in my research of the Mays Collection at the Center. Her enthusiasm, cooperation, and professionalism will long be remembered; Mrs. Leida I. Torres, Reference Librarian, and Mrs. Joellen P. ElBashir, Curator, at the Moorland-Spingarn Research Center also provided valuable research assistance for the project. The author is also grateful to Ms. Vicki C. Johns, former editor, Office of University Relations Publication Center at the University of Tennessee, Knoxville, for graciously lending her proofreading and editing skills to the manuscript. Don Williams, *Knoxville News-Sentinel* columnist, editor, and founder of *New Millennium Writings*, Dr. George Sirgiovanni, Professor of History, College of Saint Elizabeth, Morristown, New Jersey, and Mercy Cannon, Ph.D. candidate, Department of English, University of Tennessee, read portions of the manuscript and provided valuable editorial suggestions and assistance. Credit is also extended to Ms. Tammorah DeVane, a former student in the Public Administration Program at North Carolina Central University at Durham, when the author served as director, 1989-1991; Ms. DeVane typed some of the original research for this project. Ms. Brenda Roulhac, a former graduate student in communications at the University of Tennessee, typed and formatted some previous versions of Dr. Mays's speeches so that I could edit them on my computer.

Several librarians and archivists from colleges and universities where Dr. Mays delivered speeches during his career aided my research by securing materials through interlibrary loans. These include: Mrs. Carol Cooper, former assistant reference librarian at the Oak Ridge, Tennessee Public Library and Mrs. Catherine Miller, currently a reference librarian at the Oak Ridge Public Library; Mrs. Victoria Parrish, former secretary, School of Divinity, Duke University, Durham, North Carolina; Dr. Julia P. Davidson, Director of University Relations, Shaw University, Raleigh, North Carolina; Dr. Dorothy M. Haith, former

Library Director, Albany State University, Albany, Georgia; and Mr. Richard Topp, Archivist, Regenstein Library, University of Chicago.

The author telephoned and wrote to individuals who had resources or information regarding Dr. Mays. Those persons include: Winfield Curry, Assistant Archivist, United Negro College Fund Archives, Fairfax, Virginia; Tanya Elder, Archivist, The Riverside Church Archives, New York City; Whitney Miller, University Archivist, Michigan State University, East Lansing, Michigan; Rachel Canada, Public Relations Staff, University Archives, The University of North Carolina at Chapel Hill; Elizabeth Mulherrin, Resource Access Librarian, Agnes Scott College, Decatur, Georgia; DeWitt N. Martin, Jr., President of the Butler Street Young Men's Christian Association, Atlanta, Georgia; William Fowlkes, Associate Editor, *Atlanta Daily World*; Glenda J. Pence, Administrative Assistant, Rockefeller Memorial Chapel, University of Chicago; William King, University Archivist, Duke University, Durham, North Carolina; Samuel Speers, Associate Dean, Rockefeller Memorial Chapel, University of Chicago; Pierre Beffa, Director of the Library, World Council of Churches, Geneva, Switzerland; Doris Dysinger, Special Collections/University Archives Specialist, Bucknell University, Lewisburg, Pennsylvania; Minnie M. Johnson, Archivist, South Carolina State University; Paul G. Anderson, Archivist, Christ Church Cathedral, St. Louis, Missouri; Janet Olson, Assistant Archivist, Northwestern University, Evanston, Illinois, and many others.

In the final stages of preparation for the book, I was assisted by Dorothy Albritton, Homer Hickson, and Linda Bellamy. Again, thanks to all.

Acknowledgments

I would like to thank the following people, organizations, and institutions for granting me permission to publish speeches, photos, and quotes for this book.

American Baptist Convention Historical Society	Quote from oral interview with Dr. Mays by R. Dean Gordon, reprinted with permission from the American Baptist Convention Historical Society, Rochester, New York
Bucknell University	"His Goodness Was Not Enough," reprinted with permission from Bucknell University Historical Collections
Centre College	"The Challenge of the Seventies," reprinted from *Centerpiece*, Volume 11 (August 1970), with permission from Dr. Robert E. Glass, Centre College
Dr. Doris Levy Gavins	"Three Enemies of Mankind: A Challenge to the University," and "Education to What End?," reprinted from Doris Levy Gavins *The Ceremonial Speaking of Benjamin Elijah Mays*, with permission from the author, Dillard University
Duke University	"The Vocation of a Christian—In, but Not of, the World," reprinted with permission from Duke University Archives

"Martin Luther King, Jr.," reprinted with permission from Duke University Archives

Florida A & M University
"The Inauguration Address for Dr. William H. Dennis, Jr.," reprinted with permission from Dr. James N. Eaton, Black College Archives, Florida A & M University

Howard University
"An Impossible Dream Comes True," reprinted from *New Directions*, Volume 1 No. 3 (Spring 1974), with permission from Moorland-Spingarn Research Center

"Eulogy of Dr. Mordecai Wyatt Johnson," reprinted from *New Directions*, Volume 4, No. 1 (January 1977), with permission from Moorland-Spingarn Research Center

Jimmy Carter Presidential Library
"Jimmy Carter" speech

Kappa Alpha Psi Fraternity, Inc.
"The Unfinished Task," reprinted from *The Journal*, Volume 43, No.1 (February 1957), with permission from Kappa Alpha Psi Fraternity, Inc., International Headquarters, Philadelphia, Pennsylvania

Mays Collection
"A Crisis and a Challenge"
"Carolina Symposium on Public Affairs"
"Except a Man Be Born Again, He Cannot See the Kingdom of Heaven"
"Our Colleges and the Supreme Court Decision"
"The Challenge to Overcome the Major Disabilities of 341 Years in a Quarter of a Century"
"The Paradox of Life"
"Eulogy of Dr. Whitney Young, Jr."
Reprinted with permission from Moorland-Spingarn Research Center

Michigan State
University

"The Universities' Unfinished Task,"
reprinted with permission from Michigan
State University Historical Archives

Morehouse College

"Radio Address on the Seventy-Eighth Anniversary of Morehouse College," reprinted
from the *Morehouse College Alumnus*, Volume XIII (March-April 1945), with permission from Morehouse College
"Twenty-Seven Years of Success and Failure
at Morehouse," reprinted from the
Morehouse College Alumnus, Volume
XXXV (Summer 1967), with permission
from Morehouse College

Photos

Reprinted with permission from:
Black Cow Photo, Inc.
Jimmy Carter Presidential Library
Moorland-Spingarn Research Center
South Carolina State University Archives

Shaw University

"Desegregation: An Opportunity and a
Challenge," reprinted with permission from
Shaw University

Sheed and Ward

"The Moral Aspects of Segregation,"
Bradford Daniel, ed., *Back, White and Gray:
Twenty-one Points on the Race Question,*
reprinted by permission from Sheed and
Ward, an Apostle of the Priests of the Sacred
Heart, 7373 S. Lovers Lane Rd. Franklin,
WI 53123

Southern Regional
Council

"Why an Atlanta School Suit?" reprinted
from *New South*, Volume 5 (September-
October 1950), with permission from the
Southern Regional Council, Atlanta, Georgia

Spelman College

"The Advantages of a Small, Christian, Private, Liberal Arts College," reprinted from the *Spelman Messenger*, Volume 73 (May 1957), with permission from Spelman College

Talladega College

"The Liberal Arts College in an Atomic Age," reprinted from *The Talladegan*, Volume 43 (May 1946), with permission from Talladega College

University of Chicago

"In What Shall We Glory?" and "Why Jesus Called the Wise Man a Fool," reprinted with permission from the University of Chicago Library Archives

University of Georgia Press

"Eulogy of Dr. Martin Luther King, Jr." and "The Church Amidst Ethnic and Racial Tensions," reprinted from Benjamin E. Mays, *Born to Rebel*, with permission from the University of Georgia Press

WSB-TV, Atlanta, Georgia

Quotes from "Benjamin E. Mays: Man of Integrity" with permission from WSB-TV, Atlanta, Georgia

Chapter 1

Introduction

Throughout most of our country's history, many black orators emerged from the experience of slavery, subjugation, oppression, and long-standing discrimination. Black Americans' unyielding struggle for freedom, justice and equality produced spokespersons who articulated the ironic predicament of a racial minority seeking freedom and justice in a land of opportunity founded on principles of equality enshrined in the Declaration of Independence and the Constitution of the United States.

Black Americans have continually expressed displeasure with the injustices they have experienced as an ethnic group possessing unique talents for expressing eloquently and meaningfully the hopes, dreams, problems, possibilities, and promises of American life. We still wrestle with racism, racial profiling, affirmative action, gender inequality, and economic injustice as we move into a new millennium that promises technological progress via the Digital Age. We are still debating the merits of an increasingly culturally diverse society. Various groups strive to secure and maintain the intellectual, economic, and political power necessary for survival and to enjoy the technological advancements and benefits of the twenty-first century.

The black American struggle for social justice is significant in our life and culture, but the documental oratory of most blacks has been subordinated. Black American orators have not been included in publications recording the superb speeches of this nation's great orators. Instead, the major speeches of black Americans are usually compiled black anthologies. Some of those anthologies include: Alice Ruth M. Dunbar, *Masters of Negro Eloquence* (1913); Carter G. Woodson *gro Orators and Their Orations* (1925); Benjamin Brawley, *The in Literature and Art* (1930); Roy L. Hills, *Rhetoric and Race Revolt* (1964); Marcus Boulware, *The Oratory of Negro Leaders, 1900-1968* (1969); Philip S. Foner, *The Voices of Black: Major Speeches by Negroes in the United States, 1797-1973* (1973), and others. There is, however, a growing awareness of the gift of oratory through which many men and women of color have contributed to American life and culture. Martin Luther King, Jr.'s "I Have a Dream" speech,[1] delivered at the March on Washington on August 28, 1963, is commonly considered one of the great speeches of the twentieth century. It is frequently cited, especially in reference to the civil rights movement of the 1960s, in biographies of the great black leader, and in speeches on the annual Martin Luther King, Jr., holiday celebrations.

When one begins to consider the great orators of color in American history, many voices come to mind. Examples are Sojourner Truth, Harriet Tubman, Nat Turner, Booker T. Washington, Marcus Garvey, Frederick Douglass, Howard Thurman, Mordecai Johnson, Vernon Johns, Martin Luther King, Jr., Ralph Abernathy, Malcolm X, Joseph Lowery, Jesse Jackson, Adam Clayton Powell, Paul Robeson, Mary McLeod Bethune, Richard Allen, W. E. B. DuBois, Barbara Jordan, Maxine Waters, Otis Moss, Sr., and Benjamin E. Mays. These are but few of the black orators who have reminded Americans of the commonality of the human condition and of the contributions of various minorities to improving American life and culture. This book focuses on the oratory of Benjamin Elijah Mays, mentor of Nobel Peace Prize laureate Martin Luther King, Jr., and an inspiration to several generations of Americans.

The academic year 1994-95 marked the centennial of this great black American's birth. In recognition of the many contributions of this prodigious personality, year-long celebrations were staged at Bates College in Lewiston, Maine, Mays's alma mater, and at Morehouse College, where ˋ served as president for twenty-seven years. In October 1994, Bates ˋ˒ge hosted a Centennial Symposium on the life and career of Dr. ˕n addition to conducting the Centennial Symposium, the college ˋated a multipurpose building, the Benjamin E. Mays Center, ˋnor. The dedication ceremony attracted approximately 1,500 Bates College campus. ˋollege honored Mays by staging several programs that ˋd researchers from throughout the United States. ˋelebration concluded on May 21, 1995, with the ˋn E. Mays National Memorial where Mays and his wife, Sadie, were re-interred. A statue of Mays in full academic regalia was unveiled. This ceremony, held on the Morehouse College Quadrangle, was witnessed by approximately 700 people. Such celebrations are but a small token of appreciation for the significance and meaning of Mays's life and his contributions to American society.

Benjamin E. Mays was an extraordinary human being; his intellectual odyssey is one of the inspiring sagas of the twentieth century. He rose above the demeaning and oppressive conditions of his birthplace in rural South Carolina and became a personality of national and international significance. During his life and career he mastered several roles, including author, minister, teacher, civil rights advocate, orator, humanitarian, educator, and administrator.

His accomplishments are legendary; he wrote nine books, published more than seventy professional articles, and wrote chapters in fifteen other books. Dr. Mays also wrote more than a thousand articles in a weekly column for the *Pittsburgh Courier* and the *Chicago Defender*. He delivered more than one thousand speeches to audiences in the United States and in foreign countries and received more than two hundred awards as well as forty-nine honorary degrees. Named in his honor in Atlanta is a street, Benjamin E. Mays Drive, formerly Sewell Road; a high school, Benjamin E. Mays High (1982); and a dormitory on the Morehouse College campus, Benjamin E. Mays Hall. A scholarship is also named in his honor at the college. His picture hangs in the Statehouse in his native South Carolina, and he was elected to the South Carolina Hall of Fame in 1984. A stretch of Highway 178 close by his birthplace is named Mays Crossroads. A monument near the highway chronicles the highlights of the career of one the state's most famous native sons.

The Reagan Administration denied a nomination to award Dr. Mays the Medal of Freedom prior to his death in March 1984. However, in delayed recognition and compensation for this denial, Congressman John Lewis of Georgia proposed in January 1993 that a commemorative stamp honoring Dr. Mays be commissioned. Lewis also proposed a bill to award the Medal of Freedom to Dr. Mays posthumously. The Medal of Freedom resolution was sent to President Clinton, and the stamp resolution was sent to the Citizens Stamp Advisory Committee.[2] Efforts to bestow the award continue. Georgia's Democratic senators, Max Cleland and Zell Miller, recently[3] introduced a Senate resolution in the 107th Congress urging President George W. Bush to award the Medal of Freedom honor to the late Dr. Benjamin E. Mays. As of November 30, 2001, the resolution had passed both houses of Congress. The resolution is now on the desk of President Bush. When the President signs the measure, the late Dr. Benjamin E. Mays will at last receive posthumously the coveted highest civilian honor he so richly deserves.

The approval of the Medal of Freedom resolution for Dr. Mays will be a gesture in the right direction and should help dramatize President Bush's pledge to bridge the racial divide in America. Bestowing the award will concurrently acknowledge the monumental accomplishments of a man whose achievements are not as widely known as they should be.

* * *

Benjamin Elijah Mays was born on August 1, 1895,[4] to former slaves Hezekiah and Louvenia Mays in rural Epworth, ten miles from the nearest railroad station at Ninety-Six, South Carolina. Although they never pursued a formal education, Mays considered his mother and father intelligent. His mother could neither read nor write; his father could read printing, but could not read script and could not write his name. This is understandable considering the circumstances under which they were born and lived. Bennie was the youngest of eight children—five girls and three boys. His family, like most blacks of the region, were tenant farmers. Although they were never hungry as sharecroppers, they possessed meager resources and barely broke even at the end of each year, despite long hours hoeing, plowing, picking cotton, and performing other farm chores.

When Mays was born, thirty years after the end of the Civil War, lynching was widely accepted by both church and state. In 1900 there were 115 lynchings in the United States.[5] Blacks were disenfranchised and employed in such menial jobs as domestics, farm workers, sharecroppers, and renters—the predicament in which blacks found themselves after the period of slavery. Blacks lived in constant fear of physical violence. In these circumstances, blacks were considered an inferior class and not expected to aspire to lofty goals; Mays later affirmed that approximately 99.8 percent of them never did.[6] But Benjamin E. Mays was an exception; obviously he was a member of that lofty 0.2 percent.

Young Bennie realized very early his plight as a black male born in late nineteenth century rural South Carolina. At age four, he witnessed a group of white men on horseback humiliating his father by making him bow down and salute them. The young lad feared for his father's life and began to cry. Fortunately and improbably, the mob eventually rode off without physically harming his father—the cries of Mays could well have been his father's saving grace, because the mob sought blacks to lynch.[7]

This event made Mays aware that, in his native state of South Carolina, blacks existed in a hostile environment of hatred and denial of social and political rights. While other blacks experienced similar indignities, this event gave impetus to his lifelong battle against racial injustice, ignorance, and poverty. He was thereby motivated by these conditions to dedicate his life to helping the black race and, consequently, humanity.[8] As a result, he continued to speak and write about this terrifying childhood experience.

Before he began his schooling at the one room Brickhouse School for blacks in the Epworth community, Mays's oldest sister Susie taught him to spell, read, and count to one hundred. The intellectually gifted Mays was far ahead of the other students in his class when he entered the school at age six. Because of his scholastic talents he often was "Exhibit A" when visitors came to the school. Bennie was always eager to recite and usually excelled during school programs at the end of the school year. He developed a keen thirst for knowledge that lasted a lifetime.

When Bennie was about nine years old, he delivered a speech on Children's Day at Old Mount Zion Baptist Church. Susie encouraged Bennie to appear on stage. For the program he memorized a portion of the "Sermon on the Mount." After the recitation, the congregation applauded long and hard. It was a terrific ovation, especially for a nine-year-old lad who prayed while plowing with a mule for God to help him learn his speech well.[9] Based on his speech, the adults at Old Mount Zion predicted that Bennie was destined to achieve great things in life, and he vowed never to disappoint them. This event was Mays's first taste of public response to his oratory.

Mays considered his childhood characterized by frustration and doubt.[10] He had an insatiable thirst for knowledge but had to overcome his father's unrelenting opposition to his educational aspirations, and he also needed money to pursue his goals.[11] Mays wanted to rise above his oppressive racial environment, in which blacks had no civil or political rights protected by the Constitution. Their lack of equality was substantiated by the "separate but equal" doctrine enunciated in *Plessy v. Ferguson*, 1896, only one year after Mays's birth, which became the main policy in race relations until segregation in public education was declared unconstitutional in the *Brown v. Board of Education* case handed down by the Supreme Court in 1954. He wanted to dispel the prevailing myth that blacks collectively were born inferior. Although Mays felt that he had to do something about this predicament, his father wanted him to help with the farming, as large families were needed to provide the requisite supply of cheap farm labor necessitated by the prevailing share-cropper system. Mays worked against an obvious impediment: his father believed that too much education made one dishonest. Hezekiah opposed his youngest son's striving to get an education beyond that offered in the one-room school in the Epworth community; that was all any sharecrop-per needed. However, before he died in 1938, while living with his son in Washington, D.C., a wonderful epiphany occurred: the elder Mays admitted that he was wrong and that his son's accomplishments made him proud.

On the other hand, Bennie's mother was perennially more under-standing of his desire to get an education. Louvenia Mays, a deeply religious woman, believed that God answers prayers, and her convic-tions influenced Bennie. Each night she would gather all of the family for prayers. Sometimes Bennie read certain portions of the Bible to her. Louvenia Mays defiantly continued to tell her children that they were as good as anyone else. This display of prayer and belief in God and in her children laid the foundations for the religious commitments that so stead-fastly guided Mays later in life.

On some moonlit nights the youthful Bennie would walk off into the woods to pray to God for the opportunity to get an education, and his desires goaded him daily. He wanted to leave the farm to seek his mis-sion in life. The Brickhouse School, the members of Old Mount Zion Baptist Church, and his family provided the inspiration; he needed de-liverance. He had a strong foundation for his delivery. From his family he learned the value of honesty and hard work; from his school he devel-oped a profound thirst for knowledge; and from the members of Old Mount Zion he received the encouragement that motivated him to achieve his laudable accomplishments in the following years.

This type of elder-and-youth-relationship in the Epworth community is typical of black community practice and culture throughout most of American history. While it did not receive the formal labeling of "mentoring" at that time, the youth traditionally received encourage-ment from their homes, churches, and schools. The making of Benjamin Elijah Mays as one of the great men of the twentieth century is clearly a validation for this model of motivation.[12]

In 1909, Mays's pastor Reverend Marshall, and Mays's mother persuaded his father to let Bennie go to an Association School in McCormick, South Carolina, about twenty-five miles away. It was considered slightly better than the Brickhouse School. Like Brickhouse, it too ran only four months out of the year; during the other eight months youngsters like Mays were supposed to help their families do the work the farms required. After Mays spent two years at the Association School, Mays's mother recognized its limitations. She prevailed upon his father to permit him to attend the high school department at South Carolina State College in Orangeburg.[13]

In 1912, at the age of seventeen, Mays entered the high school department at South Carolina State College in Orangeburg; through hard work and diligent study, he graduated as valedictorian in 1916. While in his sophomore year at South Carolina State, he won an oratorical contest, further displaying his innate gift for inspiring speech. It was also at South Carolina State that the poverty-stricken young Mays received further inspiration to keep on striving and holding on to his dreams.[14] He gave much credit to his teachers at the college for providing the impetus needed for success, and considered them his friends. They also aggressively encouraged him to continue his education beyond the bounded high school curriculum. Bennie listened. Soon afterward, he embarked on the second step of his personal trek.

Mays matriculated into Virginia Union University in Richmond in the fall of 1916 where he spent his freshman year earning all A's. However, he continued to hear a compelling inner challenge; he wanted to test his intellect with the best and brightest of white society and to challenge the erroneous popular notion about the innate inferiority of the black race. Mays met two Bates graduates at Virginia Union—Charles E. Hadley, '14, a chemist, and Roland A. Wakefield, '16, a mathematician. Impressed by the young man's obsession to continue his education, these two men encouraged him to seek admission to Bates College and wrote letters to college President Chase in his behalf.[15] His next step was a big one indeed.

In the fall of 1917, he transferred to Bates College in Lewiston, Maine. He was initially classified as a sophomore on probation, with the understanding that he had to pass qualifying examinations in order to be classified as a full-fledged sophomore; characteristically, he did, and was duly "fledged." Mays was then only one of four blacks among the six hundred white students comprising the Bates College student body.[16]

He paid his expenses at Bates primarily by working at several low-paying jobs, and he received a scholarship after his first year.

Upon entering Bates College, Mays set high goals; he planned to excel as he had at South Carolina State and Virginia Union. He decided in advance to enter the sophomore declamation contest that he learned about in the Bates College Catalog. During the summer of 1917, while employed as a Pullman porter on the New York Central Railroad, he diligently prepared for the contest by rehearsing and learning "The Supposed Speech of John Adams." Before the contest, he was informed that Mrs. Fred Pomeroy, wife of his biology professor, was proficient in public speaking. He solicited her help, and she agreed to coach him in preparing for the contest. He won first prize.[17]

After Mays's success in winning the public speaking contest, he was approached by Professor Craig A. Beard, debating team coach, who had heard him speak, and invited him to try out for the debating team. After some reflection, he agreed, and made the team. Well known on campus, he became active in such campus organizations as the Bates Forum, the Philhellenic Council, the YMCA, and the Debating Council, and he was initiated into Omega Psi Phi Fraternity in Boston. As a graduating senior, he was elected as Class Day Orator. After a very successful tenure as an undergraduate student, he graduated from Bates with honors in 1920; fifteen years later, he was elected to membership in Phi Beta Kappa National Scholastic Honor Society.[18] Mays later enrolled in graduate school; he received his M.A. in 1925 and his Ph.D. in 1935, in divinity from the University of Chicago.

Mays excelled at Bates. In the process, he dispelled from his mind the myth of the inherent inferiority of all blacks and the inherent superiority of all whites.[19] The Bates College years were a series of liberating experiences, enabling Mays to see himself as a free person with dignity and worth. For a great part of Mays's life he fought against segregation and discrimination, and his early humiliations as a lad growing up in his native state of rural South Carolina were enough to inseminate bitterness in him. But he considered his teachers at Bates his friends; he had classmates whom he respected; and the campus atmosphere was warm. In light of these positive influences, he could no longer generalize that all white people were prejudiced.[20] Upon graduation, he had achieved, through his performance, his goal of academic excellence. He had bested most of his classmates in academics, debating, and public speaking.[21]

After graduation from Bates College, Mays married Ellen Edith Harvin on July 31, 1920, in Elizabeth City County, Virginia. Mays and Ellen had become engaged when they were students at South Carolina State. He considered Ellen to be charming and well balanced. She was the kind of woman who understood the desires of an ambitious young man like Mays who was determined to get his college degree and continue his education; accordingly, they had agreed not to marry until he had finished Bates College. In the interim, when Mays was at Bates, she remained in South Carolina and continued her education. They corresponded frequently and remained loyal to each other. When time permitted, Mays visited during his vacations from college.

At the time of their marriage, Ellen taught Home Economics at Morris College in Sumter, South Carolina. She also worked as a Jeanes Teacher, supervising black students in Clarendon County, South Carolina, under the auspices of a grant for that purpose established by Anna Jeanes of Philadelphia in 1907.[22] But the marriage was short-lived. A little more than two years after their marriage Ellen died at the tender age of twenty-eight on February 2, 1923, following a brief illness. This tragic event left Mays shocked and saddened. But he gradually overcame his sorrow through preoccupation with his busy teaching responsibilities and other professional involvements. The couple had no children.

The Mays odyssey had already turned toward sharing his hard-won knowledge. Mays began his professional career as an instructor of mathematics at Morehouse College (1921-1924); consequently, he continued with his part-time graduate work at Chicago. He was the first to teach a course in calculus at the college. He also taught a course in psychology and a course in religious studies, coached the debating team, and served a term as acting dean. Concurrently, he served as pastor of Shiloh Baptist Church, a few blocks from the campus.

From 1925 to 1926, he served as professor of English at South Carolina State College in Orangeburg where Mays's career ladder had another interesting personal rung. The love bug touched Mays once again. It was at South Carolina State that he met his second wife, Sadie Gray. Sadie was also a teacher at the college. They were married on August 9, 1926.

Mrs. Sadie Gray Mays, a beautiful and delightful lady, received her elementary and high school education in Gray, Georgia, a city named after some of her early ancestors, and at Paine College in Augusta, Georgia. She continued her education at the University of Chicago where she received the Ph.B. and M.A. degrees in social work. In addition to teaching at South Carolina State, she later taught at Spelman College and the Atlanta University School of Social Work. Mrs. Mays also utilized her skills in social work in Atlanta, St. Louis, Tampa, and Washington, D.C. She accompanied her husband on several trips abroad and became interested and knowledgeable about women and family issues in the countries they visited.

Known as a very able and inspiring speaker,[23] Mrs. Mays was often invited to deliver speeches to church, professional, and civic groups, especially during the early years of her husband's presidency of Morehouse.[24] When I was a student at Morehouse, I did not witness her deliver a public address, but I found her to be very articulate and affable in speaking to students individually and in small groups. At this time she had relinquished her career ladder and had taken on full responsibilities as "First Lady of the College" in order to aid her husband's demanding job obligations. Mrs. Mays remained her husband's closest and most devoted companion for forty-five years.[25] Mays sired no children in the second marriage. Meanwhile, he continued the journey toward his goals, receiving ever-wider recognition of his talents.

After leaving South Carolina State because the college had a policy that would not allow husband and wife to work together on the faculty, he and his new wife sought other employment.

Mays served a tenure as executive secretary of the Tampa, Florida, Urban League from 1926 to 1928. He was appointed national student secretary of the Young Men's Christian Association (YMCA) from 1928 to 1930. From 1930 to 1932, he served as the director of a Study of Black Churches in the United States, sponsored by the Institute of Social and Religious Research of New York. In 1932, he returned to the University of Chicago where he completed work for his doctorate in 1934.[26]

That same year, Mays was appointed by President Mordecai Johnson, a Morehouse College alumnus, as Dean of the School of Religion at Howard University where he served in this position until 1940. Under his direction, the enrollment of the graduate school was increased; the faculty was strengthened; the physical plant improved; and the School of Religion received cherished accreditation from the American Association of Theological Schools. His personal journey now embraced international locations. He was one of thirteen Americans to attend the World Conference of the YMCA in Mysore, India, 1937. He represented the United States at the Oxford Conference on church, community, and state at Oxford University, England (1937). He served as a leader of the Youth Conference in Amsterdam, Holland (1939).[27] These travels broadened his perspective on international issues and, likewise, his view on race relations. Through his experiences as Dean of the School of Religion he established his reputation as an effective administrator and became a national personality, thereby placing himself in a position for consideration for appointment to a higher level of academic leadership. His next career move allowed him to mold his greatest legacy as an educator, administrator, orator, mentor, and inspirational motivator of youth for over a quarter of a century.

Mays was appointed the sixth president of Morehouse College on August 1, 1940, at the age of 45. An article in the *Atlanta Journal* dated May 11, 1940, stated that Mays would replace Dr. Charles D. Hubert, who had served as acting president following the retirement of Dr. Samuel H. Archer, the fifth president of Morehouse College. Dr. Hubert would continue as director of the School of Religion at Morehouse.

Soon after assuming the presidency of Morehouse College, Mays learned that three things had to be done. He needed to secure more money to augment the institution's meager financial resources, to increase the size of the faculty, and to improve the quality of the faculty by hiring better qualified professors.[28] He achieved these goals and much more during his tenure at the college. Morehouse's enrollment doubled, its endowment quadrupled, and the faculty grew from twenty-three with only two Ph.D.s to more than sixty-five full-time faculty and an increase in the number of Ph.D.s to 54 percent during the years Mays was president of the institution.[29] President Mays also succeeded in getting a chapter of Phi Beta Kappa, the national academic honor society, installed on campus. Morehouse thus became one of three predominantly black institutions of higher learning with a chapter of the prestigious honor society and one of only four in the state of Georgia on campuses both black and white.[30]

The ladder reached higher still. Mays received significant honors and awards during the early stages of his Morehouse presidency and thereafter. In 1944, he was elected vice-president of the World Council of Churches, the first time a black man had been elected to that office, where he was viewed as a religious liberal who had not even sought to convert his Methodist wife to the Baptist faith.[31]

Mays received an honorary degree from his alma mater, Bates College, on June 15, 1947,[32] his fifth honorary degree. He was honored by the University of Chicago School of Divinity as "Alumnus of the Year" on October 19, 1949.[33]

An article written in 1950 by an *Atlanta Daily World* reporter, and also head of the Atlanta Bureau of the *Pittsburgh Courier*, William Fowlkes, paid tribute to the stature and contributions of President Mays. Fowlkes asserted that as a college head, preacher, writer, and conferee on local and national problems, Dr. Mays displayed a distinct form of dignity and honor. Fowlkes continued his assessment of the great educator thus: "When the history of the twentieth century is written there will be a niche therein carved for this militant crusader for human rights."[34] Fowlkes asserted additionally, "When Mays declared that the South worships segregation and is more concerned with maintaining it than anything else, his comments made southerners squirm; but church leaders and laymen everywhere agreed with him."

In 1954, Dr. Mays was selected by *Pulpit*, a black religious magazine, as one of the top twenty preachers in America. And in 1955, Mays was selected as one of America's Ten Most Powerful Negroes," by *Our World,* a black publication.

The great educator, minister, and orator received honors and awards throughout his professional career. During his 27 years as president of Morehouse College Dr. Mays served as a role model, a father figure, a teacher, and a great motivator to his followers. In physical stature Mays stood six feet tall, but appeared taller because of his erect posture—a habit he developed during his youth to walk with dignity and pride; he weighed approximately 180 pounds and had a full head of iron-gray hair with a contrasting dark complexion. His distinctive physical appearance complemented his towering intellectual stature. When Mays walked into a room, eyes were likely to focus in his direction. His mere physical presence attracted attention.

At Morehouse, Mays endeared himself to the world of academe and many other worlds. A student-oriented president, Mays earned the nickname "Buck Bennie" from the students for his insistence that students pay off their bills on time. *The Maroon Tiger*, the student newspaper, ran the headline "Buck Bennie Rides Again" during the early months of his presidency. Although his nickname was passed down from generation to generation, it was always with increased respect. But Mays was best known for the many acts of compassion and generosity to his students. There were numerous stories of Mays helping students to pay their bills: he often helped students find paying work on campus, and even paid bills for students who could not find the means to provide for their expenses. I personally knew of two students who were employed by President and Mrs. Mays at their home on campus, earning money to pay for their college expenses by driving the Mayses to personal engagements and assisting with household chores. One of the students also stayed at the president's home, as others had before, and would continue to do.

There was the heartwarming story of a student named Ernest Wright, a member of the Class of 1941, who could not afford the suit required for participation in the graduation exercises. Dr. Mays had one of his own suits altered to fit the student so that he could take part in the ceremony. On another occasion, Dr. and Mrs. Mays bought a suit and overcoat for a Morehouse student, who became a leader during the Atlanta University Student Movement of the 1960s, so that the student would be properly attired when representing Morehouse at student meetings and conferences.

President and Mrs. Mays also initiated an annual Christmas Dinner for students left on campus during the holidays because they lived too far to travel home or could not afford to travel home. They enjoyed a delicious traditional Christmas meal at the home of President and Mrs. Mays. The couple was greatly admired for such acts of concern for the welfare of their students. The Christmas Dinner continued throughout the Mays presidency. These stories and acts of compassion were numerous and significantly etched in the history of the Mays presidency.

In addition to his humanitarian acts in the interests of Morehouse College students, Benjamin Mays was a compassionate family man. It was fundamental to his personality. During the process of researching materials for this book among the Mays Collection at Moorland-Spingarn Research Center at Howard University, I came across numerous personal letters between Mays and some of his relatives wherein financial assistance was implied or requested, and provided by Mays. He helped six nieces and nephews through college. Typically, he never asked that they repay him, but merely asserted, "pass it on." Consequently, they were all proud of their "Uncle Bennie." He was their favorite uncle and hero. This sense of family pride in Mays's accomplishments and personality clearly showed when I met two of his nephews at the October 1994 Mays Symposium at Bates College. One of his nephews remarked to me gleefully, "You're one of Uncle Bennie's students, too." I replied, "Yes."

For most of Mays's tenure as president, weekly chapel sessions were required of all students. The students assembled in Sale Hall Chapel from 9:00-9:50 a.m. every day except Saturday. These sessions sometimes included visiting speakers of national stature such as Mordecai Johnson, Howard Thurman, W.E.B. DuBois, Mary McLeod Bethune, Channing Tobias, Jesse O. Thomas, and others. The weekly chapel programs helped to cultivate the "Morehouse Family" spirit. On Tuesday mornings of each week, President Mays spoke to the student body, that looked forward to these speeches about freedom and truth, love and justice, mercy and forgiveness, aspiration and motivation, perseverance and endurance, reform, and resistance.[35] Sometimes these sessions included discussions regarding important developments and issues related to campus life. As a great teacher, he prepared diligently for these Tuesday chapel lectures to the students. He had his greatest impact on his students through his weekly chapel sessions. His spirit of advocating academic excellence permeated the campus and endeared him to generations of Morehouse students during the 1940s, 1950s, and 1960s.[36]

In these chapel sessions, he had a great impact on the education and critical thinking of his students. Some of his former students commented on the importance of these weekly chapel sessions. Bob Moore, News Reporter, WSB-TV, Atlanta stated:

. . . Sometimes speakers were boring. But on Tuesdays, when Dr. Mays spoke, it was crowded. These chapel speeches had great influence on such famous students as Maynard Jackson, Julian Bond, Lerone Bennett, and Martin Luther King, Jr.[37]

Julian Bond noted:

When I was at Morehouse, he spoke to us in chapel and it was like sitting at the feet of a great teacher."[38]

Sere Myers, Sr. Oral Surgeon, Kansas City, Missouri, stated:

At the age of fifteen, my first year at Morehouse, Dr. Mays's speeches sent chills down my spine. He made us feel that if we could succeed at Morehouse, we could conquer the outside world. When he walked among us, it was like a Messiah had entered the room.

He further remembered the wisdom of Dr. Mays, such as:

> Morehouse can prepare you. If you make an A at Morehouse, you can make an A at Harvard. If you make a B at Morehouse, you can make a B at Oxford. . . .[39]

Tobe Johnson, professor of political science at Morehouse, referred admiringly to Mays's ability to drop maxims or quotations that stuck, or his ability to make metaphors work and make people remember them.[40]

President Mays used a variety of techniques to motivate his students in these chapel sessions.

One of his key techniques was to refer to students who had recently graduated from Morehouse and were engaged in graduate study at institutions of higher learning. He would write to the deans or chief executive officers of these institutions to see how the students were performing, and thereby assess the quality of education they had received at Morehouse. After receiving reports on some of these former students, he would say to the students in chapel:

> You remember John Doe who was here a year ago? Well, he is at Ohio State or he is at Chicago or he is at Harvard or he is at Yale. Now I am going to tell you how he is getting along. And then I would talk about this man and his record. I think I inspired and motivated more boys than you know. . . . We used all kind of instruments to stimulate and motivate students and inspire them.[41]

Martin Luther King, Jr., a student at Morehouse from 1944 to 1948, came under the influence of President Mays during these chapel sessions. King would often engage in informal discussions with President Mays; sometimes they agreed and sometimes they disagreed. Occasionally, these discussions continued into President Mays's office.

Mays was also a friend of King's father, Martin Luther King, Sr. Both Mays and King, Sr., were active participants in civic and religious organizations in the city of Atlanta and on the state and national levels. Mays was sometimes invited to the Kings' family home for dinner. These visits, no doubt, enhanced King's exposure to the great educator and his ideas. In retrospect, Coretta Scott King assessed this relationship when she stated:

Dr. Mays had a great influence on Martin Luther King, Jr. Dr. Mays
influenced his decision to become a minister. He was an example of
the kind of minister Martin could become. Dr. Mays was by example
well informed. He was a scholar. Dr. Mays was an excellent speaker.
He possessed great moral principles; was respected by his colleagues.
He was concerned about people and people issues. He encouraged
excellence in your particular endeavor. He motivated all of these young
men who attended Morehouse during his presidency to carry their excellence in their fields and make a contribution to society.[42]

After Martin Luther King, Jr., became well known after his successful leadership of the Montgomery Bus Boycott (1955-1956), he often
referred to Mays as his spiritual and intellectual mentor.[43] Dr. Mays
then began to realize the influence that he had on the most famous graduate of Morehouse College. They developed a friendship that lasted
throughout their lives. Mays reflected on his relationship with his former
student when he spoke at a Martin Luther King, Jr., birthday celebration
at Duke University in 1976. That speech is here (see pp. 103-109). Mays's
eulogy at King's funeral, a masterpiece of twentieth century oratory, is
also included in these pages (see pp. 247-253). Mays influenced an impressive number of other Morehouse students in his tenure as president.
He said to his students during his chapel sessions, "Do whatever you do
so well that no man living and no man yet unborn could do it any better."[44] He reminded his students that, "They could be poor; they could
be black; their ancestors may have been slaves; they may be discriminated against, but still be free in their minds and souls. No man is a slave
until he accepts it in his mind."[45] He counseled social engagement,
civic responsibility, and academic excellence: "Here at Morehouse we
are not just producing doctors, lawyers, engineers, and preachers, we
are turning out men," he said.[46] Mays, through his own life and career
demonstrated that one could succeed in one's chosen goals in life in spite
of seemingly insurmountable environmental factors. He exhibited a model
of his own experiences when he taught.

During Mays's tenure at Morehouse, the civil rights movement,
ranked by many chroniclers as one of the major events of the twentieth
century, spread throughout the South. Beginning in the early 1960s,
students in the Atlanta University Center decided to launch a series of
sit-in demonstrations designed to desegregate public accommodations in
downtown Atlanta. Because of his laudable stature among the students,
the leaders of the movement in the Atlanta University Center decided to

consult Dr. Mays before they launched their plan. He gave his support, and he privately worked with Atlanta's elected officials to bring a peaceful resolution to the desegregation of public accommodations in the city. Later, former mayor Ivan Allen credited Dr. Mays with helping to avoid serious violence during those turbulent days of civil rights demonstrations. He stated in a television documentary:

> I recall very vividly . . . Dr. Mays's advice made it possible for us to come out of these demonstrations unscathed. He helped to keep the lid on Atlanta. We didn't always see eye to eye. We had a few disagreements, but we overcame. He brought me down on three or four occasions. He was right and I was wrong. I took it like a man.[47]

In conjunction with the rapidly expanding social movement, Mays helped counsel Hamilton Holmes and Charlayne Hunter (later Mrs. Gault) when they sought to become the first black students to enter the University of Georgia in 1960. Hamilton Holmes was an honor student at Morehouse College and was encouraged by Dr. Mays and local civil rights leaders, along with Hunter-Gault, to desegregate the university. They succeeded through a federal court order that provided for their admission on January 6, 1961.[48] Both graduated in June 1963 and became successful in their careers. Holmes was elected to Phi Beta Kappa upon graduation, later graduated from Emory University's Medical School, and became a successful orthopedic surgeon at Grady Memorial Hospital in Atlanta. Hunter-Gault became a prominent television journalist; she was a New York-based national correspondent for *The MacNeil/ Lehrer News Hour* for several years. In an act of honor and recognition, the University of Georgia established an annual lecture in honor of the two trailblazers in 1985. They were both honored with plaques during the eighth annual lecture at the university.[49] Twenty-five years later, in June 1988, Charlayne Hunter-Gault became the first black scholar to deliver the commencement address at the university in its 203-year history—this event was symbolic of the drastic changes that took place in the South during the civil rights movement. A manifestation of the continuation of this progress occurred on January 6, 2001, when the University of Georgia held a public program to commemorate the fortieth anniversary of the admission of Holmes[50] and Hunter-Gault as the first black students to desegregate the university. On the occasion the university honored the trailblazers by renaming the academic building, the

Holmes-Hunter Academic Building. A plaque was placed outside of the renamed building to symbolize the spot where their entry took place forty years earlier.

Mays was also among the civil rights leaders who had supported Horace Ward, a Morehouse alumnus, in his earlier attempt to enter the Law School at the University of Georgia in the 1950s, but the federal court ruled against it. Later, Ward graduated from the Northwestern University Law School in Evanston, Illinois; Ward made the highest score recorded on the Georgia state bar examination. He gladly gave his assistance to the legal team[51] in the admission of Holmes and Hunter in their successful entry into the University of Georgia. Additionally, Horace Ward served in the Georgia State Senate and later became one of the first black federal judges appointed in the South under the Carter administration—a position he still holds.

***

These young student civil rights activists of the 1960s personified the kind of struggle against racial injustices that Mays had fought an intellectual battle against all his life. He was a constant foe of racial indignities and once remarked that he came out of the womb fighting against injustice. After being driven out of a dining car in 1923 when he tried to sit at a table reserved for whites only, he successfully sued the Southern Railway Company in 1942. The United States Supreme Court eventually declared segregation in Pullman cars illegal in 1950. Additionally, Mays could not exercise the right to vote until he was 52 years old, even though he had earned a Ph.D. and was a college president. This denial of the suffrage was due mainly to the white primary, declared illegal in *Smith v. Allwright* in 1944, and other devices written into southern state constitutions after the Civil War that denied blacks the right to vote.

In contemplation of times past, Mays told an audience of the American Baptist Convention meeting in Buffalo, New York, in January 1951, "In both the North and South, the church is the most segregated institution in the United States."[52] He firmly believed that discrimination and racial injustice are incompatible with the teachings of Christianity. During the civil rights movement of the 1960s, his former student and friend, Martin Luther King, Jr., registered a similar charge that, "Eleven o'clock on Sunday morning is the most segregated hour of the week."

***

The Morehouse years were the keystone of Mays's career: he was in great demand as a speaker, served on many boards and commissions, and became an advisor to presidents Kennedy and Johnson. After retiring from Morehouse in 1967 (see his commencement address on pp. 163-174), he served as the first black president of the Atlanta School Board, 1969-1981, and developed a close relationship with Jimmy Carter during this period. Carter, the 39th President of the United States, once visited the home of Dr. Mays in southwest Atlanta. Dr. Mays campaigned for Carter in the 1976 and 1980 presidential elections (see Mays's campaign speech in support of Jimmy Carter, pp. 110-115). President Carter often sought his advice on important issues and policies. Carter shed light on this relationship when he asserted:

> His lifetime of experience makes you confident of what he thinks, and what he tells you is indeed the truth. . . . Dr. Mays would send me a copy of his speeches on human rights, international affairs, and discrimination. . . . Sometimes Mays would give me a call at the White House, and later he would visit. Dr. Mays thought that it was good for me politically to emphasize a policy of noninterference with human rights, equality, freedom, and human dignity, not only to the nations of Africa, but to other nations of the world as well.[53]

When the civil rights movement continued to induce social change throughout the South, Mays witnessed the transformation in South Carolina, a place he once feared due to the mob scene and other indignities he observed during his childhood years. But during the 1970s and 1980s, Mays received numerous honors and recognitions of his achievements from his home state. As previously noted, he was elected to the South Carolina Hall of Fame; his picture was hung in the Statehouse; he became the recipient of honorary degrees from institutions of higher learning, and a monument was erected near his birthplace. Other honors were bestowed upon the native son. On three occasions I visited the area where Mays was born and reared, and any reference to the great educator became a source of great praise for him from the local citizens. One local black man remarked to me concerning Dr. Mays, "There is not a finer man to be found anywhere." This great man brought recognition and honor to his community and his state through the national and international honors he received.

Speaking in Greenwood, South Carolina, in 1970, he talked of his desire to disprove the myth of the inherent inferiority of blacks that prevailed during his childhood and urged the community to encourage its young people to be "somebodies."[54] He also summed up his philosophy of life when he stated, "If one man is richer or wiser or has more power than another, he got there either by luck, faith or the grace of God. No man is high enough to look down on another." This idea of the commonality and brotherhood of man is a perennial theme in the speaking and writing of Benjamin Mays.

When Mays was honored by South Carolina on July 12, 1980, he had reached another bell tower in his professional career. As his portrait was unveiled in the Statehouse in Columbia, South Carolina, the Honorable Richard Riley said that he had never seen so many in the Capitol auditorium, except when a new governor was inaugurated. The event was attended by the state's congressmen, state senators and representatives, members of Mays's family, other dignitaries from the state, and friends from across the land. A luncheon followed the portrait-unveiling at the Governor's mansion, and in the evening a banquet held to praise his accomplishments was attended by approximately 1,000.[55] Mays regarded this as one of the great days in his life.

Throughout his professional career, Mays used moral persuasion to attack racial inequities from the classroom, the pulpit, and the board room, and to call attention to the struggle for racial justice, and he used his pen and his voice to launch an unyielding battle against social injustice. He did not espouse violence, yet he taught America the self-redeeming value of forgiveness (see Mays's sermon on forgiveness on pp. 240-246). Mays considered his greatest contribution to society to be his investment in people. As Dr. Mays traveled around the country he often encountered former students, friends, and admirers who had heard him speak in the past. These individuals could often quote from a particular speech Mays had delivered that affected their lives. They could many times cite the time and place of the speech they recalled. These occasions brought Mays happiness and a sense of fulfillment. As a public speaker, he possessed his own unique style. Once you heard him speak, you desired to hear him again, and some of his words of wisdom stayed with the audience for a very long time.

The 1920 Bates College yearbook contained the following statement concerning the oratorical powers of Mays, the graduating senior.

Do you hear that rich mellow tone, that Southern dialect? Who can it be with that enchanting ring to his voice, that clear deliberate enunciation to his oratory. That's Bennie Mays and say can't he speak! If you hear him once you will always remember him.

* * *

Mays suggested two major prerequisites for a successful speaker: a speaker must be sure his message has real content and should say only what he believes. For Mays, this theory embodies the secret of the Gospel of Jesus Christ who spoke of his doctrines as truths.[56]

Mays did not read his speeches; he felt that one who read a manuscript word for word would lose his audience. His excellent memory aided the effective delivery of the prolific orator,[57] and he always maintained eye contact with the audience, using hand gestures whenever necessary. He did not exhibit the traditional emotional style of the Baptist Church of which he was a product. Rather, his remarks contained intellectual content, pragmatism, logic, and conciseness, and he identified with the sentiments, aspirations, needs, and problems of the audiences to whom he spoke. By enunciating certain words and phrases rather than resorting to emotional gestures Mays emphasized his crucial points. His experience in debating allowed him to stress ideas in concise and logical terms and to bring issues to satisfactory closure.

In his speeches, Mays opposed segregation in education and public accommodations. As a minister of the Christian church, he called upon humanity to accept the Lord as Creator and Father and to practice the brotherhood of man. For example, on one occasion in 1963, the famous evangelist Billy Graham stated that there was love between the races in the South. In an answering speech, Mays objected, saying that he was in a better position to speak to that point than Graham. Mays contended that it was in the South where he was slapped and momentarily blinded simply because he was a black rascal trying to look too good; it was in the South where he was almost lynched while riding in a Pullman car; and it was in the South where he had to step backward out of a dining car to keep from being beat up from the rear.[58] Both men, however, later witnessed the transformation of the South from the old to the new.

A seminal study on the oratory of Benjamin E. Mays was conducted by Doris Levy Gavins in 1978.[59] Dr. Gavins conducted interviews with Mays, his former students, colleagues, and associates to evaluate and grasp the substance and style of his oratory. In an interview with Gavins, Mays acknowledged that he never gave a sermon without using phrases or metaphors related to Biblical references, and he also cited works of Biblical scholars. Additionally, in preparation for his speeches, he made use of his own experiences and related them to known experiences of his audiences. He incorporated his educational experiences in psychology, philosophy, and poetry to illustrate ideas in his speeches.

The interviews with Mays's former students and colleagues revealed some perceptions essential to understanding his oratory and style of delivery. Some of these revelations follow:

Melvin Watson, then-professor of religion at Morehouse, viewed Mays as an impressive man—tall, thin with a strong face using passive type gestures, while permitting his voice to provide dramatization.[60]

Wendell Whalum, then-professor of music at Morehouse, said:

His eyes would make one sit up. His face does the work, his hands serve as a necessary extension of his facial expression. One feels the full impact in the raising of a finger, or a change in volume or rate. The voice is soft using a conversational tone.[61]

Samuel D. Cook, a former student of Dr. Mays, and then-president of Dillard University, stated:

Mays uses a concentrating stare, a slight move of the hands, and variation of rate and volume for emphasis. His conservative movement is merely standing on tiptoe over the podium to emphasize a point. He never paced the floor like Mordecai Johnson or used dramatics as Howard Thurman.[62]

Brailsford Brazeal, then-dean of students at Morehouse, affirmed that Mays walked the floor when he had something biting to say. Movement was a sign that he meant business.[63]

Robert Brisbane, then-professor of political science at Morehouse, saw Mays's delivery as unique in that the pauses highlight certain points, he raises the volume and changes his pitch and pace, producing a cadence distinctly different from other good speakers and preachers.[64]

Daniel Thompson, then-vice president for academic affairs at Dillard, viewed Mays's style as the most interesting of modern black orators. He used a historical approach synonymous with antebellum oratorical style. The speaker had to assume that no one could read and write, and the people were constantly tired. The speaker had to keep his speech interesting or everyone would fall asleep.[65]

These interviews reveal the unique style and impact of Mays's oratory. I had the opportunity to hear Mays speak on several occasions and observed his oratorical style as concise, analytical, and germane to the various audiences where he spoke. He possessed an almost perfect sense of timing in delivering his speeches. His addresses for general audiences, sermons, and eulogies lasted between twenty-five to thirty minutes on average, while his commencement addresses averaged about twenty minutes. He was a powerful, credible, smooth speaker, who captured his audience's full attention in the first few minutes and held it until the end.

I had the responsibility of inviting Dr. Mays down to Fort Lauderdale, Florida, when I was employed as a social studies teacher at Attucks High School in Hollywood, Florida, in the early 1960s. I was appointed chairman of the Achievement Committee for my fraternity, Zeta Chi Chapter of Omega Psi Phi Fraternity, Incorporated (Broward County, Florida). Dr. Mays was also a member of the same national fraternity founded in 1911 at Howard University.

The fraternity wanted to continue the tradition of inviting nationally prominent individuals to speak for the annual Achievement Week Program on the second Sunday in November 1960. I suggested we try to get Dr. Mays. After writing letters inviting him to speak in November 1960, he declined, indicating that he had a previous commitment to speak at a college in the Midwest on the date we wanted him to speak. We therefore decided to invite another prominent person to speak for us on that program.

When the 1960 Achievement Week Program was completed, we immediately decided to start planning for the 1961 program. I remained as chairman of the committee for a second year, and again I decided, after a lengthy discussion with the fraternity brothers, to try Dr. Mays; this time we had a year in advance to negotiate. I immediately wrote Dr. Mays, inviting him to be our speaker on the second Sunday in November 1961. I still had to do a great deal of negotiating since he had such a busy meeting and speaking schedule. After a few letters over several months, I persisted, and he accepted. Usually, we had our guest speakers fly in the Saturday afternoon before the specified Sunday because we had a banquet scheduled for Saturday evening. But Dr. Mays wrote back informing me that the particular Saturday was the date of Morehouse's homecoming celebration, and he wanted to spend that day on campus, since he was often out of town on the day of homecoming.

He further informed me that he really didn't like to fly, but I suggested he could fly down the Sunday morning before the afternoon program, which would allow him to attend the homecoming activities on campus. He accepted on those terms. He informed me that he didn't charge for speaking engagements, but he would accept an honorarium of $200, and expenses. We were happy to pay these modest fees.

Dr. Mays arrived at the Miami International Airport about 10:30 a.m., and we drove him to Fort Lauderdale where he delivered his speech at the Dillard High School Gymnasium. Later that afternoon he spoke to an enthusiastic crowd of professionals, parents, students, teachers, church members, and the public from Broward County, for which Fort Lauderdale is the county seat. There were between 800 to 1,000 in attendance. He spoke of the importance of the civil rights struggle and made specific references to the Due Process Clause of the Fourteenth Amendment, with relationship of the struggle of black Americans for first-class citizenship. The audience applauded throughout his speech. When Dr. Mays concluded, he received a standing ovation. He then stood on stage for about forty-five minutes, greeting a long line of admirers, shaking hands, and signing autographs until I approached to escort him to the next event on the agenda, a meeting with the Morehouse Alumni Club of Broward County. He spoke informally with that group for about an hour, updating us on the state of affairs at the college, and stressed the need for increased alumni donations and gathered our names and addresses to keep an updated alumni roster.

Dr. Mays had already decided to stay overnight in Fort Lauderdale before flying back to Atlanta. He said that he didn't like to fly late at night because it would break up the night; I took that to mean that he valued getting a good night's sleep.

After talking with the Morehouse Alumni Club, I drove Dr. Mays to the home of a local minister, Reverend Jethro W. Toomer, who would have Dr. Mays as his house guest for the night. Before I left Dr. Mays with the Toomers, I shook his hand and told him we appreciated his accepting our invitation to come down to speak. He was indeed pleased that such a large crowd came out on a mild and sunny Sunday afternoon to the fraternity's program. I told him they turned out because they had heard so much about his reputation as an eloquent speaker; and they were also informed about his ideas from reading his weekly column in the *Pittsburgh Courier*. When our conversation ended, he got out of the car; I breathed a sigh of relief for accomplishing an important mission—getting Dr. Mays to come down to deliver a speech after two years of very challenging efforts.

Dr. Mays's career, education, and personal experiences prepared him for his unique ability to identify with various audiences. He spoke to the learned and the unlettered, the haves and have-nots, black and white, young and old, northerners and southerners, liberals and conservatives, rich and poor. As a widely read, first-rate scholar, he had a broad perspective on the world's important issues. His own speeches contained in this book demonstrate his command of the issues and the concerns of the audiences to whom he spoke, and his uniqueness as a great orator of the twentieth century.

While a college president, he delivered almost one speech every week, and in the post-Morehouse years, he kept an equally busy speaking schedule. He ceased delivering speeches when he became too ill to accept such invitations; there were occasions when he used a wheelchair and needed to be helped to the podium, demonstrating his resolve. He quit speaking in public, only a few months before his death.

Dr. Benjamin Elijah Mays spoke to Americans about freedom, justice, equality, civic responsibility, poverty, virtue, brotherhood, forgiveness, benevolence, motivation, academic achievement, war, and peace. His speeches are treasures to be preserved.

The representative speeches of Dr. Benjamin Elijah Mays reveal the mind of a man of impeccable moral character, lofty academic achievement, perceptive intellectual insight, and exemplary compassion for the plight of the downtrodden, the dispossessed, and the common man. Throughout his professional career, he articulated society's obligation to make right the wrongs that afflicted its constituents.

Like orators, poets, prophets, and philosophers centuries before, he looked at the world and tried to make sense of the prevailing human condition and the social forces that impacted it. And because of his monumental contributions to race relations, education, and religion, we are now, and will be, spiritually richer, better informed, and more aware of the brotherhood of man and the fatherhood of God. We may never see his likeness again in our life span. Yet his expanding legacy challenges us still in continuing efforts to achieve even higher intellectual and humanitarian aspirations to make America and the world better in the twenty-first century.

Notes

1. Dr. Mays delivered the Benediction after King's spellbinding and historic address.

2. Letter from Elizabeth Douglas, secretary to Congressman John Lewis, November 11, 1997.

3. *Atlanta Journal Constitution*, February 14, 2001.

4. According to a Certificate of Birth issued by the State of South Carolina, County of Saluda, the official date listed on the document certified October 6, 1959, is August 1, 1895. Mays Collection, Moorland-Spingarn Research Center, Howard University.

5. Benjamin E. Mays, "In My Life and Times," September 27, 1966, unpublished essay, Mays Collection, Moorland-Spingarn Research Center, Howard University, p. 1.

6. Ibid., p. 3.

7. Benjamin E. Mays, *Born to Rebel* (New York: Scribner, 1971), p. 1.

8. Freddie C. Colston, "Dr. Benjamin E. Mays: Reflections on an Intellectual Giant of the Twentieth Century," a paper presented at the Benjamin E. Mays Symposium, Bates College, Lewiston, Maine, October 29, 1994.

9. Ibid., p. 16.

10. Ibid., p. 35.

11. Ibid.

12. Freddie C. Colston, "Dr. Benjamin E. Mays: Reflections on an Intellectual Giant of the Twentieth Century," a paper presented at the Benjamin E. Mays Centennial Symposium, October 29, 1994, Bates College, Lewiston, Maine.

13. Greenwood *Index-Journal*, September 7, 1970.

14. *Pittsburgh Courier*, November 12, 1955.

15. Benjamin E. Mays, *Born to Rebel*, p. 53.

16. *Atlanta Daily World*, February 22, 1987.

17. Benjamin E. Mays, "In My Life and Times," p. 8.

18. Ibid.

19. Charles V. Willie, "The Education of Benjamin Elijah Mays: An Experience in Effective Teaching," *Teachers College Record*, Volume 84 (Summer 1983): 958.

20. Dr. Benjamin E. Mays, "In My Life and Times," p. 9. See also by the same author, "Why I Went to Bates," Alumnus Issue, Series 63, No. 6, *Bates College Bulletin*, (January 1966): 1 & 2.

21. Charles V. Willie, Ibid.

22. Mays, *Born to Rebel*, p. 42.

23. *Atlanta Daily World*, October 18, 1941.

24. *Atlanta Daily World*, February 21, February 22, and October 29, 1942.

25. Mrs. Mays died in October 1969 at the age of 69.

26. Mays Biographical Sketch, Revised Edition, 1980, Mays Collection, Moorland-Spingarn Research Center, Howard University.

27. *Pittsburgh Courier*, September 8, 1962.

28. Benjamin E. Mays, *Born to Rebel* (New York: Scribner, 1971), p. 176.

29. *Atlanta Constitution*, March 29, 1984.

30. Ibid.

31. *Time*, December 11, 1944, p. 74.

32. Morehouse College Alumnus, Volume XV (July 1947): 22.

33. *Morehouse College Alumnus, Volume XVII* (November 1949): 16.

34. William A. Fowlkes, "No Ivory Tower President," *Pittsburgh Courier Magazine Section*, October 21, 1950, Mays Collection, Moorland-Spingarn Research Center, Howard University.

35. Charles V. Willie and Ronald R. Edmonds, eds., *Black Colleges in America* (New York: Teachers College Press, 1978), p. 268.

36. Lerone Bennett, Jr. "Dr. Benjamin E. Mays: The Last of the Great Schoolmasters," *Ebony,* Volume 33 (December 1977): 76.

37. WSB-TV, Atlanta, Georgia, "Benjamin E. Mays: Man of Integrity," March 9, 1981.

38. Ibid.

39. Ira Joe Johnson and William G. Pickens, eds., *Benjamin E. Mays and Martha Mitchell: A Unique Legacy in Medicine* (Winter Park, Florida: FOUR-G Press Publishers, Inc., 1996), p. 145.

40. Dr. Dereck J. Rovaris, Sr., *Mays and Morehouse: How Benjamin E. Mays Developed Morehouse College, 1940-1967* (Silver Spring, Maryland: Beckham House Publishers, Inc., 1990), p. 104. See also Benjamin E. Mays, *Quotable Quotes* (New York: Vantage Press, 1983), pp. 3-20.

41. Oral history interview with Dr. Mays by R. Dean Goodwin, August 10, 1974, Atlanta, Georgia (audio transcription), American Baptist Convention Historical Society, Rochester, New York.

42. "Benjamin E. Mays: Man of Integrity," March 9, 1981.

43. See Freddie C. Colston, "Dr. Benjamin E. Mays: His Impact as Spiritual and Intellectual Mentor of Martin Luther King, Jr.," *The Black Scholar*, Volume 23 (Winter/Spring 1993): 6-15.

44. Leonard Ray Teal, "Benjamin E. Mays, Teaching By Example, and Leading Through Will," *Equal Opportunity,* Volume 16 (Spring, 1987): 14-22.

45. Benjamin E. Mays, *Born to Rebel*, pp. 191-192.

46. Teal, Ibid.

47. "Benjamin E. Mays: Man of Integrity."

48. See Charlayne Hunter-Gault, *In My Place* (New York: Farrar Straus Giroux, 1992) for a coverage of this historic and interesting story.

49. *Atlanta Daily World*, November 1, 1992.

50. Hamilton Holmes died in 1995. He was represented at the ceremony by his wife and son—he too, graduated from the University of Georgia.

51. The group also included attorneys Constance Baker Motley, Donald Hollowell, and Vernon Jordan.

52. See *Atlanta Constitution*, March 29, 1984.

53. "Benjamin E. Mays: Man of Integrity."

54. *Greenwood Index-Journal*, September 7, 1970.

55. *Pittsburgh Courier*, August 2, 1980.

56. Ibid.

57. Sometimes, Mays made outlines and spoke from them. On other occasions, he spoke extemporaneously. In his later years, he frequently delivered speeches using 5 x 8 index cards typed in large print, especially when the aging process affected his eyesight. This partially accounts for the fact that all of his speeches are not available in a completely written format.

58. *Pittsburgh Courier*, October 19, 1963.

59. Doris Levy Gavins, *The Ceremonial Speaking of Benjamin Elijah Mays: Spokesman for Social Change, 1954-1975* (Ph.D. dissertation, Louisiana State University, 1978).

60. Gavins, p. 31.

61. Ibid., p.31.

62. Ibid., p. 32.

63. Ibid., p. 31.

64. Ibid., p. 32.

65. Ibid., p. 35

Chapter 2

General Audiences

Radio Address on the Seventy-Eighth Anniversary of Morehouse College*

Morehouse College was founded in 1867 in the basement of Springfield Baptist Church in Augusta, Georgia, by William Jefferson White and Richard C. Coulter, an ex-slave, under the sponsorship of the American Home Mission Society. Enrollment consisted of thirty-eight illiterate adult ex-slaves from Augusta. Then known as the Augusta Institute, its main purpose was to prepare black males for the ministry and for positions in education. In 1879 it was moved to Atlanta, Georgia, and incorporated as the Atlanta Baptist Seminary.

In 1897 the school was renamed Atlanta Baptist College and in 1913, under the new charter, became Morehouse College. It was named in honor of Dr. Henry Lyman Morehouse, corresponding secretary of the American Baptist Home Mission Society, a philanthropist and an avid supporter of the education of black youth. Before the beginning of World War II, the college enrollment numbered approximately five hundred students.

During February 15-19, 1945, Morehouse celebrated the seventy-eighth anniversary of the founding of the institution. The observance commenced in Sale Hall Chapel on February 15 with a recital by the

* *Morehouse College Alumnus*, Volume XIII (March-April 1945): 3-4, Morehouse College Collection, Robert W. Woodruff Library Archives, Clark Atlanta University

famous American tenor, Roland Hayes. On February 19, the Reverend William Holmes Borders, '29, pastor of Wheat Street Baptist Church, Atlanta, and Mr. T.M. Alexander, '31, president of T.M. Alexander and Company, Atlanta, delivered remarks to the alumni. At the alumni banquet, Dr. Will W. Alexander, vice president of the Rosenwald Fund, was the principal speaker.

One highlight of this five-day celebration was President Mays's anniversary broadcast (February 19) delivered from 11:05 to 11:25 p.m. over Station WSB-Atlanta, followed by the Morehouse Glee Club under the direction of Professor Kemper Harreld.

In his radio address, President Mays informed his listening audience that Morehouse was in the process of developing a philosophy of education. Accordingly, Mays maintained: "Morehouse College must develop men sensitive to the wrongs, the sufferings and injustices of society and willingness to accept social responsibility for these ills."

This address, delivered during World War II, proposed the development of good men through college curricula as a possible means of preventing future wars.

* * *

As Morehouse celebrates its seventy-eighth anniversary, it is thinking of a philosophy of education—one that may prove adequate in the turbulent years ahead.

The fundamental defect in the world today is the fact that although man's intellect has been developed to a point beyond his integrity and beyond conflicts between nation and nation, the hatreds between men and men are not exclusively intellectual issues.

It will not be sufficient for Morehouse College, for any college for that matter, to produce clever graduates, men fluent in speech and able to argue their way through, but rather honest men, men who can be trusted in public and private life—men who are sensitive to the wrongs, the sufferings, and the injustices of society and who are willing to accept responsibility for correcting the ills.

It is the function of education, and it shall be the function of Morehouse College, to define the goals of life and to supply the power of motivation to enable students to achieve their goals.

After this war and now, we shall need skills all right, but we shall need spiritual skills as much as, or more than, technical skills. We shall need skills in how to live together in harmony and good will—black men, white men, yellow men, brown men. We shall need skills in how to make it possible for all men and women who are physically fit to work and who have enough character to work, to have jobs.

We shall need skills in human trust and religious faith so that we will not be afraid to live our democracy, nor to walk our Christianity. We shall need skills in how to get rid of selfishness and how to abolish war. We shall need skills in integrity so that men in politics and high office will possess the courage to do right—without fear. And, most of all, we shall need skills on how to develop techniques by which men will not only have the mind to see the good and desire it, but men will possess the will to choose the good and act upon it. Our world is sick today not because we do not know but because we, like Pilate of old, lack the moral courage to act on what we know.

The present crisis is a moral crisis located in the will. Unless Morehouse College and other colleges and universities in America can create skills in these areas, our mechanized civilization is doomed. Morehouse College must help supply these spiritual skills. It will not be the purpose of Morehouse College to produce scholars—experts in science, history, literature, philosophy and religion: these are mere means. It will be the purpose of Morehouse College to develop first of all men: *men* who are scholars, *men* who are experts in science, history and philosophy. The words of J. G. Holland are applicable to our present needs:

> God, give us men! A time like this demands strong minds, great hearts, true faith, and, ready hands; men whom the lust for office does not kill; men whom the spoils of office cannot buy; men who possess opinions and a will; men who have honor; men who will not lie; men who can stand before a demagogue and damn his treacherous flatteries without winking; tall men, sun-crowned, who live above the fog in public duty and private thinking.

The Liberal Arts College in an Atomic Age*

Dr. Mays delivered this address at the inauguration of Dr. Adam Daniel Beittel as the seventh president of Talladega College in Talladega, Alabama. At the time, Mays had served as president of Morehouse College for about six years, and he served as a vice-president of the Federal Council of Churches of Christ in America for two years. The address was delivered at 10:30 a.m. on March 29, 1946, in DeForest Chapel on campus. Attending the ceremonies were members of the student body, college faculty, alumni, members of the Board of Trustees, representatives from thirty-six colleges and universities, delegates from learned societies, members of the college community, and distinguished guests.

Dr. Mays's speech focused on a major issue of the 1940s, the use of atomic energy. The speech followed, by seven months, the dropping of the atomic bomb on the Japanese cities of Hiroshima, August 6, 1945, and Nagasaki on August 9, 1945. President Truman ordered the dropping of the bombs to halt Japanese aggression and bring an end to World War II and to prevent the possibility of continued war casualties and further human destruction. Yet the decision created a discussion of the uses and potentially destructive capabilities of atomic energy.

* * *

Since two atomic bombs were dropped on two Japanese cities, I have heard three eminent scientists speak on the significance of the atomic bomb for our age. I have read statements on the subject by several other scientists. Though approaching the subject in their own characteristic ways, in one thing they all agree: the solution of the world's ills and man's destiny on the earth does not rest wholly in the hands of science. They all agree that if mankind is to be saved from total destruction, man must find a way whereby the peoples of the earth can live together in good will, justice, and peace. They may not admit that man must rely on religion or that he must rely on God, but when the scientist begins to speak of spiritual values, he is speaking about religion. They are all saying that science alone cannot guarantee man's continued existence on the earth.

---

* Reprinted from *The Talladegan*, Volume 43 (May 1946): 1-4, Talladega College, Talladega, Alabama

Science Seeks Religion

This is tantamount to saying that in some way the mind, the heart, the desire, and the will of man must be changed. What a revolution in the thinking of scientists! No scientist would have dared speak like that twenty-five years ago. The three scientists referred to above said in substance that it is up to the church, to religious people, to point the way out of the confusion and chaos in which man finds himself today. Perhaps for the first time in the history of scientific development, science is seeking help outside of its own area. It has discovered or created something that causes even the scientist to tremble.

Mutual Selfishness

There can be no doubting the fact that the unscrupulous use of atomic energy for destructive purposes has created a state of mutual helplessness. No man is any more secure today than another. For example, England can no longer place her trust in her Navy for security nor in her colonial possessions. The English may be just as helpless or insecure as the fifty million untouchables of India. The United States can no longer take refuge in her industrial might nor in the great expanse of the Atlantic and the Pacific Oceans. An American citizen in an atomic age may be less secure than the natives of Africa. A millionaire has no more security than a sharecropper; a Ph.D. no more than an illiterate street sweeper. As Kirtley Mather of Harvard University has pointed out, it is the unanimous testimony of several hundred scientists, including the experts in atomic physics, "that there can be no adequate military defense for us or anyone else against death and destruction from atomic explosions and products of nuclear fission. Nor is there anything we can do to prevent any one of a dozen nations from achieving within a few years the ability to do to us what we have demonstrated we can do to them." This is the state of man in this year of our Lord, 1946.

Interdependence of Nations

Less than thirty days ago, we sat in Columbus, Ohio, and listened with rapt attention to the President of the United States as he addressed the Special Session of the Federal Council of the Churches of Christ in America. The President followed in the footsteps of the scientists. With unmistakable clarity, the President declared that the future of man is not in the atomic bomb. He literally cried out for an Isaiah or a Saint Paul to bring light and hope to a diseased world. Thus, science and government are bewildered and confused and are groping for spiritual values and spiritual insight to lead us to a better day. As Kirtley Mather says in another connection, "We had been thinking that interdependence meant the necessity of acquiring rubber from the East Indies, tin from Malaysia, coffee from Brazil, pineapples from Hawaii, the opportunity to sell typewriters, sewing machines, vacuum cleaners, and zippers in Belgium, China, Peru, and Turkestan. We now know that future peace and prosperity of the United States depend upon the intelligence and good will of the governments and people of foreign lands, as well as upon our own wisdom and good intentions. The interdependence of man, which a few prophets and seers have proclaimed for centuries, is being driven home to everyone with explosive violence.

Education in an Atomic Age

What does all this mean for liberal arts colleges? What does it mean for Talladega? What does it mean for any college or university or technical school? I know of only two ways by which mankind can be improved or made better: one is through education, whether formal or informal; the other is through the impact of religion. Since this is an academic occasion and since only fools rush in where angels fear to tread, I shall attempt to define what it seems to me ought to be the aims and goals of education in an atomic age.

There seems to have been a tacit assumption within recent decades that if the mind was developed and if one was trained to think clearly and logically, sound integrity of necessity would follow. The crisis through which the world has just passed and is passing should banish forever from our minds such erroneous ideas. I make bold to assert that one of the fundamental defects in the world today is the fact that man's intellect has been developed beyond his integrity and beyond his ability to be good. The conflict between nations, the hatred between races, and the ill-will between man and man are not exclusively intellectual issues. We know more science, religion, philosophy, and literature than we have ever known. And yet we stand nearer the brink of a catastrophe than at any period in our history.

The great Socrates was obviously wrong when he advanced the idea that if men knew what was right they would do it. Saint Paul had greater insight than Socrates when he advanced the idea that men do that which they know they ought not to do, and they fail to do that which they know they ought to do. Paul was simply saying that intellect alone is not enough. The trouble with the world lies basically in the area of ethics and morals: the failure of man to recognize any sovereignty beyond himself, any power beyond the state, and a failure to recognize a moral law in the very nature and structure of the universe. At this point, American education stands condemned. In its humanistic, mechanistic, and secularized emphasis, it has led men to believe that they can lift themselves by their own bootstraps and that moral law is wholly relative and a creation of man's mind. Even the great Harvard report, in the final analysis, is nothing but a humanistic document. The goals of education must be defined in terms other than secular.

Good Men the Goal

It will not be sufficient for the liberal arts college like Talladega, or any other college for that matter, to produce men technically trained, clever graduates, men and women fluent in speech, able to argue and think their way through, but rather will be sufficient only when it can produce honest men who can be trusted both in public and private life—men who are sensitive to the wrongs, the sufferings, and injustices of society and who are willing to accept sane responsibility for correcting them.

Teachers and students should be more than good scholars; they should be good men and good women.

Wanted—International Morality

Unless men of this type can be trained in our colleges to assume leadership in the economic, political, and international life, the future of the world is indeed precarious. And I make bold to assert that the time is short. It is one thing to develop men who are sane—so honest, so just, so understanding, so truthful, that they will never want to drop the bomb. Make no mistake. To develop the former without developing the latter is suicidal, and it is like placing a loaded shotgun in the hands of a fool. It should be one of the goals of a liberal arts college to develop the latter without neglecting the development of the mind. We need men of honor and integrity in the industrial world. We need men of honor and integrity in political life. We need men of honor and integrity in education and religion. We need that which, for the most part, we do not now have—an international morality. A morality, for example, which will not encourage Russia to break her treaty with Japan and praise her for breaking it, on the one hand, and then pull our hair and wring our hands when Russia breaks her treaty with Iran. A parent cannot teach its child to lie in one situation and expect it to tell the truth in another.

Sir Richard Livingstone is correct when he refers to our era as an "Age without Standards." He is also correct when he says: "The efficiency of a community will depend on its technical and vocational education, its cohesion, and largely on its social and political education. But the quality of its civilization depends on something else. It depends on standards, its sense of values, its ideas of what is first-rate and what is not. The vocational and social aspects of education are essential, but the most fatal to omit is its spiritual aspect; fatal, because its absence may be long unperceived, and as an insidious disease, a state may suffer from it and be unconscious of its condition till the complaint has gone too far to cure. Our knowledge of the sciences, natural or social, fixes the limit of the course within which the yachts on which humanity is embarked must sail, but does not indicate their voyage, still less supply the wind to fill their sails." It is the function of a liberal arts college to define the goals of life and supply the power of motivation to enable students to achieve the goals.

Spiritualizing Science

As important as are technical skills, and marvelous as are the wonders of a mechanized civilization such as ours, the emphasis is one-sided. In the postwar world, the emphasis must be on the spiritual as well as the material. The natural sciences must be spiritualized. Subjects like chemistry must be more than technical, more than a means of making a living, of increasing our comfort or increasing our profit, and certainly more than a means of destroying humanity. All subjects must be liberalized in the sense that constructive goals must be defined and sought, and these subjects used to enrich life and to make men better. The professor of any subject, whether it is history, English, sociology, mathematics, religion, biology, chemistry, or physics, should know, through study and vicarious living, what the problems of life are and what the purpose of living is. This being true, all teaching should point to ways in which a particular subject can contribute toward a solution of the complex problems of life and ways in which living can be improved and humanity made better.

To this end liberal education should dedicate itself. If such is accepted as the major objective of education, then a hard and fast distinction between technical and liberal education proves to be false. What Sir Richard Livingstone says on this point is pertinent: "Take French. A man may study it in order to be able to order his meals in a French restaurant, or for business purposes; then it is technical education. He, as a man, is no better for being able to talk to a French waiter, or to order goods in the French language. But he may study French to extend his knowledge of the thoughts and history and civilization of a great people; then it is liberal education. He, as a man, is no more complete for that knowledge. Or take carpentering: its study may be a means to making a living or to making furniture or boats or other objects; then it is technical education. He, as a man, is no more complete for that knowledge. But it may also give a clearer eye, a finer sense of touch, a more deft hand, and insofar make a better human being; then carpentering is liberal education."

Skills in Living in Harmony

We certainly need technical skills. But we need spiritual skills as much as or more. We need skills in how to live together in harmony and good will—black men, white men, yellow men, brown men. We need skills in how to make it possible for men and women who are physically fit to work, and those who have enough character to work, to have jobs. We need not be afraid to live our democracy and not be afraid to walk our Christianity. We need skills in how to get rid of selfishness and how to abolish war. We need skills in integrity so that men in politics and in high office will possess the courage to do right without fear. And most of all, we need skills in how to develop techniques by which men will not only have the mind to see the good and desire it, but that they will possess the will to choose the good and act upon it. Our world is sick today not because we do not know but because we, like Pilate of old, lack the moral courage to act on what we know. The present crisis is a crisis located in the will. It is naive to say that our destructive, prejudicial behavior is based wholly on ignorance.

Unless liberal arts colleges and other colleges can create skills in these areas, our atomic civilization is doomed, and we make bold to assert that it ought to be doomed. Talladega College must help to supply these spiritual skills. It should not be the purpose of the liberal arts college to produce scholars—experts in science, history, literature, philosophy, and religion: these are mere means. It should be the purpose of the liberal arts college to develop first of all men: men who are experts in science, history and philosophy. But the end should always be to develop good men.

Why an Atlanta School Suit?*

Founded at the Butler Street YMCA in Atlanta in 1945, the Hungry Club was a weekly public forum luncheon that grew out of an observation made by Dr. Ira D. Reid, then chairman of the Sociology Department at Atlanta University. Dr. Reid recognized that there was no regular open forum in Atlanta where pertinent public issues could be discussed in a desegregated setting. Credit was given to Dr. Reid and Mr. John C. Calhoun, then a city councilman, for getting the organization started. Mr. Warren R. Cochrane, President of the Butler Street YMCA, offered the YMCA facilities and volunteered to help find speakers.

Dr. Reid suggested the name for the forum, the Hungry Club, which gave both food for taste and food for thought. In a telephone interview conducted on February 18, 1999, Mr. William Fowlkes, associate editor of the *Atlanta Daily World* and a founding member of the organization, indicated that the Hungry Club was a place where one could eat a meal and enjoy hearing a speaker for about $4 or $5. It was open to the public and continues to this date.

On October 4, 1950, Dr. Benjamin E. Mays spoke to the group regarding a suit that had been filed on September 19, 1950, in the Federal District Court on behalf of 200 black parents seeking to bring about equal educational facilities in the Atlanta public school system. Dr. Mays served as chairman of the Education Committee of the Atlanta NAACP at the time the suit was filed. The audience for the forum on the school suit included about 350 people, among whom were Auburn Avenue business people, local citizens interested in what Dr. Mays had to say, and students from Emory University, Georgia Tech and the Atlanta University Center. The speech was delivered between 12:00-1:00 p.m. and aired on radio Station WERD thirty minutes later.

* * *

The suit filed September 19th by 200 Negro patrons of the public schools against the Atlanta School Board has attracted more attention and discussion than any other suit in recent years. The suit has been

---

* Reprinted from *New South*, Volume 5 (September-October, 1950): 3-4, Southern Regional Council, Atlanta, Georgia

condemned by the Atlanta Press and some Negroes have condemned it. It is very difficult for people to speak and write on the subject of race with calm and objectivity, especially when the question of segregation is a sacred institution in our native South.

I think it was the great Woodrow Wilson who said that an educated man is one who can lend more light in an argument than heat. It seems to me that since September 19th, we have generated more heat on the subject than light. I hope I can shed light not heat. If I should succeed in helping clarify a difficult issue, I will have rendered my community a distinct service. Whether I succeed or fail, believe me, my intentions are good.

The purpose of this address, therefore, is to give what I conceive to be the motives that lie behind the suit and to place it in its proper perspective. To argue that the suit makes an attack on segregation because the initiators of the suit want Negro children to go to school with white children is to miss the point entirely. Mixed schools is not the heart of the suit. Negroes opposed the curtain and the partition of the dining cars not because they wanted to eat with white people, but because the curtain and the partition were embarrassing to Negroes and because they set Negroes off as inferior persons. This the Negro resented. Eating with white people on the diner was not the issue.

Separate but Equal

The motive behind the Atlanta suit represents the growing conviction, rightly or wrongly, among Negroes everywhere that there can be no equality under segregation—the growing belief that the "separate but equal" theory is a myth. Even the Negroes who argue that the suit was ill-timed are likely to say when talking among themselves that segregation means inequality. There is a growing conviction among Negroes that if one racial group makes all the laws and administers them, holds all the public money and distributes it, it is too much to expect that group to deal fairly with anyone but its own. If a Negro were a part of the policymaking body, the situation might be different—but as things are now, the Negro has grave doubts that equality in education can be reached.

There is also a growing conviction that the gulf of inequality is so wide that in order for the Negro schools to be brought up to the standard of white schools, appropriations for Negro schools must be increased over a long period—beyond the appropriations of the white schools. This would mean that the rate of improvement in white schools would have to be speeded up. The conviction exists among Negroes that the school board will hardly reverse the appropriations in this way and that it would not accelerate the improvement in Negro schools sufficiently to bring them up to the standard of white schools within a relatively short time.

The Negroes who believe this way may be in error, but there is one thing that sustains their belief. The history of segregation is a history of inequality. History seems to be against the idea of "separate but equal."

Supreme Court Rulings

The Supreme Court seems to say as much. It seems to say in both the *McLaurin* and the *Sweatt* cases that segregated education could not be equal. It stated that even if the school at Houston were equal in faculty and facilities, it would not be comparable to the Law School at the University of Texas. The *McLaurin* Case at the University of Oklahoma seems to say something similar. McLaurin's education at the University of Oklahoma under segregated auspices was not adjudged to be equal education.

I am convinced that the emphasis in the Atlanta suit has been wrongly placed. The emphasis has been placed on the phase of the suit which speaks of white public schools being opened to Negroes. The emphasis, if rightly located, would be placed upon the reason why the suit has been filed as it was. It says clearly that the conviction exists that this is the only way Negro children of Atlanta can have equal educational opportunities. The stress is not on mixed schools but on the inequality that results from the dual educational systems. The responsibility, therefore, rests upon those in power to provide equal educational opportunities for all of Atlanta's children. Since our laws plainly say that there must be separation, but equality under separation, it should never have been necessary to file suits anywhere in the South to get what the law provides. The law should have been obeyed from the beginning. Now our own laws and, speaking as a minister, our own sins, are catching up with us.

Comparative Facts

Honestly, I do not believe that it sheds much light on the subject to talk about the great improvements that have been made in Negro schools in recent years without at the same time pointing out the improvements that have been made in white schools in a comparative period. For, after all, in a dual civilization such as ours, which insists theoretically upon "separate but equal," one does not run the race alone. It is always a biracial issue. We should take a second step. After making the comparison and if we find, as we surely will, that the Negro schools are in the main inferior to the white schools, we should find out in dollars and cents how much it will take to equalize the Negro schools.

We should face this problem honestly and courageously. And if a careful, scientific study should reveal that several million dollars are needed to bring the Negro schools up to the white, we should accept the findings in good faith and with good intention. It has been estimated that it would cost the State of Georgia anywhere from $100 million to $175 million to equalize Negro schools. Is the State of Georgia willing to spend $100 million or $175 million to equalize Negro schools? Are citizens of Georgia willing to be taxed for this purpose? If not, what is the solution? Then a third step should be taken. We should find out how long it will take to bring the Negro schools up to the standard of white schools. If it will take ten years or twenty-five years or a century, that would suggest one thing. If it would take two, four, or five years that would be different. We could improve Negro schools for a half century and not make them as good as the white schools. Honestly, democracy and the Christian religion all require that we face the situation with a determination to give every child in Georgia an equal educational opportunity. The burden of proof is upon the South to prove to the world that it can have two separate but equal school systems.

If we believe in the democratic way of perfecting social change, we should be willing to trust the federal courts. This is the machinery which our founding fathers have set up as one of the ways to resolve differences and to adjust grievances. Negroes should not be criticized too severely if they take advantage of the democratic way which our founding fathers have bequeathed to us in the United States Constitution. The Negro has always relied upon the machinery of the law and the courts to gain his objective, the machinery which the white man has created.

Faith in the South

I have another conviction and that is this: when the Supreme Court of the United States hands down a decision, that decision will be respected and obeyed. When the brightest court of the land speaks, the South, like the rest of the country, obeys. At this point, I have faith in my native South. When the United States Supreme Court said the University of Texas had to admit Sweatt, the University of Texas admitted him. When the Supreme Court ruled against segregation of McLaurin, the University of Oklahoma obeyed the court and stopped segregating him. When the University of Virginia barred a Negro in July, the Attorney General said that the action of the University would not stand up in court, and it did not. The officials at the University of Virginia accepted the ruling and admitted the Negro. The Attorney General of the State of Tennessee has recently ruled that Negroes can attend the graduate, the law, and the dental schools of the University of Tennessee. The people of Tennessee will accept the Attorney General's decision. When Day Law was amended in Kentucky, the colleges of Kentucky opened their doors to Negroes. Negroes are in the University of Arkansas by the voluntary act of the university.

When in King George County, Virginia, ten Negro children tried to enroll in the white schools in the fall of 1948 because the King George schools official had not followed a federal court order of the year before to equalize schools, the parents of the children took the official to court. In order to equalize the facilities, the local judge suggested that the white school drop science. The white parents rose up in arms. As a result, the white school got back its science, and the Negroes got a new high school. When the Supreme Court ruled against the curtains and partitions on the dining cars, the South took down the curtains. When the Supreme Court ruled against disenfranchising the Negro, the South permitted the Negro to vote. The South does not flout the decisions of the United States Supreme Court. I have faith to believe that we in Georgia will respect the decision of the federal courts.

If the Negroes were resorting to illegal, unconstitutional, undemocratic means to achieve their rights, they should be greatly condemned. But as long as they trust the peaceful ways of the federal courts, we should be calm and poised and wait with patience the decision of the court. There is no need to be panicky; there is no need for rabble-rousing; there is no time for fear. For when we get through rabble-rousing, the question will still be: can there be two separate but equal school systems?

I conclude, as I began. Let us not confuse the issue. The question is not mixed schools; the question is—can there be equality in segregation?

Our Colleges and the Supreme Court Decision*

Dr. Mays presented this speech at the United Negro College Fund Convocation at the Metropolitan Opera House in New York on March 20,
1955. The Convocation concluded a three-day, fund-raising visit to the
city by the presidents of the thirty-one predominantly black colleges that
comprised the Fund's membership. Dr. Mays's speech came about ten
months after the Supreme Court decision in *Brown v. Board of Education*, May 17, 1954, outlawing segregation in public education in the
United States. His address directed attention to the issue of the new
desegregation policy as it related to predominantly black institutions of
higher learning in the country.

The Convocation Committee that sponsored the fund-raising event
included the Honorable Robert F. Wagner, Mayor of New York as honorary chairman; C. D. Jackson, vice president of Time Life, Inc., who
chaired the committee; and John Foster Dulles, Secretary of State, a
guest speaker along with Dr. Mays. Leontyne Price, renowned soprano,
performed at the event, and the Tuskegee Institute Choir rendered musi-
cal selections for the occasion. Among others making remarks were C.D.
Jackson; Dr. Frederick Patterson, president of the fund; and William J.
Trent, Jr., executive director. Dr. Harry V. Richardson, president of
Gammon Theological Seminary, Atlanta, gave the invocation and the
benediction.

The convocation audience of approximately 3,600 included the presidents of the thirty-one predominantly black colleges, UNCF sponsors,
contributors, alumni of UNCF member institutions, and invited guests.

* * *

Dr. Chairman, Ladies and Gentlemen:

You are sharing with us in tonight's Convocation, an occasion of
great moment . . . one that has been one hundred years in the making. It
goes back to the founding of Lincoln University in Pennsylvania—the
first college for Negroes in the United States, which came into being in
the year 1854. A century later, on May 17, 1954, the Supreme Court of
this land made its momentous decision against segregation in educa-

---

* United Negro College Fund Archives, New York City

tion . . . declaring that to separate some children from "others of similar age and qualifications solely because of their race . . . may affect their hearts and minds in a way unlikely ever to be undone."

You are sharing with us tonight, then, the beginning of a great new century in our history—a day in which the American ideal of equality of opportunity for all of the people has taken on new meaning.

The Supreme Court decision will enable the thirty-one colleges that make up the United Negro College Fund to fulfill the mission which is inherent in their nature. Custom made them segregated institutions. The charters of many of the thirty-one colleges were all-inclusive from the very start. And where circumstances made it necessary to designate restrictions in order for the colleges to be born, steps have already been taken to remove such restrictions.

The vast majority of these colleges were interracial in origin. Devoted, competent, saintly church people, imbued with a sense of mission, graduates of the best colleges and universities in the land, left their comfortable environments of the North, went into the heart of the South and founded Hampton, Virginia Union, Bennett, Fisk, the Atlanta group, Talladega, and the rest. They lived with the Negro students and taught them with great affection and love. They saw their students not as sons and daughters of slaves, but as human beings of intrinsic value, worthy of respect and a chance to develop to the status of full-grown men and women. The faculties soon became integrated, and these institutions have never lost their interracial character.

For more than three-quarters of a century for some, and more than a half century for others, these thirty-one colleges have carried the torch of freedom and interracial good will for the South. When the churches were closed to interracial gatherings, and other institutions were barred against them, it was on the campuses of Negro colleges that Negroes and white people of good will and prophetic insights met to discuss their common problems and to lay foundations which helped to pave the way for the momentous decision of May 17, 1954. So it is the genius of the so- called Negro private colleges to welcome in their confines all classes and races of men. The Supreme Court decision, therefore, will enable these colleges in time—free in soul, heart, and mind, but restricted by custom and law—to do in full force what up to now they have been forbidden to do: open their doors to all qualified students who seek admission.

The May 17th decision of the Supreme Court will, when the climate is ripe, enable these colleges to compete in the open market and be judged wholly on the basis of the quality of their work. The question has been repeatedly asked—what will happen to these thirty-one colleges now that the Supreme Court has declared segregation in the public schools unconstitutional? I make bold to assert that the same thing will happen to these thirty-one colleges that will happen to the other colleges that have practiced segregation for three-quarters of a century. They will be judged on the basis of the quality of their work.

There are only two criteria, perhaps three, by which any educational institution has a right to survive and a right to approach the public for support. The first question is this. Are these thirty-one colleges needed now and will they be needed in the future? The fact that all of them have as many students as they can adequately teach and provide for is sufficient evidence to say that they are fulfilling a need which without them would not be met. The Supreme Court can abolish the legal basis for the imposed segregated existence of the thirty-one Negro colleges, just as it can abolish the segregated character of hundreds of white colleges in the South. But the Supreme Court cannot abolish the educational need nor the desire for an education on the part of millions of young Americans.

There are two and one half million young people enrolled in our colleges and universities. The colleges and universities are just about filled to capacity, and some are overcrowded. Experts tell us that in 1970, fifteen years from now, there will be five million young people in our colleges and universities. Where will we put them? Can we double the dormitories, the teachers, the classroom space, the laboratory facilities, the endowments, and the libraries in fifteen years? It seems logical to say, therefore, that whether segregated or desegregated, all colleges will be needed in the years ahead. The Supreme Court decision cannot abolish the need.

The second test as to whether a college has the right to live is the quality of its work. The regional and national rating boards demand that all institutions meet their requirements before they can be appraised as first-rate. The question is: do these thirty-one colleges meet the standard of excellence as set forth by regional and national rating boards? At the present time they do. Since the need is there and since these colleges meet the standard of excellence required of them, they will survive in the desegregated tomorrow, whether that tomorrow be next year, ten years hence, or a quarter of a century—just how long it will take in the deep South I am not wise enough to say.

I hope I may be pardoned if I point out that these colleges have met the challenge in the past. It is hardly an accident that of the thirty-one college presidents in the Fund, twenty-two of them are graduates of one of the thirty-one colleges and that eleven of the land grant state college presidents are also graduates of colleges in the Fund. These colleges have given to America Booker T. Washington, Robert Russa Moton, Mordecai Johnson, John W. Davis, and Mary McLeod Bethune in education; Howard Thurman, Channing Tobias, James Robinson, and George Kelsey in religion; Charles Johnson, E. Franklin Frazier, and Ira Reid in social science; James Weldon Johnson, Walter White, Frank Yerby, and Langston Hughes as authors and poets; Louie Wright, T. K. Lawless, and Peter Marshall Murray in medicine and surgery; P. B. Young, Robert Vann, Robert Abbott, Carter Wesley, and the Scotts and Murphys in journalism; and James Nabrit, Thurgood Marshall, and Judge Stevens in law. At this very moment, graduates work in our leading universities, including Columbia, Harvard, Yale, and the University of Chicago.

As wonderful as the decision of the Supreme Court is, it cannot remove the fact that at present, and unfortunately for a long time to come, the Negro people will be a disadvantaged economic group. This will be true long after every vestige of legal segregation has disappeared from the American scene. Whether in the North, where no legal segregation exists, or in the South, where it does exist, the economic status of Negroes is far below that of white people. The median income for the white family in the U.S. in 1950, according to the U. S. Department of Commerce, was $3,445; the median for the nonwhites was $1,869. The average Negro family has as annual income of 50 percent or 60 percent of that of the white family.

In Alabama in 1949, the median family income for whites was $2,056, for Negroes $882; in Georgia, it was $2,159 for the white family and $909 for the Negro family; in North Carolina, it was $2,215 for the white family and $1,056 for the Negro family; in South Carolina, the median income for the white family was $2,391 and for the Negro family, $790; in Mississippi, it was $1,614 for the white family and $601 for the Negro family.

Despite tremendous gains, in 1952 Negro wages and salaries were 52 percent of that for whites. Forty percent of all Negro families had incomes of less than $2,000 a year in 1952, compared with 16.5 percent for whites. Only 10 percent of the colored families made more than $5,000 a year, while 35 percent of whites did. Approximately one-half of Negro men and two-thirds of Negro women are still below the semi-skilled levels. Against this, only about one-sixth of the white men and women are. Forty percent of Negro farm families still have incomes of less than $500 a year.

It will take a long time for the decision of the Supreme Court to close this gap. The economic struggle for a Negro boy to go to college is approximately from two to three times as hard as it is for a white boy. Although great improvements are being made in this area, no one would be naive enough to predict that this gap will be closed almost overnight. How long will it take to bring the income of the Negro family up to that of the white family? Here again, I am not wise enough to say. But the time is not yet.

In one of the colleges in the Fund, a survey was made of parents of the students enrolled. In this particular college, and I believe it is typical of the thirty-one, only 14 percent of the parents were paying the student's full bill, and only 22 percent of the parents were able to pay the entire cost of the education of the children. The vast majority of the Negro students, 75 percent or more, must work during the school year and summers in order in order to go to college.

What does all this mean? It means that for many years to come, these thirty-one colleges must set their fees low enough for Negro students to be able to attend. The total annual cost must be kept at $750 or $800 rather than $1,200, $1,500, or $1,800. The low fees will also prove an advantage to many white students. If the fees in private Negro colleges were raised to compare with the fees in the white private colleges, the cost would be prohibitive to a high percentage of Negro students. It will take a long time for a group which started behind in the race of life to compete economically with a group that began the race centuries ahead. I have faith to believe that an understanding American public will not forget this fact when our society is completely desegregated.

Finally, it will be a great tribute to American democracy when a future historian writes that between 1854 and 1900, scores of private church colleges were established mainly to educate the sons and daughters of slaves, but by a certain year in the twentieth century, America had abolished all forms of segregation based on race and color, and that these colleges formerly founded for Negroes had made so great an imprint on American life and were so adequate when segregation was abolished, that students from the four corners of the earth, irrespective of race, were studying within their walls. It will be an exciting and thrilling story. Where else could it happen? Nowhere, except in the United States.

The Inauguration of President
William H. Dennis, Jr.*

On November 3, 1955, in Albany, Georgia, Dr. Mays spoke at the inauguration ceremonies for William H. Dennis, Jr., the third president of Albany State College. Dr. Mays took the opportunity to praise the choice of Dr. Dennis as president, discussing the problems and prospects of the job of a college president in eloquent and concise terms, and drawing heavily on his own experiences as a college administrator. The audience included members of the Georgia Board of Regents, representatives from forty-six institutions of higher learning, representatives from thirteen learned and professional societies, college faculty, students, alumni, community leaders, and friends of the college. At the time, Albany State College was one of several institutions of higher learning with an alumnus of Morehouse College serving as president.

The investiture made by the chairman of the Board of Regents, Dr. Caldwell, expressed gratitude to the citizens of Albany and the vicinity for support and cooperation given to the college in years past.

After Dr. Mays's address, President Dennis presented his inaugural statement. He examined the purposes of higher education in America and the trends in the South, and he outlined his plans for the development of the College.

Dr. William Dennis was educated in the public schools of Brunswick, Georgia, and received his B.A. degree from Morehouse College in 1931. He earned the M.A. degree from Atlanta University in 1942, and he engaged in further graduate study at New York University and Indiana University.

Dr. Dennis joined the faculty of Albany State College in 1946 as an associate professor of education. Prior to his appointment as president of the college, he served as Director of Teacher Education in 1953, and became acting president on July 1, 1954.

* * *

Mr. Chairman, Chancellor Caldwell, Members of the Board of Regents, President Dennis, Members of the Faculty, Students and Friends:

---

* Black College Archives, Florida A. & M. University, Tallahassee, Florida

We have assembled here today, on this auspicious occasion, to inaugurate the third President of Albany State College. We are here, state officials and friends, to certify that we look forward to a bright future for this institution and to assure Doctor Holley that his labors here have not been in vain and to say to Doctor Brown that his years of service are appreciated.

Though I humbly accept the honor to give the inauguration address, I think it is altogether proper and fitting that I should be invited to do so, not because of any merit of my own, but because I, by chance, happen to be President of Morehouse College, the institution from which President Dennis received his bachelor's degree. So an invitation to give this address is tantamount to saying to me, "It is a command. You must." And so that's why I am here.

Once in a great while, I, like other college presidents, engage in the innocent luxury of bragging. In the inauguration of President Dennis today, I am happy to say that he is one of the ten Morehouse graduates who at the present time are serving as presidents of institutions of higher learning in the South, stretching from Washington, D.C., to Marshall, Texas. A total of eighteen institutions have had and have now Morehouse men as presidents.

I hope the audience and President Dennis will pardon me if I take a few liberties in this talk this afternoon. I am going to assume that a man who, by God's grace, has weathered the storm in a private college for fifteen years, whose job it is to respectfully ring doorbells for money from Maine to Texas, and who has passed the half century mark, has earned the right to give advice. My talk this afternoon, though meant for all, was composed with the President in mind. I congratulate you, President Dennis, and the Board of Regents for your being chosen the third President of this institution. It is a high honor, one of trust and responsibility, one that will come to but few men.

I suppose your most difficult task will be in that nebulous area called public relations. But your public will be your students, your faculty and your staff, your Board of Regents, your community, local, state and national, and last, but by no means least, your alumni. In some honest way, without deceit and without hypocrisy, you will be called upon to satisfy all five groups. Although it is humanly impossible to satisfy everybody, every time, the satisfaction must be sufficient to get the job done and to keep a president on the job. Deep-seated dissatisfaction in any one of the five areas could prove adequate to make an administration short-lived.

As I see it, there is no scientific formula that one may adopt that will guarantee good public relations which will satisfy completely all parties concerned. And yet there are a few things which to me are indispensable in good college administration.

The first thing that I suggest is the most difficult to achieve. It would be a mighty fine thing, Sir, if your administration should prove to be one that the Board of Regents, the Governor, the alumni, the community, the faculty, and students would all learn to trust completely not necessarily your intellect, for no man is infallible—not even every idea or program you espouse, for some of them may be too visionary and impracticable— but rather complete confidence in your good heart, your good intentions, your integrity, your intellectual honesty, your wisdom in administration, and your judgment to make wise decisions.

It is not always easy to get students and faculty to trust the administration and not easy to get students to understand that administration and faculty are their friends, not lined up against them. Nor is it easy for an institution to develop a philosophy of education which says more in deeds than in words that this institution is not an organization but an organism where each component part is valuable and indispensable to the whole, just as each organ of the body is valuable and serves the whole. The component parts of an institution must work together, including trustees, Board of Regents, president, deans, professors, students, secretaries, cooks, maids, and janitors. They all must be made to feel that they are important, somebody, persons, not things, and that they are making a fine contribution to the educational program of the college.

This ideal may never be completely achieved. But a program designed to approximate the ideal will bring large dividends in good campus morale and in building up trust and confidence, without which no administration can be wholly successful. It is just as important to keep an appointment with a student as it is to keep one with a dean, with a secretary as it is with a professor; it is just as important to keep your word with the janitor as it is to keep your word with a banker in the town. They are all important. A college cannot run without cooks and the people who keep up the buildings and grounds. The tone for such a campus life must be set by the president of the college.

In dealing with the larger community, consideration, tact surcharged with wisdom, will be needed. The community and your alumni, your friends and your enemies—for you will have both—will be ready to weigh every word you utter and to prove or condemn everything you do. Many of these comments will be favorable and complimentary: when they are complimentary, rejoice and be exceedingly glad, but do not weep too much if you find yourself at times not so favorably spoken of, even when you have done the very best you could do under adverse circumstances; and do not be surprised when the criticisms come from unexpected quarters. A man who cannot take it on the chin should not accept the presidency of a college.

I believe the same principle holds in dealing with the public as in dealing with faculty and students. Tact without deception, complete candor and intellectual honesty in every public relation, and courage, supported by the soundness of your program and the justice of your cause, will bring the school support and friends.

It is my considerable judgment that in your public relations, whether on the campus or off, with students or teachers, with your peers or your supervisors, it is better to be straightforward and honest than to be deceptive and hypocritical. The most important thing confronting any man in high position, whether in private or public life, in education or religion, in business or in politics, is to maintain the integrity of his own soul. I like those words of Henry Van Dyke in the story of the other wise man. When the search seems frustrating and fruitless, Henry Van Dyke makes the other wise man say: "It is better to follow even the shadow of the best than to remain constant with the worst. He who would see great things must often be willing to travel alone."

There will probably be no substitute for hard work and long hours. You will discover to your dismay that you had far less work to do as a professor and far less responsibility to carry. You will more than once yearn for the good old professorial days when you had nothing to do but prepare your lessons, read books and magazines, teach your classes, hold conferences with your students, grade your papers, and serve on two or three committees. Those days will not return as long as you serve in this position. You will have to fight mighty hard to keep abreast with what is happening in the world and to keep intelligently literate and alive.

If things are to hum at this college, you will be compelled to work harder than any of your colleagues on the faculty and staff. A good administrator will surround himself with competent people, if he can find them, and will delegate authority. But you will find that much will be left undone unless you, yourself, follow through on much of that which you have delegated. As good as your teachers and administrative officers may be, you will be a lucky man if you find a few among them who can and will carry willingly great responsibility without the necessity of your having to follow up—lucky indeed if you find a few who will stick with you when the going is tough and risky. When you find such a person or persons, hang on to them with cords of steel and give them every encouragement, for they are rare. These are your true friends.

I am sure I speak for the other college presidents when I say to you that we welcome you to a lonely position. Your concern for the welfare of Albany State College, the budget, the plant, the quality of teaching and student performance, can never completely be shared by your colleagues. You verbalize your concern, and they may verbalize theirs in return, but to actually experience the responsibility which is yours, the disappointment at the slow movement of things, and the seeming lack of serious concern on the part of teachers, students, and trustees, must be carried mainly by you and you alone. It isn't that they aren't fine people. They are. It simply means that people know thoroughly and feel deeply only those things which they themselves actually experience and for which they are responsible. So, today, you are officially and responsibly entering into a new experience in your educational career. In this sense, then, we welcome you to a lonely job. Even most of the campus gossip, good, bad, and indifferent, may reach you last or not at all. Much of this, of course, will be good riddance. Faculty members may even avoid normal social contact with you and yours because they fear they may be accused by their colleagues of courting favors.

I suppose one of the first things confronting a new administrator is to learn his job well and know more about his institution than anyone else: its needs, aims, its role in education, and the place his institution is to play in a society that is ever changing. This is important because whether in private institution or tax supported one, your trustees or Board of Regents will require that you justify every new program you propose, every new building or piece of equipment you request and every salary item you wish to increase, to the dotting of the i's and the crossing of the t's. Their confidence in and respect for you will grow in proportion as they become convinced that they have a man at the head of Albany State who knows his job, is honest and straightforward, and who knows where his institution is going. You must supply the leadership for Albany State College.

The challenge that confronts you does not differ, in broad outlines, from the challenge that confronts all other college presidents. As I see it, there is but one task before you, and that task is to take a good institution and make it the best. And this means that year by year, we all must strive to improve the quality of our students, the efficiency of our teachers, the adequacy of our equipment, and the moral tone of our campus life.

As far as it lies within your power, see to it that you have an adequate plant, building, books, and laboratory equipment, but keep in mind the fact that a college is no better than the men and women who teach in it and who administer its affairs. The plant may be ever so fine and the equipment ever so outstanding, but without competent, consecrated teachers, an institution cannot be first-rate. For many decades now, many of us have played with this thing we call education. Not only have our buildings and equipment been inadequate, but much of our teaching has been second, third, or even fourth-rate. We have been satisfied to do a shabby job. Too many teachers have felt that they had finished their education when they earned a second or first-rate A.B., A.M., or Ph.D. Few articles were read. Few books were read and mastered and no articles and books written. College has taken a sort of a winter resort where students come to have a good time.

Too many teachers require too little of their students. They sympathize unhelpfully with the students whose backgrounds are poor and whose opportunities have been limited. Seldom do they challenge their students so as to make their brains perspire. To use the taxpayers' money or the money from philanthropy to do a second-rate job is dishonest. To play around and not give students a first class education is immoral. It will be hard enough for many when they are thoroughly prepared; it will be trebly hard if they are poorly prepared. In too many of our institutions, social life is far more important than a stiff academic program, and a winning football team purchased at the expense of good education is more important than a Class A rating by the Southern Association of Colleges and Secondary Schools. Your main job will be to make a good institution better, and a better institution the best.

I apologize for reminding you that we are serving a group of people who started behind in the great race of life: two hundred and forty-four years of unrequited toil and ninety years of battling against the odds. So bear in mind that he who starts behind in the race of life must forever remain behind or run faster than the man in front. We started behind in the race of life. Certainly we cannot afford to allow sand to burn under our feet. We must step along. Great progress has been made, and more progress will be made. But only the naive will contend that we have proved our case in American life.

Mr. President, lest you are so deeply depressed by now that you are ready to resign before being officially installed, I bring you good news and glad tidings. Those of us who "squawk" about our hard jobs as college presidents wouldn't give them up for hardly anything in the world. You seldom hear of one resigning voluntarily. The cursed job grows on you. It seizes you, challenges you, possesses you, consumes you, so that you find yourself doing the work as if God sent you into the world at this precise moment in history to do this particular job. It's a thrilling experience. You will find some satisfaction and joy in your work. And these will come from three principal sources.

There will be joy and satisfaction in seeing an idea take wings and a dream fulfilled. As you project your program into the future—one year, five years, ten years, and twenty-five years—you will find some of your dreams coming true, no longer mere blueprints but massive structures; a better faculty, no longer a dream but a happy reality; a more carefully selected and a more serious minded student body, no longer ideas but actualities; and better human relations, not just something to be devoutly wished for but experiences concretized in the town. These accomplishments will bring you satisfaction and joy. They will enable you and your staff to mount up with wings as eagles, to run and not grow weary, to walk and not faint. As you move along, building a greater institution, improving the educational status of the great Commonwealth of Georgia, the state officials will express to you and your staff their sincere gratitude for work well done. Your faculty, students and alumni will tender their appreciation. All these things will warm your heart and make the load easier to carry. But it would be unwise to rely too much upon public acclaim and praise to furnish the momentum you need to do a constructive job. The best inspiration may come from the friendly criticism of your friends and the stumbling blocks placed in your path by your enemies. You will get both. The call to duty, as you see it, must be the motivating factor, whether you receive praise or blame.

Finally, your most satisfying experience may come in creating ideas you will never fully implement and in choosing ideals you will never capture. It is new ideas and ideals that keep one alive. There is nothing more powerful than an idea and nothing so real as a dream. A college presidency, as much as anything I know, has the potentials of keeping a man alive and of keeping before him a vision of the ideal. This ideal can keep you chasing it right here in Albany State College.

In my limited mind, an ideal is something that haunts you, teases you, tantalizes you, keeps you forever dissatisfied with the ordinary, beckons you on to nobler things, but the nobler things are never completely achieved. It is evasive, elusive, slightly deceptive, but honest. It allows no sand to burn under your feet while you lie or sit complacently at rest.

An ideal goes before you, takes its position on a high hill, and calls to those below to "Come on up and possess me." Those below begin the journey with swift feet, to find the spot where the ideal sat, only to discover that the ideal has flown higher, this time to a lofty mountain. Its tantalizing voice is heard again: "Come up and possess me." The travelers strike out again and succeed a second time in reaching the spot where the ideal was. But again the ideal has fled, taking a different position, this time on a mountain loftier than the last—still inviting the weary travelers to "Come up and possess me." The searchers continue the chase but never succeed in capturing the ideal.

Browning describes the ideal in his poem "Andrea del Sarto." Andrea, the faultless painter, had reached perfection in art. Boasting about it, Andrea said: "I have arrived. I do not have to stretch any more. To imagine is to achieve. All I have to do is to pick up my brush and paint." But Browning, sensing the tragedy of satisfaction, makes Andrea del Sarto say: "Ah, but a man's reach should exceed his grasp, Or what's a heaven for?"

Lowell pictures the ideal in dramatic language when he says:

Just beyond, forever burn
Gleams of a grace without return;
Upon thy shade I plant my foot,
And through my frame raptures shoot;
All of thee but thyself I grasp;
I seek to fold thy luring shape,
And vague air to bosom clasp.

Emerson in his poem "The Forerunners" describes the ideal as happy guides but elusive and evasive guides:

Long I followed happy guides,—
I could never reach their sides;
Their step is forth, and, ere the day,
Breaks up their leaguer, and away.
Keen my sense, my heart was young,
Right goodwill my sinews strung,
But no speed of mine avails
To hunt upon their shining trails.
On and away, their hasting feet
Make the morning proud and sweet;
Flowers may strew,—I catch the scent;
Or tone of silver instrument
Leaves on the wind melodious trace;
Yet I could never see their face.

Sidney Lanier socializes the ideal in the "Song of the Chattahoochee."
The ideal is expressed in the waters of the Chattahoochee:

High o'er the hills of Habersham
Veiling the valleys of Hall,
The hickory told me manifold
Fair tales of shade, the poplar tall
Wrought me her shadowy self to hold,
The chestnut, the oak, the walnut, the pine.
Overleaning with flickering meaning and sign,
Said, Pass not, so cold, these manifold
Deep shades of the hills of Habersham,
These glades in the valleys of Hall.
But oh, not the hills of Habersham,
And, oh, not the valleys of Hall
Avail: I am fain for to water the plain.
Downward, the voices of Duty call—
Downward, to toil and be mixed with the main,
The dry fields burn, and the mills are to turn,
And a myriad flowers mortally yearn,
And the lordly main beyond the plain
Calls o'er the hills of Habersham,
Calls through the valleys of Hall.

If we ever catch up with our ideals, if we ever become complacent
and satisfied with second-rate things, if we ever cease to dream and

build air castles for a better college, a better state, a better nation, and a better world, it's time to die.

The beauty of an ideal lies in the fact that it is bound by neither time nor space, circumscribed by neither nation nor race, restricted by neither class nor caste. The Y.M.C.A. developed out of the slums of London. Tuskegee blossoms in the woods of Alabama. Jesus was born in a manger in Bethlehem of Judea. Albany may be as good a place to dream and build as Tuskegee and as challenging as stuffy New York or London. I close with the poem "Goshen."

"How can you live in Goshen?"
Said a friend from afar,
"This wretched town
Where folks talk little things all year,
And plant their cabbage by the moon?"
Said I:
"I do not live in Goshen,—
I eat here, sleep here, work here:
I live in Greece
Where Plato taught,
And Phidias carved,
And Epictetus wrote.
I dwell in Italy,
Where Michael Angelo wrought
In color, form and mass;
Where Cicero penned immortal lines,
And Dante sang undying songs.
Think not my life so small
Because you see a puny place;
I have my books; I have my dreams;
A thousand souls have left for me
Enchantment that transcends
Both time and place.
And so I live in Paradise,
Not here."

The Moral Aspects of Segregation*

Dr. Mays joined William Faulkner and Cecil Sims in addressing the twenty-first annual meeting of the Southern Historical Association on November 10, 1955, at the Peabody Hotel in Memphis, Tennessee. Historians, writers, students, researchers, and invited guests constituted the audience.

William Faulkner of Oxford, Mississippi, a Nobel Prize-winning novelist who was strongly opposed to segregation, spoke to the crowded, racially mixed group. He was one of three panelists who gave remarks on the previous 1954 Supreme Court's decision at the Phi Theta banquet climaxing the first day of the annual meeting. Mr. Cecil Sims, a lawyer from Nashville, presented the legal point of view on the issue, while Dr. Mays, president of Morehouse College, gave remarks from a sociological and moral perspective.

In his remarks, Dr. Mays made the compelling assertion, "No group is wise enough, good enough, to restrict the mind, circumscribe the soul, and to limit the physical movement of another group. To do this is blasphemy." His overall argument claimed segregation as immoral, and he provided a compelling set of reasons to support his claim of immorality.

Some friends of the educator feared for his life after such a provocative attack on the status quo in race relations in the South, but no acts of violence occurred against him. It is a great testament to his wisdom and courage that he said what he honestly believed, in the face of implicit threats to his personal safety.

* * *

Whenever a strong dominant group possesses all the power, political, educational, economic, and wields all the power; makes all the laws, municipal, state and federal, and administers all the laws; writes all constitutions, municipal, state and federal, and interprets these constitutions; collects and holds all the money, municipal, state, and federal, and distributes all the money; determines all policies for government, business, political, and education; when that group plans and places heavy

---

* Reprinted from Bradford Daniel, ed., *Black, White, and Gray: Twenty-one Points on the Race Question* (New York: Sheed and Ward, 1964), pp. 170-176

burdens, grievous to be borne, upon the backs of the weak, that act is immoral. If the strong group is a Christian group or a follower of Judaism, both of which contend that God is creator, judge, impartial, just, universal, love and that man was created in God's image, the act is against God and man—thus immoral. If the strong group is atheistic, the act is against humanity—still immoral.

No group is wise enough, good enough, strong enough, to assume an omnipresent and omniscient role; no group is good enough, wise enough to restrict the mind, circumscribe the soul, and to limit the physical movement of another group. To do this is blasphemy. It is a usurpation of the role of God.

If the strong handicap the weak on the grounds of race or color, it is all the more immoral because we penalize the group for conditions over which it has no control, for being what nature or nature's God made it. And that is I believe tantamount to saying to God, "You made a mistake, God, when you didn't make all races white." If there were a law which said that an illiterate group had to be segregated, the segregated group could go to school and become literate. If there were a law which said that all people with incomes below $5,000 a year had to be segregated, the people under $5,000 a year could strive to rise above the $5,000 bracket. If there were a law which said that men and women who did not bathe had to be segregated, they could develop the habit of daily baths and remove the stigma. If there were a law which said that all groups had to be Catholic, the Jews and Protestants could do something about it by joining the Catholic Church. But to segregate a man because his skin is brown or black, red or yellow, is to segregate a man for circumstances over which he has no control. And of all immoral acts, this is the most immoral.

So the May 17, 1954, decision of the United States Supreme Court and all the decisions against segregation are attempts on the part of the judges involved to abolish a great wrong, which the strong have deliberately placed upon the backs of the weak. It is an attempt on the part of federal and state judges to remove this stigma, this wrong, through constitutional means, which is the democratic, American way.

I said a moment ago that if the strong deliberately pick out a weak racial group and places upon it heavy burdens, that act is immoral. Let me try to analyze this burden, segregation, which has been imposed upon millions of Americans of color. There are at least three main reasons for legal segregation in the United States.

1. The first objective of segregation is to place a legal badge of inferiority upon the segregated, to brand him as unfit to move freely among other human beings. This badge says the segregated is mentally, morally, and socially unfit to move around as a free man.

2. The second objective of segregation is to set the segregated apart so that he can be treated as an inferior: in the courts, in recreation, in transportation, in politics, in government, in employment, in religion, in education, in hotels, in motels, restaurants, and in every other area of American life. And all of this has been done without the consent of the segregated.

3. The third objective of legalized segregation follows from the first two. It is designed to make the segregated believe that he is inferior, that he is nobody, and to make him accept willingly his inferior status in society. It is these conditions which the May 17, 1954 decision of the Supreme Court and other federal decisions against segregation are designed to correct—to remove the immoral stigma that has been placed upon 16 million Negro Americans, as these are the reasons every thinking Negro wants the legal badge of segregation removed, so that he might be able to walk the earth with dignity, as a man, and not cringe and kotow as a slave. He believes that this is his God-given right on the earth.

Segregation is immoral because it has inflicted a wound upon the soul of the segregated and so restricted his mind that millions of Negroes now alive will never be cured of the disease of inferiority. Many of them have come to feel and believe that they are inferior in that the cards are so stacked against them that it is useless for them to strive for the highest and the best. Segregate a race for ninety years, tell that race in books, in law, in courts, in transportation, in hotels and motels, in the government that it is inferior—it is bound to leave its damaging mark upon the souls and minds of the segregated. It is these conditions that the federal courts seek to change.

Any country that restricts the full development of any segment of society retards its own growth and development. The segregated produces less, and even the minds of the strong group are circumscribed because they are often afraid to pursue the whole truth and because they spend too much time seeking ways and means of how to keep the segregated group in "its place." Segregation is immoral because it leads to unjust brutality and lynching on the part of the group that segregates. The segregated is somebody who can be pushed around as desired by the segregator. As a rule, equal justice in the courts is almost impossible for a member of the segregated group if it involves a member of the group imposing segregation. The segregated has no right that the segregator is bound to respect.

The chief sin of segregation is the distortion of human personality. It damages the soul of both the segregator and the segregated. It gives the segregated a feeling of inherent inferiority which is not based on facts, and it gives the segregator a feeling of superiority which is not based on facts. It is difficult to know who is damaged more—the segregated or the segregator.

It is false accusation to say that Negroes hail the May 17, 1954, decision of the Supreme Court because they want to mingle with white people. Negroes want segregation abolished because they want the stigma of inferiority removed and because they do not believe that equality of educational opportunities can be completely achieved in a society where the law brands a group inferior. When a Negro rides in an unsegregated Pullman, he does it not because he wants to ride with white people. He may or may not engage in conversations with white people. He wants good accommodations. When he eats in an unsegregated diner on the train, he goes in because he is hungry and not because he wants to eat with white people. He goes to the diner not even to mingle with Negroes but to get something to eat. But as he eats and rides, he wants no badge of inferiority pinned on his back. He wants to eat and ride with dignity. No Negro clothed in his right mind believes that his social status will be enhanced just because he associates with white people.

It is a false accusation to say that Negroes are insisting that segregated schools must be abolished today or tomorrow, simultaneously all over the place. As far as I know, no Negro leader has ever advocated that, and they have not even said when segregation is to be a finished job. They do say that the Supreme Court is the highest law of the land and that we should respect that law. Negro leaders do say that each local community should bring together the racial groups in that community, calmly sit down, and plan ways and means, not how they can circumvent the decision, but how they can implement it and plan together when and where they will start. They will be able to start sooner in some places than in others and move faster in some places than in others, but begin the process in good faith and with good intent. To deliberately scheme, to deliberately plan through nefarious methods, through violence, boycott, and threats to nullify the decision of the highest law in the land is not only immoral, but it encourages disregard for all laws which we do not like.

We meet the moral issues again. To write into our constitutions things that we do not intend to carry out is an immoral act. I think I am right when I say that most of our states, certainly some of them, say in their constitutions "separate but equal." But you know as well as I do that on the whole, the gulf of inequality in education has widened with the years. There was no serious attempt nor desire in this country to provide Negroes with educational opportunities equal to those for whites. The great surge to equalize educational opportunities for Negroes did not begin until after 1935, when Murray won his suit to enter the law school of the University of Maryland. It is also clear that the millions poured into Negro education in the last twenty years were appropriated not so much because it is right, but in an endeavor to maintain segregation.

We brought this situation upon ourselves. We here in the South have said all along that we believe in segregation but equal segregation. In 1896 in the Louisiana case, *Ferguson v. Plessy*, the United States Supreme Court confirmed the doctrine "separate but equal." When Murray won his case in 1935, we knew we had to move toward equalization. Since 1935, many suits have been won.

It would have been a mighty fine thing if we had obeyed the Supreme Court in 1896 and equalized educational opportunities for Negroes. If we had done that, the problem would have been abolished, and we would have been saved from the agony and fear of the hour. We didn't obey the Supreme Court in 1896, and we do not want to obey it now.

Let me say again that the May 17, 1954, decision of the Supreme Court is an effort to abolish a great evil through orderly processes. And we are morally obligated to implement the decision or modify the federal constitution and say plainly that this constitution was meant for white people and not Negroes. Tell the world honestly that we do not believe the part of the Declaration of Independence which says, in essence, that all men are created equal, that they are endowed by their creator with certain inalienable rights, that among these are life, liberty, and the pursuit of happiness.

We are morally obligated to abolish legalized segregation in America or reinterpret the Christian Gospel, the Old and New Testaments, and make the Gospel say that the noble principles of Judaism and Christianity are not applicable to colored peoples and Negroes. Tell the world honestly and plainly that the fatherhood of God and the brotherhood of man can work where the colored races are involved. We are morally obligated to move toward implementing the decision in the deep South or lose our moral leadership in the world. If we do not do it, we must play the role of hypocrite, preaching one thing and doing another. This is the dilemma which faces our democracy.

The eyes of the world are upon us. One billion or more colored people in Asia and Africa are judging our democracy solely on the basis of how we treat Negroes. White Europe is watching us too. I shall never forget the day in Lucknow, India, when nine reporters from all over India questioned me ninety minutes about how Negroes are treated in the United States. I shall remember to my dying day the event in 1937, when the principal of an "untouchable" school introduced me to his boys as an "untouchable" from the United States. At first it angered me. But on second thought, I knew that he was right. Though great progress has been made, for which I am grateful, I and my kind are still untouchables in many sections of the country. There are places where wealth, decency, culture, education, religion, and position will do no good if one is a Negro. None of these things can take away the mark of untouchability. And the world knows this.

Recently a group of colored students from Asia, Africa, the Middle East, and South America were visiting an outstanding Southern town. All the colored people except those from Africa and Haiti could live in the downtown hotels. The Africans and Haitians had to seek refuge on the campus of a Negro college. That incident was known to all other colored students and it will be told many times in Europe, Asia, Africa—and it will not help us in our efforts to democratize the world.

Not long ago a Jew from South Africa and a man from India were guests of a Negro professor. He drove them for several days through the urban and rural section of the state. The Negro, the host, a citizen of the United States, could not get food from the hotels and restaurants. His guests, one a Jew and the other an Indian, had to go in and buy food for him. The man who introduced me in India as an untouchable was right. The Negro in America is untouchable.

Two or three years ago, a friend of mine was traveling in Germany. He met a German who had traveled widely in the United States. He told my friend that he hangs his head in shame every time he thinks what of his country did to the Jews—killing six million of them. But he told my friend that after seeing what segregation has done to the soul of the

Negro in the South, he has come to the conclusion that it is worse than what Hitler and his colleagues did to the Jews in Germany. He may be wrong, but this is what he is telling the people in Germany.

Make no mistake—as this country could not exist half slave and half free, it cannot exist half segregated and half desegregated. The Supreme Court has given America an opportunity to achieve greatness in the area of moral and spiritual things, just as it has already achieved greatness in military and industrial might and in material possessions. It is my belief that the South will accept the challenge of the Supreme Court and thus make America and the South safe for democracy.

If we lose this battle for freedom for 15 million Negroes we will lose it for 145 million whites, and eventually we will lose it for the world. This is indeed a time for greatness.

Carolina Symposium on Public Affairs*

Dr. Mays delivered this address at the University of North Carolina in Chapel Hill on March 11, 1956, almost two years after the Supreme Court adjudicated the *Brown v. Board of Education* decision outlawing segregation in public education in the United States. The audience included university administrators, faculty, students, alumni, guests, and local townspeople.

The symposium involved a week-long schedule of activities, March 11-16. The events commenced on Sunday evening at 8:00 p.m. in Memorial Hall on a campus that was filled to capacity. Dr. Mays was one of three speakers who spoke on the first evening of the program; the others were A. (Pete) McKnight and William Fletcher Womble. The speakers focused on the topic: "The Supreme Court's Challenge to the South: A Progress Report."

Dr. Mays used his extensive knowledge of black history in presenting a discussion of the legal and historical background of the *Brown v. Board of Education* decision. He cited several court cases that led to the landmark decision.

* * *

Really, the history of the May 17, 1954, decision of the Supreme Court declaring segregation in the public schools unconstitutional reaches back to 1619, when the first slaves landed in this country in Jamestown, Virginia. For 200 hundred years or more, the Negro was not a problem. He became a problem when agitation began for his emancipation in the first half of the nineteenth century. He was not a problem because he was not a legal person. He was chattel—like cats and dogs, horses and mules, houses and land—to be bought and sold at the will of the master.

The Negro became a real problem in 1865. Chattel slavery was over. The Negro could not be used in that capacity any longer, so as a free man he became a problem, no longer wanted. There were at least four proposals: send them to Africa; colonize them; leave them alone and they will die out, for they will never be able to compete in this complex American civilization. It is fair to say that this proposal was never taken

---

* Mays Collection, Moorland-Spingarn Research Center, Howard University

seriously. The fourth proposal was to segregate them and educate them unequally.

Africa and colonization proved impracticable. The Negro multiplied instead of dying. So, soon after emancipation, the various movements arose designed to segregate the newly emancipated people. I think it is fair to say that segregation is the only program that this country has ever strongly considered for the Negro. Segregate him by law in the South, and segregate him by custom in the North. Unlike other racial and cultural groups from Europe, it has not been the purpose for the Negro to become integrated into the totality of American life. The basic program for the Negro has been one of separation.

Let me say here, in order to keep the Negro straight, that it is historically inaccurate to say what some writers and speakers are saying, that the Supreme Court is upsetting a way of life that has been centuries in the making. In my calculation, we cannot include the slave era which ended in 1865. It must be the segregated way of life, which began approximately, in some areas, ninety years ago. Let me trace briefly the history of segregation in the South, including disenfranchisement. Around 1868 and 1869, the Reconstruction Constitutions of the southern states, under northern supervision, extended the ballot to the Negro. Between 1877 and 1890, local means were employed in the South to keep the Negro from voting. Beginning with 1890, the southern states began to adopt constitutional amendments to restrict Negro suffrage. Mississippi took the lead in 1890. South Carolina followed in 1895, Louisiana in 1898, North Carolina in 1900, Alabama in 1901, and Georgia in 1908. By 1912, the Negro in the great majority of the southern states had been completely disfranchised.

By 1899, the cruel, iron hand of segregation had settled upon the Negro as a great nightmare, stigmatizing the race with the badge of inferiority. Beginning with Tennessee in 1881 and ending with Oklahoma in 1907, fourteen southern states had segregated Negro passengers on the railroad. Beginning with West Virginia in 1863 and ending with Delaware in 1875, sixteen states had separate education for Negroes and whites. By 1899, no one dared challenge segregation.

So you see that it was not until 1907, forty-nine years ago, when segregation on the railroad was an accomplished fact in Oklahoma. The ballot was legally taken from the Negro in Georgia in 1908. He regained it through the federal courts in 1946. So you see, the Negro was deprived of the ballot in Georgia for only thirty-six years. Segregation in the public schools in some areas is only eighty-one years old, the longest ninety-two years old. Let me say again, then, that segregation as a legal institution is less than one hundred years old.

Let me move now into what I consider to be the most serious part of this brief, inadequate history leading up to the May 17, 1954, decision of the Supreme Court. Although I did not have time to check the state constitutions of the southern states, I think it is safe to say that all of them make some reference to equality before the law through stipulating segregation for Negroes and whites. The doctrine "separate but equal" became famous and was confirmed by the Supreme Court in a transportation suit in 1896 in the case of *Plessy v. Ferguson.*

It is unfortunate to have on record the fact that though the various state constitutions call for racial equality under the law and the Supreme Court confirmed the doctrine of "separate but equal" in 1896, there was no serious effort put forth to equalize educational opportunities for Negroes until suits began to be filed in the courts, beginning in 1936. In other words, the southern states, for the most part, did not obey the United States Supreme Court in transportation or education. From 1896 to 1936, a period of thirty-nine or forty years, little, if anything, was done to equalize educational opportunities for Negroes in the South. Let me document this statement. Thirteen southern states in the school year 1918-19 spent $12.91 per capita for each white child of school age, $4.42 for each Negro child—a difference of $8.49. In the school year 1924-25, these thirteen states spent $27.95 per capita for each white child of school age, for the Negro child $9.52—a difference of $18.43. In 1931, these thirteen states were spending per capita for each white child of school age $40.92, for the Negro child $15.78—a difference of $25.14. In other words, from 1919 up to 1931, the per capita expenditure for the white child increased $28.01; for the Negro child, $11.36. So, dollar wise, the gap of inequality widened instead of closing.

. . . If we here in the South had begun in 1896 to try to equalize educational opportunities for Negroes, the May 17, 1954, decision of the Supreme Court would have taken a different complexion, and the decision would have been more acceptable to the South. The situation which we face now is due in part to our failure to obey the decision of 1896 and a failure on our part to obey our state constitutions, laws which we ourselves made.

The 1896 decision was not challenged until 1935, when Murray sued to enter the law school of the University of Maryland. The great strides taken to equalize educational opportunities for Negroes were taken within the last twenty-five years, resulting mostly from court decisions that the "separate" must be made "equal." Of course, many communities moved to equalize educational opportunities and facilities without being sued, because it soon became evident that if inequality was found to be based on race or color, the suit could and would be won in federal court.

Murray won his suit in the courts of Maryland to enter the law school of the university of that state. This was a clear warning to state universities and to the public school systems of the South that they had to get busy to equalize salaries, educational opportunities, and facilities if segregation were to be maintained.

The next important case in the separate but equal doctrine was *Gaines v. Canada* in 1938. In the Gaines case, the Supreme Court made it clear that a state cannot meet its obligations to Negro students by giving them out-of-state scholarships; it can only do so by providing equal opportunity for education within its own borders. To meet the demands of the Supreme Court, the state of Missouri opened a separate law school for Negroes in St. Louis. Following the Missouri pattern, segregated law schools for Negroes were established in Louisiana, North Carolina, and South Carolina. It was attempted in Oklahoma and Texas. In the meantime, Negroes began to win suits against local school boards whereby the federal courts ordered local school boards to equalize educational opportunities on a segregated basis. So within the past twenty years, great progress has been made in this direction.

The next most significant case was that of Miss Lois Sipuel (later Mrs. Fisher). She sought admission to the law school of the University of Oklahoma and was denied. She appealed to the federal court. After several years of litigation, the Supreme Court settled the Fisher case in 1948 by ordering the state of Oklahoma to provide Mrs. Fisher with equal educational opportunities within its borders "and to do so as soon as it did for applicants for any other group." This was tantamount to saying that no further white students could enter the university law school until Mrs. Fisher was admitted. The state knew that they could not provide a law school for Mrs. Fisher equal to the one at the University of Oklahoma in the time required, so she was admitted to the University of Oklahoma.

Two more significant cases must be reviewed in this history, another one in Oklahoma and in Texas. In *G. W. McLaurin, appellant, v. Oklahoma State Regents for Higher Education*, the federal court ruled that

the university had to admit McLaurin and provide him with the education he sought as soon as it provided that education for applicants of any
other group. The court said further that "to the extent that Oklahoma
statutes denied him admission, they were unconditional and void." The
Oklahoma legislature amended these statutes to permit Negroes to enroll
in the institutions of higher learning attended by white students if the
courses were not available in Negro institutions. The amendment said,
however, that the instruction had to be on a segregated basis.

McLaurin was admitted on a segregated basis and was required "to
sit apart at a designated desk in an anteroom adjoining the classroom; to
sit at a desk on the mezzanine floor of the library, but not to use the desk
in the regular reading room, and to sit at the designated table and to eat
at a different time from the other students in the school cafeteria."

The applicant objected to such treatment and filed a motion to modify
the order and judgment of the district court. The court held that such
treatment did not violate the 14th Amendment. An appeal followed, and
in the interim, the treatment afforded McLaurin was altered. For a while
the section of the classroom in which the appellant sat was surrounded
by a rail on which there was a sign—"reserved for coloreds." Later, this
was taken away, and he was assigned a seat in the classroom in a row
specified for colored students, given a table on the main floor of the
library, and permitted to eat at the same time in the cafeteria as the white
students but assigned a special table.

The Supreme Court finally ruled in 1950 that once the University of
Oklahoma had admitted McLaurin, he must receive the same treatment
at the hands of the state as students of other races.

In the same year, 1950, the Supreme Court ruled on the Sweatt case.
His application was rejected. He sued. The state in the meantime provided a law school, for Sweatt refused to enroll in the segregated law
school. The Sweatt case came nearer to striking down segregation than
any other case prior to May 17, 1954. The Supreme Court said that
whether the University of Texas Law School is compared with the original or new law school for Negroes, we cannot find substantial equality in
the educational opportunities offered white and Negro law students by
the state. In terms of number of the faculty, variety of courses and opportunity for specialization, size of student body, scope of library, avail-
ability of Law Review and similar activities, the University of Texas
Law School possesses to a far greater degree those qualities which are
incapable of objective measurement but which make for greatness in a

law school. Such qualities, to name but a few, include: reputation of the faculty, experience of the administration, position and influence of the alumni, standing in the community, traditions, and prestige. It is difficult to believe that one who had a free choice between these law schools would consider the question closed.

The forerunner of the May 17, 1954, decision of the Supreme Court was the Clarendon County (South Carolina) case where a dissenting judge ruled that segregation per se is unconstitutional. The five cases outlawing segregation in the public schools on May 17, 1954 were: Clarendon County, South Carolina: Prince Edward County, Virginia; Topeka, Kansas; Wilmington, Delaware; and the District of Columbia.

In concluding these cases, the Supreme Court ruled on May 17, 1954 "that in the field of public education the doctrine of 'separate but equal' has no place."

As for now, every southern state has admitted Negroes to state universities except South Carolina, Georgia, Alabama, Florida, and Mississippi. It is unfortunate, though, that in the other southern states except Kentucky and Arkansas, Negroes were admitted as a result of court orders, including the University of North Carolina; that outside of the deep South, desegregation in public schools is moving forward. Segregation is also out of the dining cars, in interstate travel, and in the armed forces.

Interestingly enough, the Supreme Court gave the South what some southern states requested. It did not uproot segregation overnight, as some people would believe. It set no specific time when desegregation was to begin, no specific time when desegregation must be an accomplished fact, and left the implementation to the District Court. The Supreme Court simply says in essence that the job of desegregation should be taken and completed in good faith and with honest intent within reasonable time. We are not being unduly coerced.

May I say in closing that it is also discouraging and deeply to be regretted that in almost every case, top Negro leadership in the various communities have been ignored, and they have not been asked to help the school boards to plan ways and means of implementing the decision.

The Unfinished Task*

This challenging and provocative speech was delivered by Dr. Mays before an estimated crowd of 1,500 in Sisters Chapel on the Spelman College campus on December 26, 1956. According to Dr. Dellie L. Boger, a professor at Morehouse and a member of the Kappa Alpha Psi Fraternity, writing in the *Kappa Alpha Psi Journal* in February 1957, "This public program was conducted at the forty-six Grand Meeting of the Kappas' convention held jointly with the Alpha Kappa Alpha Sorority and was an enjoyable and thrilling success." Following his address, Dr. and Mrs. Mays held a reception for the Grand Chapter in the lounge of the Chemistry Building on the Morehouse College campus.

Dr. Mays declared, "Our task is to improve the human product." Mays saw this as the challenge for education and religion.

* * *

I am defending the thesis tonight that we of this generation know more facts, and we have more accumulated knowledge than our ancestors knew we had, and that our minds are better trained than theirs. Our most outstanding scholars are more learned than the top scholars of past ages.

Our geniuses in mathematics know more about calculus than Newton and Leibniz, who invented it. Our modern atomic and hydrogen physicists, Niels Bohr, the late Albert Einstein, and Max Planck, knew more physics and chemistry than the physicists and chemists of ancient days. Our great minds in biology know more about evolution and life than Darwin and Mendel. Our brilliant economists are better versed in economics than Karl Marx, the God of the communists, and leading sociologists know more about society and population trends than Malthus.

They Could Learn

If Plato, Socrates, and Aristotle were suddenly raised from the dead, they could learn a great deal sitting at the feet of our eminent philoso-

---

* Reprinted from Kappa Alpha Psi Fraternity, *The Journal*, Volume 43, No. 1 (February 1957): 7- 12.

phers in our great universities. Certainly our experts in religion and theology are much better trained than the prophets of the 8th and 7th centuries—better trained than Amos and Moses, Micah and Malachi, Isaiah and Jeremiah. They have more formal training than Jesus and Paul.

We have the highest rate of literacy in history. We have more schools, colleges and universities, professional schools, than any previous era. In fact, we are the most degreed people in all history: A.B.s, A.M..s, Ph.D.s, M.D.s, D.D.S.s, D.S.s, LL.D.s, Litt.D.s, all kind of Ds. There is no doubting the fact that we know more than our ancestors.

Our Scientific Era

When it comes to applied sciences, we know more than our forefathers. We walk and run faster than they walked and thought. They were making good speed when they traveled six miles an hour in a buggy or wagon. Today, in an automobile, a sane man can drive sixty miles an hour; an insane man can drive ninety. It took Columbus sixty-nine days to cross the Atlantic, but we make it today in five days on *Queen Mary* and *Elizabeth* and less than five on the *W. S. United States*. It took Magellan many months to circumvent the globe. We do it now in three days.

Science has extended our arms. We throw and shoot farther than our ancestors. Within a few hours, we carry a bomb across the Pacific and kill thousands in Nagasaki and Hiroshima. And the bombs of 1956 are far more deadly than the bombs of ten years ago. One hundred scientists told us this past summer that radioactivity can cause an increase in cancer, can increase the number of deformed children, can reduce the life span and destroy the human race if testing of nuclear weapons ever became unlimited. On October 25, 1956, the Federation of American Scientists reaffirmed this conviction in the *New York Times*. Science has extended our ears. We hear farther than our forefathers. We gather the news in an instant from around the world: Tokyo, Cairo, Paris, New York. Science has extended our eyes. We can see farther than our foreparents could see. The telescope has revealed planets millions of miles away, and with the microscope we can see what the naked eye could never see. Through television, events happening hundreds of miles away are brought home to us in our parlors. Our muscles are stronger. Without strain, we lift tons upon tons in constructing bridges and building skyscrapers.

The Highest Standard

In the field of medicine, diseases are being conquered. It is no longer necessary to die of yellow and typhoid fever; of pneumonia and tuberculosis; of gonorrhea and syphilis. The average life span in the United States is from sixty-eight to seventy years. Man has invented the brain machine, and with it he can solve the most difficult problems in mathematics faster and with greater accuracy than the mere human mind. In America, science has given us the highest standard of living to be found anywhere in history.

Years ago Shakespeare marveling at the mind of man said: "What a piece of work is man. How noble in reasoning, how infinite in faculty. In form in moving, how express and admirable. In action how like an angel, in apprehension how like a god." What would Shakespeare say in 1956? Yes, we know more than our forefathers. But what kind of people are we?

We Are Not Better

Though convinced that we know more than our forefathers, I am not convinced that we are any better than they; not convinced that we are more peace loving, honest, and true; not convinced that we are more moral or ethical in human relations. It can be argued with great eloquence that man in 1956 is just as brutal, dishonest, hypocritical, and mean as he was in 3000 B.C. We have developed a technique for improving the mind, for increasing the comforts of life, for extending the life span, but we have developed no sure technique for applying the heart, purifying the soul, and refining the spirit. We know more, but it is not equally clear that we are better. And to increase our knowledge and develop our minds without at the same time increasing man's ability to become better is a dangerous thing. It is like placing a hydrogen bomb in the hands of a fool. Let me document the point.

The War Record

In the past 3,000 years we have fought 3,300 wars. We know how to make war, but we do not know how to make peace. Three thousand or more years ago when the Egyptians, the Babylonians, and the Assyrians couldn't settle their differences around the conference table, they fought it out on the battlefields of the ancient world. Many centuries later, when the British colonies in America couldn't settle their differences with Britain, they fought it out in the Revolutionary War.

In 480 B.C., when the Greeks and the Persians couldn't get together, they fought it out at Thermopylae. Between 1914 and 1918, we fought to the death on the battlefields of Europe. The Romans and Carthaginians fought it out between 364 and 146 B.C. Twenty-three centuries later, between 1939 and 1945, we fought it out on the battlefields of Europe, Africa, and Asia. Today, war clouds hang heavily over our heads in the Middle East; war threatens between the Israeli and the Arabs; there is war in North Africa, smouldering hatred in South Africa, revolution in Poland and Hungary; and we spend more for war than for any other single item. We know more than our ancestors, but we cannot swear that we are any better than they.

And when war comes, we are as brutal as the Pharoahs and Alexanders, the Neros and the Caesars. When war comes, we lay our religion, ethics, and democracy aside; for the only thing confronting a nation at war is to win. It cannot be with the Golden Rule or the Sermon on the Mount. If it takes lying to win the war, we lie; if it takes hypocrisy to win, we deceive. If it takes the winking at the rape of women and girls in order to keep the morale of the soldiers, we wink at it; and if it takes the dropping the bombs on Nagasaki and Hiroshima, we justify it. It isn't a question of what is right or wrong. It is a question of what it takes to win the war.

Human Relations Record

Let us see if we are any better in the area of human relations. In 64 A.D., Nero burned Christians alive. It is said that in order to escape suspicion of having himself set fire to Rome, he blamed it on the New Sect of Christians and "ordered one of the cruelest persecutions ever known." "Victims were dipped in pitch," and allowed to burn at night like "torches for the delight of the populace." Nineteen centuries later in history, Adolph Hitler outdid Nero and caused six million Jews to be put to death.

In the first century of the Christian Era, the Jews and the Samarians did not like each other. The hatred was so great that an orthodox Jew traveling from Judea in the south of Galilee to the north would not go through Samaria, but instead would go to the extreme east or west and travel on the fringes of Samaria. In 1956, there is prejudice against the Jew in every part of the world. At this moment, the government of South

Africa is seeking to destroy the bodies, the minds, and the souls of the Bantus, the Indians, and the colored people. After 335 years of residence in North Africa, sixteen million Negroes are battling today for the status of first class citizenship in the United States. Segregation based on race and color exists in education, housing, hospitals, recreation, and employment. We in the deep South are seeking every legal and illegal mean, every moral and immoral means, to maintain a segregated society. The white citizens' councils, the state's righters, and organizations for the preservation of constitutional government are determined to defy the May 17, 1954, decision of the Supreme Court. The hundred or more southern congressmen who signed the Southern Manifesto have taken their stand with the White Citizens' Council.

Political and Social Sciences

In politics, we find men resorting to foul play in order to get elected. The two major parties in the United States spend millions of dollars in order to get power. Votes are bought and sold. As in war, the main object in all too many campaigns is to win. Win fairly, if possible, but by all means win.

Our values are twisted. We spend as much as $60 billion dollars a year for defense in the U.S.A. If we spent $60 billion, we would be able to endow 1900 colleges and universities in the United States with $31 million each. But no amount of logic or eloquence could persuade the United States Congress to appropriate that amount of money to endow education. We spent more than $9 billion a year for alcoholic beverages. For every dollar we spend for the churches, we spend eight for alcoholic beverages. We spend more for tobacco and cosmetics than for religion and education. Church membership is at an all-time high. There are more college graduates than ever before. And yet our jails and penitentiaries are crowded. Men and women from all walks of life are there. They are there from the slums and from the mansions of the wealthy. Doctors, lawyers, teachers, preachers, governors, and legislators are domiciled in our jails. We will spend thousands for parties and dances but only a few dollars for freedom. Politicians kick us around. They will tell us to our faces that they are going to keep us jim crowed. A Georgia congressman recently referred to Negroes as big hound dogs. And yet the vast majority of Negroes will not register and vote. Our values are twisted.

What then is our unfinished task? Our task is to produce a man who will be an improvement to the human product. How to make men better is our job. It is not bigger and better bombs that we need. It is bigger and better men.

Unfinished Business

Our unfinished business is to discover how to develop businessmen who will not exploit the poor, who are more interested in people than in profit. In politics, our task is to provide a man who will not lie on his opponent in order to get elected, who would prefer to be right than to be prime minister of Britain or President of the United States. In education, our job is to create an environment so that democracy can be lived and Christianity walked, where both will come as natural to us as breathing: an environment where a Catholic will not dislike a Protestant nor a Catholic a Protestant; where there will be no prejudice against a Jew, none against a Japanese or Mexican, none against a black man and none against a white man; an environment where each individual is looked upon as a child of God, born in his image, possessing a personality sacred unto God. In international affairs, our task is to produce men who will seek the ways of peace and not war.

Ladies and gentlemen, I am trying to make it plain that knowledge alone is not enough. Prophets and poets have known this for centuries. Paul knew it when he said in essence, "I find myself doing that which I ought not to do." Paul is saying that knowledge alone is not enough. My mind doesn't help me. I know the truth, and yet I lie. I see the light but cannot always walk in it. I see the high road beckoning to me, but I take the low road. I know the good, but I choose the evil. I know that peace is better than war.

Tennyson sensed the same thing when he said: "Let knowledge grow from more to more but more of reverence in us dwell. That mind and soul, according well, may make one music as before, but vaster." John Drinkwater was conscious of this when he wrote: "Knowledge we ask not,—Knowledge thou has lent. But, Lord, the will,—there lies our bitter need. Give us to build above the deep intent, the deed, the deed." This is what Jesus meant when he said to Nicodemus: "Except a man be born again, he cannot see the kingdom of God."

If knowledge is not enough and if our task is to improve the human product, to make a man better, the question logically arises: "How is this to be done?"

The first challenge is to the home. The home is the great educator. After a child reaches high school and college, he has been conditioned to hate or love certain people and things, to be honest or dishonest. What he learns by association with parents in the early formative years determines to a large extent what kind of citizen he is going to be. The person who is prejudiced against capital or labor, Protestant or Catholic, Gentile or Jew, Negroes, whites, Japanese or Chinese, developed his prejudice in his early years. The home should be a place where Christianity and democracy function best and where the proper attitudes toward life are developed.

A New Research Field

In this task of making men better, the national governments should be concerned. We spend millions in research seeking ways and means of making war more destructive. Our governments seek the most brilliant minds in physics, chemistry, biology, and mathematics, put them to work to find out how to make instruments of war more deadly. I propose that the national governments of the earth seek psychologists, psychiatrists, and economists, philosophers and theologians, subsidize them to the tune of millions to the end that they might discover techniques of making men more honest, true, Christian, and democratic. The governments spend millions helping physical scientists to experiment on how to make bigger and better bombs. If we can experiment and spend millions in an effort to make men hate, to teach them to destroy, we ought to be equally concerned with research designed to improve the human product, to experiment in good living. In this connection, let us urge our government and our people to support the United Nations. The small nations and big nations have their say, and world opinion is formed. As a result of the United Nations, even mighty Britain and France cannot have their way in Egypt, and mighty Russia is condemned by world opinion for her aggression in Hungary. The third challenge, therefore, is to support and make strong the United Nations.

The fourth challenge is to our colleges and universities. The aim of education today is to develop skills in the various disciplines in order to enable the students to get ahead in the world. The purpose of education is primarily to develop skills in philosophy, literature, science, and religion for the express purpose of enabling the student to be successful in his chosen field, make a living, accumulate wealth, live in a fine house, and ride in expensive cars. The process should be reversed. Our aim in physics should be to develop a good man who is an expert in physics. Not to develop experts in chemistry, but good men who are experts in chemistry. Our aim in economics should not be to develop experts in economics, but rather good men who are experts in economics. In religion, the aim should not be to develop eloquent preachers, but good men who are eloquent preachers.

Educators should define the kind of world we are trying to build. After defining the kind of society we want to build, we should develop that kind of citizen. We should begin in the kindergarten to develop students who believe in our Christian principles and democratic ideals. Goodness is as important as literacy.

The Challenge of the Church

The final challenge is the church. The first task of the church is to reestablish a belief in God. Modern nations do not believe in the Christian God. We trust our industrial might, no sovereign beyond ourselves. The problem confronting the world is not political, not economic, not war. The problem confronting the world today is the problem of God. As long as nations set themselves up as the ultimate authority, and as long as men give their supreme allegiance to the political or economic system, we are going to have catastrophe and war. The words of Sinai are more significant today than ever before: "Thou shalt have no other gods before me."

The church must also rededicate itself to the task of making new creatures, of calling men to repentance. The church must make it clear that man is not autonomous, that he is not able to lift himself by his own bootstraps. For no man is good enough, no man is wise enough, and no man is strong enough for mankind to put its trust in him. The Romans trusted the Augusti and the Caesars, but the Roman Empire fell. The people trusted Alexander the Great, but his kingdom fell apart, and he died in a drunken stupor in Babylon. The French trusted Napoleon, but he died a prisoner of war on St. Helena. The Germans trusted Hitler, but he lost the war and committed suicide with his mistress, Eva Braun. The Italians trusted Mussolini, but he was killed by his own countrymen, and his body, along with that of his mistress, was hanged up for ridicule on the streets of Milan. Stalin was worshiped and idolized as a god, but he died or was killed, and now he is being discredited. As Tennyson has well said: "Our little systems have their day. They have their day and cease to be. They are but broken lights of these. But thou, O God, are more than they."

Repentance

The church must call all men to repentance: the great and the small, the rich and the poor, the high and the low, the learned and the illiterate. As a rule, the evangelists and often the churches call little sinners alone. We call the little gamblers, not the men at the top. The learned and the powerful are considered beyond the need of redemption. The masses of Germany and Italy needed to be reborn, but Hitler and Mussolini needed it more than they. The masses in America need to be redeemed, but the men at the top who hold the fate of men in their hands need it more than the masses.

But I hear no misgivings. I hear you say that human nature cannot be changed, that man has always been a warmonger and always will, that the strong have always exploited the weak and always will, and that race prejudice is as old as hills and cannot be eliminated. But I would remind you that in less than a generation, Hitler changed the nature of the German youth. In less than a generation, Hitler turned the German nation against the Jews, and six million of them were exterminated. In less than a generation, Mussolini made the Italian people fascists. Between 1870 and 1910, we in the United States completely segregated the Negroes in the South and made them untouchables. If Hitler, Lenin, and Mussolini could change human nature for the worse, we can change it for good purposes. I refuse to believe that war is inevitable, that the strong must always dominate the weak, that a man must be kept down because he doesn't belong to a particular race. I believe that man can be born anew.

I hear you complain further. Who am I to set the South right, to set America and the world right? I am one lone teacher, businessman, minister, doctor, or lawyer; I must be careful. I've got to live. I need my job. What can I, as a lone A.K.A. or a Kappa do? I am one woman, one man. There is nothing I can do to set the world right.

Never to the Multitude

But I would remind you that the call to do great things always comes to the individual person and never to the multitude. The call to make the Jews a great people did not go to a thousand men. It went to Abraham.

The call to lead the Jews out of Egyptian bondage did not go to the Jewish people. The call came to Moses. The call to build the ark so that the remnant might be saved from the flood did not go to the crowd. The call came to Noah. The call to be God's men and save the world from sin did not go to the Scribes and the Pharisees. The call came to Peter and Paul. The call to religious freedom and to declare the doctrine of the universal priesthood of believers did not go to the multitude. It came to Martin Luther. The call to free the Negro slaves did not come to the four million slaves. It came to individuals: Harriet Beecher Stowe, Fred Douglass, William Lloyd Garrison, and others. The call to free women for the ballot and for a college education did not come to the crowd. It came to Susan B. Anthony. The call to free India from the yoke of Britain and to free fifty million untouchables did not come to the four hundred million of India. It came from Mahatma Gandhi. All of these were one person, one man, one woman.

Specifically, what can you do? You can help in words and deeds to democratize America. You can take your stand with the federal constitution, the nine justices of the Supreme Court who have declared that segregation based on color or race is unconstitutional, un-American, undemocratic. You can take your stand, in words and deeds, on the side of love and good will and nonviolence. We can take our stand against white supremacy, the Ku Klux Klan, the White Citizens' Council and against all those who would make our democracy and religion a mockery in the eyes of the nations of the earth.

We can register and vote and work until every qualified Negro in our community is a registered voter. We can work for and support the National Association for the Advancement of Colored People, an organization that has won 36 out of 39 civil rights cases it has argued before the Supreme Court; and if the fascist forces put the NAACP out of business, we can carry on the fight for freedom through the churches and other agencies, as the Negroes in Montgomery have done under the leadership of your brothers, Rev. Abernathy and Dr. King.

A Precious Thing

Freedom is a precious thing. It has never been given. It has always been won. We can sacrifice our time and energy for it. We can spend less on luxury and more for freedom. We can encourage the timid and the coward to stand without fear, and never before have we had so many on our side in the fight to be men. Millions in America and throughout the world work and pray that America might prove worthy of the world leadership which has been thrust upon her. We can make it plain that we fight not for sixteen million Negroes, but rather we fight for the soul of the United States, the greatest country on earth. We struggle that men everywhere might be free. In North and South Africa, behind the iron curtain and those of us who toil in the deep South.

We can have faith that we cannot lose, for our cause is just, our fight is righteous. The sun, the moon, the stars, Jupiter, Neptune, Mars, and even God, fight on the side of justice and right.

This is our task: for government and public schools, for colleges and universities, for religion and the churches, for the home, for the Kappas and A.K.A.s. If we cannot do this, if we cannot make man better, if we cannot be redeemed, if we cannot abolish war, if we cannot abolish the poisoning of race prejudice, if we cannot live and help to live, nothing else matters. Our learning will make us mad. Our science will destroy us. Our religion will rise up in that day to condemn us. If we cannot improve the human product, may God have mercy on our souls. As teachers of our youth, as ministers of Christ's church, this is our task. I close with the words of Edwin Markham:

Why build these cities glorious, if man unbridled goes?
In vain we build the world, unless the builder grows.

The Advantages of a Small, Christian, Private, Liberal Arts College*

In 1881, sixteen years after the Civil War, the Atlanta Baptist Female Seminary was founded by two New England women, Miss Sophia B. Packard and Miss Harriet E. Giles. Miss Packard served as the first president of the institution from 1881 to 1891. The institution later changed the name to Spelman Seminary in honor of Mr. and Mrs. Spelman, parents of John D. Rockefeller. The seminary was later discontinued and the name Spelman College adopted.

The celebration of the seventy-six anniversary of the founding of Spelman College commenced on April 9, 1957, with an 11:00 a.m. assembly in Sisters Chapel on campus, featuring Dr. Mays as speaker.

The audience for the Founders' Day celebration included students, faculty, members of the Board of Trustees, distinguished guests, visiting friends, alumni of the college, and local community people.

Spelman, an all-female student body, had long been considered the sister institution of the all-male Morehouse College student body. The two institutions enjoyed a cordial and cooperative relationship in providing academic programs and social activities for an extensive period of time, since the campuses are located just across the street from each other. Dr. Mays was, at the time of the speech, serving the seventeenth year of his Morehouse College presidency.

* * *

I feel so close to Spelman College that I almost forget when I come to this platform that I am not actually speaking to men at Morehouse. In fact, when Spelman women and Morehouse men have their temporary social misunderstandings and temporary tensions develop, I have been accused of taking the side of the Spelman women. The relationship is both historic and close.

Recently, I spoke at the International House in New York, and on that occasion, Miss Brawner, a graduate of Spelman, sang, and Mr. Evans, a graduate of Morehouse, played. I said in my introductory re-

* Reprinted from the *Spelman Messenger*, Volume 73 (May 1957): 16-24, Spelman College, Atlanta, Georgia

marks that there was nothing unusual about Miss Brawner and Mr. Evans cooperating because Morehouse and Spelman have been cooperating since 1881. I remarked to Miss Read once that I understood that the Morehouse men helped to move Spelman from the basement of Friendship Baptist Church to its present site, and that ever since that time, Morehouse men have been moving Spelman women.

I have been requested to use the subject, "The Advantages of a Small, Christian, Liberal Arts College." I want to add the word private: "A Small, Christian, Private, Liberal Arts College." The first part of the assignment is difficult enough, but the second part is almost impossible. Also suggested was "What Men Expect of Women and Wives, Mothers and Homemakers." It is difficult because I speak from experience and a degree of authority on only two aspects of the latter topic. It is difficult again because I can only speak for Benjamin Mays and not for all men in the United States or the world. It makes no difference how learned women may become, I predict that most of them will become wives, mothers, and homemakers. From these responsibilities women can hardly escape. Nature has decreed it.

It might be well to define a few terms. When is a college "small"? For the purpose of this address, I shall consider a college "small" if its enrollment is one thousand or fewer. This is certainly small when we consider universities with ten, twenty, thirty, or forty thousand enrolled. A college is Christian when its conception of God and man is based on the Christian view of God and man; when the college accepts the idea of the Christian God as Creator, Judge, Redeemer and Father, a God who is the Father of all mankind, irrespective of nationality, class, culture or race; and when it accepts the fact that the human family is one family and that all men are brothers. In the Christian view, the life of each and every child is precious in God's sight, and the relationship of God to man is so close and so delicate that we cannot do injury to the least individual without doing injury to God, no more than one can do injury to a mother's child without doing injury to the mother. The Christian college accepts further the fact that God revealed himself through Jesus Christ, and through him, men may be saved.

For my purpose, a college is liberal when, in addition to providing the students with skills to make a living, it also provides him with ways and means to enrich life and to improve the human product. You can clearly see that in my definition of a liberal arts college or liberal education, I draw no sharp line of distinction between liberal and technical.

It is the function of the liberal arts colleges to define the standards or goals of life, to supply the motivation for achieving these goals, and to develop in the student the capacity to know what is first-rate and what is not. This is not necessarily the function of a technical or vocational school. It is the responsibility, therefore, of the liberal arts college to supply the spiritual aspects of education, without which all education is faulty and without which all education will lead ultimately to catastrophic ends. In this sense, however, all education may be liberal. What I am saying is supported by Sir Richard Livingstone. Several years ago, Sir Richard referred to our era as an "Age without Standards." What he said in that connection defines clearly what a liberal arts education is, and shows why and how all education may be liberal, or how all education may be technical and vocational. I quote Mr. Livingstone: "The efficiency of a common will depends on its technical and vocational education, its cohesion and duration largely dependent on its social and political education. But the quality of its civilization depends on something else. It depends on its standards, its sense of values, its ideas of what is first-rate and what is not. The vocational and social aspects of education are essential, but the most fatal to omit is the spiritual aspect: fatal, because its absence may be long unperceived, and, as an insidious disease, a state may suffer from it and be unconscious of its condition till the complaint has gone too far to cure. Our knowledge of the sciences, natural or social, fixes the limit of the course within which the yachts on which humanity is embarked must sail, but does not indicate the goal of their voyage, still less supply the wind to fill their sails."

Thus, in a liberal arts college, all subjects should be spiritualized. The natural sciences as well as the humanities must be more than technical, more than a means of making a living, of increasing our comfort, or increasing our profit, and certainly more than a means of destroying humanity. All subjects must be liberalized in the sense that constructive goals must be defined and sought, and these subjects used to enrich life and to make mankind better. The professor of any subject, whether it is history, English, sociology, mathematics, religion, biology, chemistry or physics should know, through study and vicarious living, what the problems of life are and what the purpose of living is. This being true, all teaching should point to ways in which a particular subject can contribute toward a solution of the complex problems of life and ways in which living can be improved and humanity made better. To prove further that any subject may do this, I quote once more Sir Richard

Livingstone: "Take French. A man may study it to order to be able to order his meals in a French restaurant, or for business purposes; then it is technical education. He, as a man, is no better for being able to talk to a French waiter, or order foods in the French language. But he may study French to extend his knowledge of the thoughts and history and civilization of a great people; then it is liberal education."

If we accept these definitions as valid, what are the advantages of the small, Christian, private, liberal arts college? First, we are going to defend the thesis that the most important factor in the education of the student is the teacher, and that the spiritual values and good human relations are exemplified best when they are concretized in a person; and that these values can be achieved and implanted best in a community that is small enough to be called a "fellowship of the concerned." If the teachers are well chosen, the goals of education clearly defined and accepted by the students and teachers, if each teacher seeks to implement the aims of education in his or her own discipline, a true liberal education is much more likely to be attained in a community of five hundred or one thousand than in a community of five, ten, or twenty thousand.

Here in this community, in this "fellowship of the concerned," where practically everybody knows everybody else, where the joys and sorrows of one are the joys and sorrows of all, and where the student-teacher relation is close and wholesome, you have a climate, an atmosphere, a frame of reference for instilling in the students the virtues inherent in liberal education and the qualities that will develop the kind of spiritual leaders so badly needed in a highly technical, militarized age. This can hardly be true in a situation where the enrollment is so large that the individual is almost negligible and is looked upon as just another student. This can hardly be true in a technical or vocational school, where the emphasis is primarily one of developing skills in order that the student may become economically secure.

A liberal arts college is also concerned with education that will enable a student to make a living. But it is equally interested in developing in the student a sense of values, a wisdom that will enable her to know what is first-rate, and what is not. The liberal arts college accepts all the skills of the mechanized world. . . .

The liberal arts college is interested in building the man as well as providing technical skills.

In a small college, the average student has a better chance to bud and flower forth. The contact is more personal, and the teachers are more likely to encourage the average student than is likely to be the case in a large student body. I, for example, was encouraged more in small Bates College, as an undergraduate, than I would have been at Harvard, Yale, or New York University. Coming out of the South, where I had gone to school only three or four months out of the year, I needed encouragement.

For example, a Bates professor, after hearing me speak in a declamation contest, would never let me rest until I agreed to go out for intercollegiate debating. I was convinced that I did not have the time and insisted that I would never make the team. Professor Baird believed otherwise. He thought I had the time and he thought I had the ability to make an intercollegiate debater. I doubt that would have happened if I had done my undergraduate work in a large university.

In a small college, more friendships are formed. You are likely to know every member of your class by name, and every teacher is likely to know your name. The rich friendships that I made at Bates thirty-odd years ago have lasted through the years; it was good to be greeted as "Bennie" by all the teachers at Bates. It was and is an affectionate greeting for all my old teachers to call me "Bennie." I believe such advantages are more numerous in a small college than in a large university.

My University of Chicago contacts were most helpful to me, and I value them highly, but the great abiding friendships were formed at Bates College, where there were about six hundred students. The men at the University of Chicago were scholarly. They had written more books, but the personal contact and the warmth of friendship were more meaningful at Bates.

I believe the opportunity for religious and spiritual and religious growth is greater in the small, private, Christian, liberal arts college. The larger the number, the smaller the percentage of students who may be revitalized by a meaningful religious experience. Here again, in the small, private, Christian, liberal arts college, we meet almost as a family unit. We worship almost as a family. In a small college, we speak of the Spelman family or the Morehouse family. It would sound ridiculous to speak of the New York University family. The unity and oneness experienced in a small college are hardly possible in a large university.

The private college has the advantage not available to the tax-supported institution. Academic freedom and discussion are inherent in the privately supported colleges. Destroy liberal arts education in America and we would destroy free inquiry and discussion. Wherever state and municipal money goes, there is control, and there is some fear, and when it comes to debatable social issues, freedom is almost completely stifled in many tax-supported institutions. Harvard is freer than the University of Massachusetts. Chicago is freer than the University of Illinois. Emory is freer than the University of Georgia, and the private Negro colleges are the freest colleges and universities in the South.

For example, there is not one publicly supported institution in Georgia where there can be held a meeting to discuss desegregation in the public schools, unless the meeting is to condemn integration and praise segregation. No teacher in a tax-supported institution in the deep South could openly advocate the implementation of the May 17, 1954, decision of the Supreme Court and hold his job.

Only in private Negro colleges in Atlanta can we have Christmas Carol Concerts where all races come and sit where they can find seats and stand where they can find room.

Taking all factors together—small, private, Christian, and liberal— it is hardly an accident that the vast majority of the top Negro leadership has come out of the small, private, Christian, liberal arts college. It is hardly an accident that DuBois, Charles Wesley, and Roland Hayes came out of Fisk University; that Walter White, James Weldon Johnson, and H. A. Hunt came out of Atlanta University; that Robert Abbott, Robert Russa Moton, Booker T. Washington, and Dorothy Maynor, came out of Hampton; that Thurgood Marshall, Langston Hughes, and the Premier of Ghana are graduates of Lincoln; that Charles S. Johnson, Howard Long and Eugene Kinckle Jones came out of Virginia Union; that Mattiwilda Dobbs came out of Spelman and Mary McLeod Bethune came out of Barber Scotia; that Howard Thurman, John Davis, Martin Luther King, and Mordecai Johnson came out of Morehouse. This type of leadership can hardly come from tax-supported institutions.

The fact that the college is small makes it possible for a better selection of students. It is a fact that there are only a limited number of top minds in our group. As the elementary and high schools improve, the number of top flight Negro students will increase. The first-rate college whose enrollment is kept relatively small can restrict the number of students admitted to those at the top of the high school graduates. A careful screening of students in this way guarantees a better quality of education in the small, liberal arts college. Spelman is uniquely qualified to play this role of providing a superior type of education. And with small classes, a better quality of teaching is also one of the assets of the small college.

Everything I have said up to now applies to both men and women. Fortunately for now, you are heirs of the sacrifices and sufferings which women of former generations endured in order that you might have the right to go to college and vote on the same basis as men.

I, for one, am glad that there is no restriction on your education and that Spelman women will become, more and more, leaders in every phase of American life: religion, medicine, law, education, the arts and sciences, business, and politics.

But over and above business, politics, and the professions, you Spelman women will be called upon to be wives, mothers, and home-makers. You will be called upon to be good in all these areas. In one sense, it makes your task a double one and more difficult than that of men. The husband and father will make exacting demands of you, and he will expect certain things of you in spite of your training and degrees. If both of you are earning, he is likely to expect you to share the eco-nomic burden. Even if you should be so fortunate as to marry a man who is able to pay for the house, pay for maintenance, buy and pay for the furniture, pay the taxes, the maid, buy the food, and buy you dresses, shoes, and furs, if you are earning, he will expect you to share the economic load. In fact, it will make for much better relations if all things are shared.

The husband will require you to make the home comfortable, a place where he delights to come and relax. Despite your busy life, he will probably insist if there are children, that they not be neglected because you happen to stand high on the social register, or because you insist on working at the neglect of the child when there is no urgent need that you work. He will expect you to be more concerned for the rearing and training of your children than for social prestige or jobs.

Men will expect women not only to be educated but refined and intelligent. I think, certainly I hope, that the day has long since passed when men prefer beauty irrespective of brain. Men will expect women and their wives to be able to cope with complex problems that will al-ways confront the world. Even if the circumstances confine the wife mainly to the home for rearing the children, he will expect his wife to be well-informed, cultured, and refined so that the children will have every advantage which comes from a well-prepared mother. I would argue for a college education for women even if they spend all their time rearing and training their children. No living person has as much to offer a child as an intelligent, devoted mother.

Finally, the husband will expect sympathy, understanding, and encouragement from his wife—when he succeeds and when he fails. The great success that many men achieve can be traced directly to the influence of their wives—to the sympathy, understanding, and encouragement that they receive from their wives. On the other hand, wives who lack these noble virtues have contributed to the miserable failure of their husbands. Husbands may, and many of them do, succeed without the needed support of their wives, but the men succeed best who receive inspiration, understanding, and encouragement from their wives.

These are my challenges to the small, Christian, private, liberal arts college, and these are my challenges to the Spelman women.

Desegregation: An Opportunity and a Challenge*

Dr. Mays delivered the Founders' Day address at Shaw University in Raleigh, North Carolina on November 18, 1966. An article in the *Raleigh News* reported the next day that approximately 1,000 persons attended the ceremony held in Spaulding Gymnasium on campus. In attendance were trustees of the university, administrators, students, faculty, alumni, and members of the community. Dr. Mays received the honorary degree of Doctor of Humane Letters at the ceremony. In the address, Dr. Mays praised the work of the university president, Dr. James E. Cheek, performed in such a short time.

Mays noted that most predominantly black institutions such as Shaw were started by missionaries who had fewer resources and expectations in the humble beginning. He also spoke of the struggle and sacrifices endured through the civil rights movement to achieve a desegregated society.

Dr. Mays reminded the young students in the audience, "There is no substitute for preparedness and professional competence." This represented classic "Mays style": to challenge and motivate young students to excel in whatever goals and professions they pursued.

* * *

Shaw University has passed the century mark. One hundred years is a short time when compared with Oxford University, founded in the 13th century, and with Harvard University, established in 1636. But when considered in the context of Negro freedom, Shaw is an ancient institution—much older than the University of Chicago. Your graduates have done much in these hundred years. I can say of Shaw what I say of Morehouse: "Few institutions, if any, have done so much with so little, and so few." So I salute you and your president, who has done so much for Shaw. Few men could have done what your president did in so short a period of time. Shaw and the predominantly Negro colleges similarly situated have wrought mighty deeds in education, religion, business, and professions, so much with so little and so few. Virtually all private Ne-

---

* James E. Cheek Library Archives, Shaw University, Raleigh, North Carolina

gro institutions started as missionary schools. And as missionary schools, they were expected to survive and thrive on less than white institutions. This philosophy has prevailed since the Civil War, and during the 246 years of slavery, that which is built for Negroes doesn't have to be as good as that which is built for white Americans. This accounts in part that under a segregated economy, virtually everything built for Negroes was decidedly inferior and deliberately planned to be inferior. All public facilities for Negroes were inferior and no place of any consequence was allowed them in local, state, and federal governments. These conditions existed until Negroes themselves rose up recently in rebellion through federal courts and demonstrations, which led to congressional legislation abolishing segregation in most areas of American life. This belief that what was meant for Negroes didn't have to be first-rate permeated the thinking of many of the missionary teachers who taught in the early years at Shaw, Morehouse, Fisk, Howard, and other institutions.

Please do not misunderstand me: I thank God for the white teachers from the North and a few from the South who left comfort and social standing to cast their lot among the newly emancipated people. There was no doubt in many of their minds that they were called of God to educate the Negro. They were socially ostracized and looked down upon by Southern whites. Whereas the majority of the people considered the Negro incapable of learning, those pioneers thought that given a chance, the sons and daughters of slaves could master the upper branches of knowledge. One illustration of this is the fact that many of our schools were called universities when they were nothing but grade schools. These teachers gave the Negro hope, and without them, the Negro's plight would be more dreary than it is.

Despite meager support and the conviction that Negro schools needed less than white schools, Shaw and other predominantly Negro colleges have prepared Negroes for outstanding leadership. I am sure that 90 percent or more of all Negro college graduates graduated from predominantly Negro colleges like Shaw and Morehouse. Easily 90 percent or more of all Negro doctors, lawyers, and dentists took their undergraduate work at schools like Shaw. I would wager that 95 percent of all Negro teachers in our public schools and colleges came out of predominantly Negro colleges. The vast majority of Negroes in business and skilled trades are graduates of our colleges.

We are proud of outstanding Negroes who have graduated from predominantly Negro colleges: proud of the Solicitor General of the United

States who came from Lincoln and Howard, Senator-elect Brooke of Massachusetts who graduated from Howard; proud of John Hope Franklin, professor at the University of Chicago, who came out of Fisk; of Martin Luther King, Jr., Nobel Peace Prize winner, and the Nabrit brothers who came out of Morehouse; proud of our Negro judges and of Negroes who are teaching in eighty or more predominantly white colleges and universities. We are proud of James Cheek, Angie Brooks, and Benjamin Quarles of Shaw.

Of course, we are proud. But bear in mind that the vast majority of Negro families are living on three thousand dollars per year or less, that thirty-five million Americans are living on the brink of poverty, and many of them are Negroes. This is the soil on which the seeds of revolution sprout. I wager that the rioters are poor and unemployed. We are proud of the desegregated society, but—lest we forget—along with desegregation goes a heavy responsibility, and the more we clamor, the more obligated we become to carry our full weight in the community, state, and nation. All knowledgeable men know that coercion of some kind must be applied to uproot entrenched wrongs supported by law, custom, and religion. It is clear as day that most of the social changes that have come about recently came through court and congressional action or some kind of demonstration. The man who profits—or thinks he profits—by keeping another man down is not good enough to voluntarily stop exploiting him.

But as our young friends demonstrate and riot in Chicago, Cleveland, Brooklyn, Mississippi, and other places, let us make it clear to them and ourselves that there is no substitute for preparedness and professional competence. There is no dichotomy in the civil rights struggle. The young men and women who never sat-in and never demonstrated, but stuck to their academic work, were and are part and parcel of the civil rights struggle. For example, Hamilton Holmes did not go to jail in 1961-62 in Atlanta, he did not sit-in at restaurants, but he did sit in and stand in the libraries and laboratories at the University of Georgia, graduating Phi Beta Kappa. This is part of the civil rights struggle.

We had to demonstrate to get hotels, motels, and restaurants open, but tell it on the mountains and everywhere that this is only half of the story. Tell the people about Brooke, running for the United States Senate from Massachusetts, now Senator-elect; two Negro senators in the Georgia State Legislature; Weaver, a member of the President's cabinet; Sam Nabrit, a member of the Atomic Energy Commission; Donald

Hopkins, a Morehouse graduate, graduating in the top third of his class at the University of Chicago Medical School. The Johnson Publishing Company in Chicago; the marvelous headquarters of the North Carolina Mutual in Durham; the Atlanta Life in Georgia; the work of outstanding Negro citizens in Raleigh; Martin Luther King, Jr., winner of the Nobel Peace Prize; Thurgood Marshall, Solicitor General of the United States; Willie Mays, Hank Aaron, starring in baseball—all these and more are part of the civil rights struggle. At the moment, the greatest contribution that Shaw students can make to the civil rights struggle is to do your work so well that when you finish, jobs will be calling you, and graduate and professional schools will be seeking you.

Desegregation and eventually integration will present a special challenge to Negroes and especially to Negro youths. Remember that no allowance will be made for our shortcomings because for 246 years our ancestors were slaves and for another one hundred years we were enslaved again through segregation by law and by custom.

No allowance will be made for poverty in that the average income of the Negro family is only about 55 percent of that of the average family. When competence is needed in science, whether government, industry, or education, no allowance will be made for inferior schools that Negroes have had to attend for decades upon decades. The only comment you will hear: "Negroes are not qualified. They failed the test." When a man of experience is needed to fill a certain post, no allowance will be made for the fact that the Negro has never been given a chance to get the kind of experience needed for that job. This is where "hire on the basis of competence" breaks down. He will be passed by and the only comment—"No Negro could be found with the proper qualifications."

Get it across to your sisters and brothers; tell it to your friends that they will never get into the main stream of American life by dropping out of school, by playing around, by graduating at the foot of their class, by cursing America or the white man for 246 years of slavery and 100 years of segregation. He may be at fault, but cursing him will do no good.

Make it clear to yourselves and to Negro youth that with low incomes, poor academic backgrounds, unfortunate home conditions, handicapped ancestors for three and a half centuries, we are now required to compete in the open market with those who have been more favorably circumstanced than we for several centuries.

What can we do? There is only one thing we can do as new opportunities open to us. We can accept as valid the Chinese proverb: "It is better to light a candle than to curse the darkness." The only thing left for a poor man to do to overcome his poverty is to find a good job, work hard, and save. The only thing a sick man can do to gain health is to follow the doctor's advice and be sensible. The illiterate man who would overcome his ignorance must study as we protest and demonstrate for justice and equality.

Such is your plight and mine. For he who starts behind in the great race of life must forever remain behind or run faster than the man in front. The man who is handicapped by circumstances over which he has no control must work harder than the man who has no such handicaps to overcome. Deprived of the best schools, reared in homes economically below standards, denied the opportunity to read good books in elementary and high school, robbed of opportunities to qualify for the best jobs, our young people are, almost overnight, challenged to meet the toughest competition of the modern world. Protest? Yes, and demonstrate when necessary. But remember, there us no substitute for excellence in performance.

Whether we like it or not, Negroes must read more and socialize less, do more research and play less, write books and articles and become recognized in our respective fields. It is better by far to be known by the articles we write than by the bridge we play, by the books we publish than by the houses we live in. It is better to have our colleagues envious of our scholarship and research than of our houses and land.

I am sure Marion Anderson is economically secure, but Marion Anderson will be known not by her wealth but by her songs. John Fitzgerald Kennedy was a millionaire, but he got into history not by his millions but because he taught America that if things need to be changed, we don't have to wait a hundred years to change them; we can change them now. Nobody cares how Socrates dressed, whether he wore shoes or walked barefoot. But the name of Socrates is immortal. Nobody cares how Mahatma Gandhi dressed or if he rode half-naked or third class. History will claim him as one of the greatest men of all times.

Jesus was a despised Jew and a carpenter, but He is known as the Son of God and the Savior of the world. Nobody thinks of George Washington's wealth. He is the father of the country. Nobody worries about Lincoln's poverty; he is the great emancipator. Shakespeare is known for *Hamlet* and *MacBeth*, Milton for *Paradise Lost*, Darwin for

The Origin of Species. W. E. B. DuBois for the *Souls of Black Folk*, James Weldon Johnson for *God's Trombones*, and Booker T. Washington for Tuskegee.

My dear young friends, let us go into a desegregated society standing on our feet and not cringing, kowtowing, and crawling on our bellies. Let us not go into a desegregated society, even when we lick de facto segregation and win the right to live anywhere we can buy, steeped in the inferiority complex. Let us not forget that we are what we are. Let us not be swept off our feet by the glamor of an integrated society. By all means, enjoy the swankiest hotels, eat in the finest restaurants, live on the boulevards, but let us never forsake that which we ourselves have built with sweat, blood, and tears. Let us not look down on banks, insurance companies, newspapers, churches, colleges, universities, real estate agencies, that Negro genius and brain have established. We can live in a desegregated society physically free but mentally slaves. Let us not become a race of employees, only looking for a soft bed somebody else has made up. But let us also become a race of employers, blazing new paths and building new enterprises. As we look forward to invading our churches, our schools, our banks, and our insurance companies, size alone is not the criterion of excellence.

As desegregation gives us larger and larger opportunities, let us not forget that these bring with them larger responsibilities. Negroes under crippling conditions have done exceedingly well, but not well enough to pass. We are still looked upon as boys. The confidence we need in all these areas is not yet there. And yet the "boy's" future in America is brighter than ever before. I dare not look to the future in despair. I look to the future with the courage and hope of Tennyson in "Ulysses."

Come, my friends,
'Tis not too late to seek a newer world.
Push off, and sitting well in order mite
The sounding furrows; for my purpose holds
To sail beyond the sunset, and the baths
Of all the western stars, until I die.
It may be that the gulfs will wash us down;
It may be that we shall touch the Happy Isles,
And see the great Achilles, whom we knew.
Though much is taken, much abides; and though
We are not now that strength which in old days
Moved earth and heaven, that which we are, we are—

One equal temper of heroic hearts,
Made weak by time and fate, but strong in will
To strive, to seek, to find, and not to yield.

I challenge you to a life of dissatisfaction as set forth by Louis Untermeyer in his poem "The Prayer."

God, though this life is but a wraith
Although we know not what we use,
Although we grope with little faith,
Give me the heart to fight—and lose.
Ever insurgent let me be,
Make me more daring than devout;
From sleek contentment keep me free,
And fill me with a buoyant doubt.
Open my eyes to visions girt
With beauty, and with wonder lit—
But always let me see the dirt,
And all that spawn and die in it.
Open my ears to music; let
Me thrill with Spring's first flutes and drums—
But never let me dare forget
the bitter ballads of the slums.
From compromise and things half done,
Keep me with stern and stubborn pride;
And when at last the fight is won,
God, keep me still unsatisfied.

An Impossible Dream Comes True*

To celebrate the 107th anniversary of its founding, Howard University invited the renowned Dr. Benjamin E. Mays to speak to an audience of administrators, faculty, students, alumni, university trustees, distinguished guests, and members of the university community. The address was delivered on March 1, 1974.

This event occurred amidst the historic Watergate scandal during the presidency of Richard M. Nixon, which eventually led to his resignation on August 9, 1974. The day after the ceremony, *The Washington Post* carried a lead story reporting the indictment of nine Watergate conspirators. Much of the news of the anniversary celebration at Howard was overshadowed by this impending political crisis in Washington.

The educator informed the audience that the university located in the nation's capital plays a major role in improving the freedom of black people. Accordingly, he affirmed that the ground work for the Brown decision was laid at Howard with black lawyers like Thurgood Marshall (then serving on the Supreme Court) and Dr. James Nabrit, Dean of the Howard University Law School, one of his former students when he taught at Morehouse in the 1920s.

Dr. Mays challenged the audience to help solve the problems facing American society and the world by maintaining a standard of excellence at Howard in all disciplines.

* * *

Howard University was born to serve all nations, all races, and all groups. But the University was also founded to play a special role in bringing a larger degree of freedom to black people: a role which if Howard University and other colleges similarly circumstanced do not play, will hardly be played. Located here in the nation's capital, where representatives of all nations converge, Howard is uniquely qualified to serve the nation and the world and besides to address itself to the peculiar needs of black people.

Someone has said: little drops of water, little grains of sand, make the mighty ocean and the barren land. The words are applicable to Howard University as we view it in the beginning of 1867 and see it now in 1974.

---

* Mays Collection, Moorland-Spingarn Research Center, Howard University

On this 107th anniversary of Howard, the drops of water and grains of sand have multiplied many thousands of times, and I wager that Howard is the most integrated University in the United States. Ninety countries are represented in the student body. Students are here from North and South America, Europe and Asia and Africa, and five of the six continents. The Near, Middle, and Far East are represented. The enrollment is approximately 10,000 students. Of these, 23 percent are from 90 countries, and 73 percent are from the United States. On the Board of Trustees, you have black and white. Your student body—like the faculty—is well integrated.

Beginning with no graduates in 1867, in 1974 Howard has graduated 35,000 men and women who have received diplomas, degrees, or certificates, and more than 14,000 of the 35,000 hold graduate and professional degrees. The campus, building, and equipment are valued at more than 90 million dollars. Seven hundred fifty thousand volumes are housed in its library.

A careful study of universities in this country and abroad would probably reveal that Howard is the most integrated university in the United States and the world. The drops of water and grains of sand have become an ocean and a great, fertile land.

Howard has a double commitment to serve the people of the United States and the world, and a special commitment to serve black people. If Howard University doesn't assume this commitment, it may be that no other university will.

It was at Howard University that black lawyers developed skills in law that paved the way for the attack on segregation. Throughout the 1930s and 1940s, we were dealing with the "separate but equal" doctrine as set forth in *Plessy v. Ferguson* in 1896. Whenever it was established that the separates were not equal, the case was won. But the constitutionality of segregation itself had never been tested in the United States Supreme Court. It was left to a Howard University-trained lawyer to take the lead in presenting the case against segregation, which brought forth the May 17, 1954, decision of the United States Supreme Court that declared segregation in public schools as unconstitutional based on the 14th Amendment.

It is significant to note that the ground work for the 1954 decision was laid in the law school at Howard and that the case was won by black lawyers Thurgood Marshall, Jim Nabrit, and others.

The situations affecting blacks have not changed drastically since 1954. The days of equality have not yet been achieved. As long as black people make a profession of killing each other, we are the most victimized in the drug trade, are hired last and fired first. A higher percentage of blacks are on welfare than that of any other group. As long as more blacks live in slums and ghettos of our cities than any other race or ethnic group, as long as our jails are filled mostly with blacks, as long as black people die faster than whites, a search for the solution to these problems must rest primarily with schools like Howard, where many of the students have their roots deep in the conditions described.

If black people, like black colleges and universities and black churches, do not take up a cudgel to change these conditions, I doubt any other centers of learning will.

Our condition as black Americans is a bit similar to that of Jewish people. The Jews have suffered for more than 3,000 years, and they have never abandoned their responsibility to the Jewish people wherever they reside on the earth. It is easy, in a matter of hours, for Jews to raise millions of dollars for Israel, never denying their Jewish ancestry. I suppose this allegiance to Jewish people goes back to Moses and before, when he preferred to suffer with his people than be the son of Pharaoh's daughter.

A university like Howard can hardly escape from this dual role and be true to its mission. Though open to all racial and ethnic groups from the beginning, Howard has always had a special mission to perform among blacks. As far as I can look into the future, this will be true for decades to come.

Howard must be as competent in all disciplines inherent to western civilization as any university in the nation and as knowledgeable in the economics of free enterprise and capitalism as any university. But Howard should know the special economic needs of black people living in the slums and ghettos of our cities and, through first-hand knowledge and research design programs, to remedy conditions they face.

It is not enough for a few of us to rise above poverty and by this token, cut ourselves off from our fellows. We should seek to build bridges of communication and understanding between the most gifted and wealthy among us and those who live at the bottom of the economic ladder, with a view of lifting them out of their poverty. Welfare must not be considered a permanent condition among black people. Studies and programs aimed at alleviating these conditions must be a special concern of black colleges and universities.

Howard graduates in medicine must be as knowledgeable in medicine as the graduates of any medical school. In addition, working with the people in sociology and social work, Howard must have special concern for diseases peculiar to blacks and how the life span of blacks can be extended. Howard's courses in English literature and poetry must be comparable to the courses found in any great university; experts in the knowledge of literature, poetry, and drama of black people must be equally important.

The homicide rate and crimes committed by black people are exceedingly high. The majority of inmates in our jails across the country are black men and women. While many blacks call each other "sister" and "brother," and say they hate whites, the truth of the matter is they hate whitey, and they kill blackey.

There may be little that universities can do about homicides and jails filled with blacks, but it is a challenge to the university serving blacks to be especially concerned with a problem that seems to be peculiar to black people—not only those of us who are native Americans, but black people everywhere.

Of the ninety countries represented in Howard's enrollment, twenty-nine (approximately one- third) of them are in Africa. Since Africa until recently has been dominated by European nations, and perhaps because they are black, the African nations have not been a special concern of our government. The European nations have been our first concern, the Asian nations second and the African nations third.

Africa, more and more, must become exhibit "A" in our concern, and Howard can play a hand in turning the attention of this country to Africa.

Virtually all these problems are deeply rooted in the life of the people in Washington, D.C.—a city owned and operated by the federal government. Maybe Howard University can get the federal government to make Washington the showplace of all the capitals of the world. It doesn't look right for Washington, the richest and most powerful capital in the world, to be surrounded by the conditions that defy its affluence.

If the University can lead the way in helping to solve these perplexing problems, while at the same time maintaining its standard of excellence in all other disciplines, another impossible dream will come to fruition, and all America will be deeply in the University's debt.

Martin Luther King, Jr.*

Dr. Mays made this presentation at the annual Martin Luther King, Jr., birthday celebration at Duke University Chapel, in Durham, North Carolina on January 11, 1976, before an audience of approximately 1,000 students, faculty, visitors, and townspeople.

Dr. Mays recounted his close friendship with the slain civil rights leader, beginning with their discussions after his Tuesday morning chapel speeches at Morehouse when King was a student. Their friendship continued throughout King's graduate studies and his leadership of the civil rights movement up until his death. Dr. Mays discussed his personal knowledge of developments in the civil rights movement and his relationship with King in these activities.

Dr. Mays acknowledged, "It must be said in full candor that I feel that Martin Luther King, Jr., did as much for me, if not more, than I did for him." Mays continued, "Had the city officials in Montgomery been more enlightened—or sensible—the life of Martin Luther King, Jr., would have been different."

Dr. Mays's speech regarding his role as friend and mentor of Martin Luther King, Jr., was eloquent and informative, and according to the Duke University student newspaper, Dr. Mays's remarks even evoked some laughter from the audience, as he referred to the stubborn behavior of the Montgomery city officials.

* * *

One never knows what it is that triggers a response, but I am convinced that it was my contact with Martin Luther King, Jr., in chapel at Morehouse that brought us close together. There we began a real friendship which was strengthened by visits to his home and in my office. Many times, during his four years at Morehouse, he would linger after my Tuesday morning address to discuss some point I had made—usually with approval, but sometimes questioning or disagreeing. I was not aware how deeply he was impressed by what I said and did until he wrote *Stride Toward Freedom*, in which he indicated that I had influenced his life to a marked degree. In public addresses, he often referred to me as

---

* Duke University, School of Divinity Archives

his "spiritual mentor." Since his death, several persons, especially those seeking data for an article or book, have asked me whether I knew in what way I was influencing Martin's life. The answer is an unqualified "no." There is no way one can know the degree of influence one has upon another.

It must be said in all candor that I feel that Martin Luther King, Jr., did as much for me, if not more, than I did for him. Perhaps if I had not known Martin through the Morehouse chapel, and if his father had not been elected to the Board of Trustees of Morehouse College, our friendship would not have reached such a meaningful depth. Our friendship continued to grow during his years of study at Crozier Theological Seminary and Boston University, during his pastorate at Montgomery, during the years when he joined his father as co-pastor of Ebenezer Baptist Church in Atlanta, and throughout the civil rights struggle.

When Martin Luther had almost completed his doctorate at Boston University, I offered him a position on the faculty at Morehouse. After giving serious consideration to my invitation, he decided that he should accept the pastorate of the Dexter Avenue Baptist Church in Montgomery, Alabama. When he returned to Atlanta as co-pastor of Ebenezer Baptist Church, I again offered him work as a part-time professor, hoping that someday he would be with us at Morehouse full-time for many years. So great were the public demands on his time, however, that after one semester he had to give up his seminar on nonviolence. Had he accepted my offer to teach at Morehouse, he would no doubt be alive today, but his name would not be among the immortals few who have achieved real greatness.

Furthermore, had the city officials in Montgomery been enlightened—or even sensible—the life of Martin Luther King, Jr., would have been a different story. Then, too, had Mrs. Rosa Parks behaved as she was "supposed to," and as Negroes generally had behaved for decades—that is, if she had gotten up and given a white man her seat—there would have been no Montgomery Bus Boycott. Had the city officials met the simple demands of The Montgomery Improvement Association, perhaps the world would have never witnessed Dr. King's capacity for magnificent, selfless leadership in the interest of mankind. The demands of the Montgomery Improvement Association were all reasonable—too reasonable—and all within the segregation pattern. It also seems that any sane city official would have agreed to permit Negroes to keep their seats if, when entering from the rear, they filled the bus, in which case whites would have to stand. The reverse would be true if whites filled the bus first. Sensible officials would have been willing to hire Negro bus drivers, certainly in predominantly Negro areas, and would have instructed white drivers to be civil in their treatment of black customers. All these demands were denied, hence the year-long Montgomery Bus Boycott.

It is highly probably that Martin Luther King, Jr., was the only man who could have led the Montgomery Bus Boycott for an entire year without violence instigated by white people. Without Dr. King's charisma, his brilliant mind, and his unquenchable spirit, Negroes would hardly have stuck it out. For Dr. King, it was the beginning of an incredible pilgrimage which was to bring him worldwide honor and acclaim—and death. From that moment of the boycott until his assassination on April 4, 1968, he moved steadily from height to height, loved by his friends and hated by his enemies. I am sorry he did not come to Morehouse, but no college could have provided such an opportunity for leadership, a leadership so needed by all mankind and one for which he was so eminently qualified.

Of the countless incidents I could relate about Martin Luther King, Jr., I have chosen three because it seems to me that they illustrate so perfectly the quality of the man's soul—his vision, his courage, his magnificent capacity for self-denying love.

The first of those concerns Rosa Parks, who was arrested December 1, 1955. Nobody knows just why, on this particular occasion, she didn't choose to obey the bus driver's order to get up so a white man might sit down. Perhaps she was tired after working all day; perhaps she was just tired of being pushed around all her life by white folks. At any rate, she sat—and—and the Boycott was on!

When the Montgomery officials discovered that violence could not stay the protest or stop the Boycott, they resorted to mass arrest, using an old state law against boycotts. Dr. King, who was in Nashville at the time, knew that if he returned to Montgomery he would be arrested too. En route to Montgomery, he stopped overnight in Atlanta. His father, frantic for his son's safety, assembled a group of friends to consult with them about the wisdom of Martin Luther King, Jr.'s immediate return to Montgomery. It was on February 22, 1956, that we met at the residence of Martin Luther King, Sr., and according to Martin Luther's own book, *Stride Toward Freedom*, the following persons were present: A. T. Walden, a distinguished attorney; C.R. Yates and T.M. Alexander, both prominent businessmen; C.A. Scott, editor of the *Atlanta Daily World*;

Bishop Sherman L. Green of the A.M.E. Church; Rufus Clement, President of Atlanta University; and Benjamin E. Mays, President of Morehouse College. As I myself remember, Attorney Dan Duke was also present.

Reverend Martin Luther King, Sr., stated his reason for calling us together and expressed his conviction that his son should not return to Montgomery right away. In *Stride Toward Freedom*, Martin Luther King, Jr., writes that after his father's statement:

> There were murmurs of agreement in the room and I listened as sympathetically and objectively as I could while two of the men gave their reasons for concurring. These were my elders, leaders among my people. Their words commanded respect. But soon I could not restrain myself any longer: "I must go back to Montgomery—my friends and high associates are being arrested. I would rather be in jail ten years than desert my people now. I have begun the struggle, and I can't turn back now. I have reached the point of no return." In the moment of silence that followed, I heard my father break into tears. I looked at Dr. Mays, one of the great influences in my life. Perhaps he heard my unspoken plea. At any rate, he was soon defending my position strongly.

I had to defend Martin Luther's position. Here was a man of deep integrity and firm convictions. "How could he have decided otherwise than to return to Montgomery? How could he hide while his comrades in nonviolent arms were being carried to jail?" In essence, this was what I said.

As for the second event, the officials in Alabama, and particularly in Montgomery, took great delight in harassing Martin Luther King, Jr., even after the Montgomery Bus Boycott ended in 1957. When Ralph Abernathy was being tried on some trumped-up charge, the Montgomery courtroom was almost full. When Dr. King wanted to get in, the officers refused him permission, and upon his insistence, he was arrested. Twisting his arms, they pushed and kicked him into a cell. Before Mrs. King and others could plan a strategy for getting Dr. King out, he was suddenly released. At the trial, he was convicted of loitering and given the choice: he could serve time or pay a fine. Here came the great decision. Convinced that he had been unlawfully arrested and unjustly convicted, and therefore could not in good conscience pay the fine, Dr. King announced that he could serve his time in jail. This pronouncement shocked and stunned the court. I understand that the judge almost begged

Dr. King pay the fine. Some person—at the time unknown—paid it. Later it was learned that Clyde Sellers, the Chief of Police, had paid it, remarking that it would be cheaper to pay the fine than to have Martin Luther King, Jr., in jail at the city's expense.

Dr. King's decision not to pay went almost unnoticed at the time, but to me it was one of the most momentous decisions of his whole civil rights career. It made a tremendous impression on me. He would obey an unjust verdict. But by serving time rather than paying a fine for something he should never have been convicted of, he registered for the whole world his protest against injustice. His great decision has motivated, and will continue to motivate, the actions of others as we pursue this long journey up the precipitous hill toward racial justice, democracy, and Christian living in this country.

A third incident will dramatize Martin Luther King, Jr.'s high regard for the law, even for unjust laws. Those who have condemned him for admonishing people to break unjust laws have not realized that when he himself violated them he was not being irresponsible, it was his way of seeking to achieve social change without instigating physical violence. If he had violated the law and then cried for amnesty, his action, in a sense, would have been irresponsible and would have indicated disrespect for law. But when Martin Luther violated the law, he did so consciously and deliberately and thought the law was blatantly unjust. He was willing to suffer for a righteous cause in the firm belief that this kind of suffering was redemptive.

I saw him demonstrate this belief on October 29, 1967. President Glenn H. Leggett had invited a group of distinguished Americans to Grinnell College to confer honorary degrees. Dr. King and I were among them—he to give the convocation address in the morning before the conferring of degrees in the afternoon, and I to introduce him. His schedule was so tight that he warned Grinnell that he might not be able to get there, so an official of the College asked me to stand in if he couldn't make it. An emphatic "no" had to be my answer to this request—this huge crowd had come to hear Dr. King, not me. No substitute would have been adequate. To make his appearance, Dr. King had to come by a private plane provided by a friend. The crowd that had waited patiently for ninety minutes for his arrival gave him a standing ovation when he appeared, and applauded long and loud when he finished speaking.

This was the speech Martin Luther King, Jr., made just before he returned to Alabama once more to serve time for contempt of court. He had a heavy cold, and I was greatly concerned when he left me in Grinnell to go to Birmingham. He could have ducked another ordeal by staying out of Alabama, but true to his character, he would not run and hide, even though he knew he was being punished unjustly. Only one who has the highest respect for the law is willing to serve time for violating laws, whether just or unjust. This man never cried for mercy; he never asked for amnesty.

The Grinnell experience was five months and eight days before his assassination. My next public speech about Martin Luther was the eulogy I gave at his funeral on April 9, 1968.

Martin Luther King, Jr., was a powerful man, and I was, and still am, so inspired by his integrity, his courage, and his commitment that I have never been quite objective about him. I was wholeheartedly in accord with most things he did. Even when I had reservations about a certain course of action, I hesitated to criticize him because I could never doubt the sincerity of his purpose. It angered me to hear him accused of being insincere or of doing things for the plaudits of the crowd. Many, for example, condemned his stand on the Vietnam War. Even some civil rights leaders and other Negroes in high places were harsh in their criticisms. In conversations, on public platforms, and in my weekly articles in the *Pittsburgh Courier*, I found myself in the happy position of defending his stand on this and many other issues.

Why should Dr. King have confined his work to civil rights and left Vietnam to the government experts and military professionals? I learned long ago that there are no infallible experts on war and that no leader has ever been able to confine his leadership to one area, a point I made in the *Pittsburgh Courier* on May 20, 1967:

> I do not agree with the leaders who criticize Dr. King on the ground that he should stick to civil rights and not mix civil rights with foreign policy. If the critics differ with him because of his stand on the Vietnam War, let them say it. No leader leads in one particular area. I think most civil rights leaders speak on other issues as well. I see nothing wrong with a man speaking out on three or four different issues. He may be right in his stand on Vietnam and he may be wrong. History will finally record the verdict.

It should be noted here that what Dr. King is doing now is consistent with his philosophy of nonviolence. He was a follower of Mahatma Gandhi before he led the Montgomery Bus Boycott.

He has expounded this philosophy on the home front, and it is logical that he would expound it on the international front. I think they should at least make their criticisms of Dr. King on the major issues. . . .

Long before the world paid tribute to Martin Luther King, Jr., by awarding him the Nobel Peace Prize, Morehouse College conferred upon him the highest honor. We wanted to be the first college or university to recognize his leadership in the Montgomery Bus Boycott. The Boycott had continued all through 1956, and our first commencement after that was in June, 1957. In April, I proposed that we honor Dr. King on June 4th by conferring upon him the honorary degree of Doctor of Humane Letters. The faculty and board of trustees accepted my recommendation unanimously. It gave me great joy to confer the degree when the day came.

The eulogy which I gave at the funeral services for Martin Luther King, Jr., at Morehouse College, on April 9, 1968, was my last tribute to a great and good man.

Jimmy Carter*

Dr. Mays delivered this oration on October 19, 1980, at the sixty-fifth annual meeting of the Association for the Study of Afro-American Life and History, Inc., at the Marriott Hotel in New Orleans. The audience was composed of scholars, professors, researchers, students, local politicians, and professionals interested in the study of Afro-American life and history. Dr. Mays once served as a vice president of this organization, founded by Dr. Carter G. Woodson in the 1920s. Mays's remarks were actually a campaign address supporting the reelection of President Carter, with whom he had developed a personal and professional relationship when Carter was governor of Georgia.

The appearance by Dr. Mays at the convention came as a part of an overall strategy of the Democratic Party's campaign blitz to carry the state of Louisiana in the upcoming election on November 4, then only two weeks away. Coretta Scott King appeared at Dillard University and made a campaign speech in support of the Carter-Mondale ticket just five days before Mays on October 14. President Carter made his first campaign visit to New Orleans on October 21, two days after Dr. Mays's speech.

To provide a rationale for why blacks should support the reelection of President Carter, Dr. Mays pointed out the names and positions of the record number of blacks who were appointed to government positions during the Carter presidency. Accordingly, Dr. Mays maintained that no president in history had appointed such a large number of blacks to public office before Carter. Mays cited further the commitment and accomplishments of President Carter in the field of civil rights and human rights.

Dr. Mays also viewed President Carter as a decent and honest man who was genuinely concerned with the problems of poverty, racial discrimination, and unemployment—fundamental aspects of Dr. Mays's personal philosophy and commitment.

* * *

* Letter, Sally Warner to Louis Martin, October 24, 1980. Jimmy Carter Presidential Library, Atlanta, Georgia

African-Americans in the Carter Administration:

Cabinet: Patricia Roberts Harris
              Secretary of Health and Human Services
              Donald McHenry
              Ambassador to the United Nations

Ambassadors (15):   Romania
                       Diplomat in Residence
                       German Democratic Republic
                       Republic of Senegal
                       Ambassador-at-large for Liaison with State and
                          Local Governments
                       Botswana
                       Trinidad and Tobago
                       Algeria
                       Mali
                       Haiti
                       Kenya
                       Deputy Negotiator, West Bank and Gaza Autonomy
                          Negotiations
                       Alternate Representative for Special Affairs in the
                          United Nations
                       Spain
                       Malaysia

33 Federal Judiciary (Federal District and Circuit Courts)
8 District of Columbia Local Judges
17 Regulatory Boards and Commissions
11 Army Military Generals and Admirals
10 Air Force Commanders
1 Navy Commander
1 Marine Corps Commander
6 United States Attorney Generals
16 United States Marshals
52 Sub-Cabinet Level Appointees
27 White House Staff
300 Senior Level Appointees to Federal Agencies

Even if Jimmy Carter has not kept his promises to blacks one hundred percent, no president in the history of the nation has done all that he wanted to do in four years. But one fact is clear: no man in the history of the nation has done as much for black Americans as President Carter has done. And he promises to do more. His executive order authorizing every branch of government to examine their budget and set aside an amount of money for black colleges is proof of this, so that we will be assured that black colleges will get their share of money, not only to keep them viable, but sufficient funds to make them equal to the best colleges and universities in the nation.

I was with the President (August 8, 1980) when this executive order was signed and responded to the president's order for the United Negro College Fund presidents.

Beginning January 1, 1981, we will have a president in the White House, and one fact is clear—whoever the President may be, he will never match what Jimmy Carter has done for black Americans. That's history—even if Jimmy Carter is not reelected, his record cannot be erased.

But we must look beyond today and look to the future of our nation and the next one hundred years and see what kind of nation we will have.

Politically, we are just about where we were in the Reconstruction days when the federal soldiers occupied the South after the Civil War. In fact, we are not where we were because we did have blacks represented in the United States Senate, after the Civil War when federal troops occupied the South. Negroes were in the Senate and the House of Representatives in several southern states. From the Hayes-Tilden Compromise in 1876 through 1910, there were Negroes in state and federal government.

I want to compare these statistics with the present situation. In the seventeen southern states, including the District of Columbia, there are twenty-two black state senators, and in the whole United States, there are seventy black state senators. In the whole southern states—sixteen, and the District of Columbia—there are about 3.4 percent blacks. In the whole United States, there are approximately 2000 blacks which represent 3.6 percent. Taking the nation as a whole, we represent easily 11 to 12 percent of the population in this country. If we had 11 percent represented, we would have at least three times more representatives, more congressmen, and more senators than we have now.

Though we have a right to rejoice, nobody clothed in his right mind would say that we are adequately represented in the governance of this nation. The percentage would be even smaller when we take into account black mayors in the United States. It is wonderful that we have able black mayors in Los Angeles, California; in Detroit, Michigan; in Gary, Indiana; Newark, New Jersey; Washington, D.C.; New Orleans, Louisiana; Atlanta, Georgia; Birmingham, Alabama. This is a small percentage when we take all of the cities in the United States and they run into the thousands. Now let me tell you that every chance we can get to get an able black person in the state houses of the nation is a gain for blacks in the nation.

A lot of things will be done in state government and national government which will determine the destiny of the United States for centuries to come. We ought to be a part of the law-making body. Senator Brooke, from Massachusetts, was an able senator and now, through dirty politics, he was defeated, and it may be a long time before we retrieve Senator Brooke's seat.

Mayor Bradley in Los Angeles is perhaps the only black mayor who has been elected when a majority of the people in Los Angeles are non-black. As popular as Maynard Jackson is in Atlanta, to be sure of his election, he had to have at least 22 percent white people voting for him. I really think a larger percent voted for Maynard, but in most of these situations, you must have the assurance that black people will make up the number of votes that will guarantee black elections. The most precious thing that a man can have in a democracy like ours is to be able to cast the ballot for the mayor, for the state representative, state senators, and for representatives and senators in Washington, whether we like politics or not we cannot avoid it. It is one of the greatest things that a black man or a black woman can do—to be a part of the government that determines his or her destiny.

As indicated by Bayard Rustin, "Our future in the balance," "Voters' apathy appears to be particularly pronounced among blacks, for whom ironically this election is of critical importance. Those blacks, and others who sit this election out, will merely be allowing others to determine what kind of government they will have for the next four years."

Most voters recognize that President Carter is a decent and humane man who is concerned about the problems of poverty, racial discrimination, and employment. Moreover, most workers are aware that the President has shown himself to be a friend of labor in his support for the efforts to achieve labor law reform, in his successful restructuring of the Occupational Safety and Health Administration, and in his support for the Humphrey-Hawkins Full Employment Bill.

Yet despite all this, I still hear the "common wisdom" that it doesn't make any difference who is elected. The evidence of history tells us something different. In 1968, there was a close race between Richard Nixon and Hubert Humphrey. Many liberals deserted the Humphrey candidacy because they were dissatisfied with the candidate's view on Vietnam. Many of them argued then, as now, that there was no difference between Nixon and Humphrey. Of course, not only were there differences, they were profound. Those liberals who today are abandoning Carter and those who say it doesn't matter who wins would do well to remind themselves of 1968.

Ronald Reagan is not simply a traditional Republican candidate, he is an ultraconservative who is now attempting to cover his anti-union and anti-worker pronouncements in a bid to attract blue-collar votes. This deception will not hold water with those who examine his stands on the issues closely. But where Reagan stands to gain most is from those who believe that it does not matter who our next president is. All of the polls show that those who are least likely to vote are the poor, blacks, and lower income workers; in other words, those who are most likely not to vote for President Carter.

Our country has entered into a turbulent and challenging decade; we face the challenges of international instability, the growth of Soviet imperialism, and promises of re-industrialization and modernization. All of these problems require a unified country. Voter apathy, alas, will not lead to greater unity, no matter who wins, because those who do not vote will continue to feel that the government is not their own.

Our futures are in the balance. At the time when our country needs to respond intelligently and compassionately to the needs of the poor, the unemployed, the elderly, and the young, our government must be committed to action. Ronald Reagan preaches the politics of less government and greater profits for big business. President Carter, on the other hand, has shown his capacity to bring together government, labor, and business in a partnership designed to address the needs of our country.

The 1980 election will be of great significance for our futures. It would be a great tragedy if voter apathy resulted in the defeat of a president who listens and is sensitive to the needs of the people. Only through a massive turnout can blacks and other people demonstrate that the coalition for social progress and economic justice still exists. Only by re-electing President Carter can we save ourselves from four years of the inhumane and disastrous policies of Ronald Reagan.

I am a world citizen. I have traveled through most of Europe, the Middle East, and the Far East. I have no prejudice against any man because he is white, red, yellow, or brown. But I have tremendous pride in black people. I love the great singers such as Schumann-Heink, Kate Smith, and other great white singers. But I love Roland Hayes, Marion Anderson, Leontyne Price, and Warfield more than I do them—because these black artists are mine. I admire William Shakespeare, Alfred Lloyd Tennyson, H. W. Longfellow, and Ralph Waldo Emerson, but I love Langston Hughes, Claude McKay, Paul Lawrence Dunbar, and James Weldon Johnson. I love these more than I love the white poets because these black poets are mine. I love the great baseball players, Babe Ruth, Lou Gehrig, Joe DiMaggio, Pete Rose, Johnny Bench, and the Neikro brothers. But give me Willie Mays, Hank Aaron, Reggie Jackson, Jackie Robinson, and Vida Blue—because these are mine. I respect all the justices of the United States Supreme Court, but give me Thurgood Marshall—because Thurgood is mine. I appreciate all the politicians in the United States, white and black, but give me our black congressmen, our black Representatives, our black mayors, and our black judges—because they are mine. I love the white historians, but give me Carter G. Woodson and John Hope Franklin and W.E.B. DuBois—these are mine. Thank you and goodbye!

1. Benjamin E. Mays as
a high school student.
(Courtesy Moorland-
Spingarn Research
Center)

2. Benjamin E. Mays, A.B.,
A.M., on the faculty at South
Carolina State College, 1926
Yearbook. (Courtesy South
Carolina State University
Archives)

3. Benjamin E. Mays was born in this house in Epworth, South Carolina, on August 1, 1895. (Photo by F. C. Colston)

4. Old Mount Zion Baptist Church, Epworth, South Carolina. (Photo by F. C. Colston)

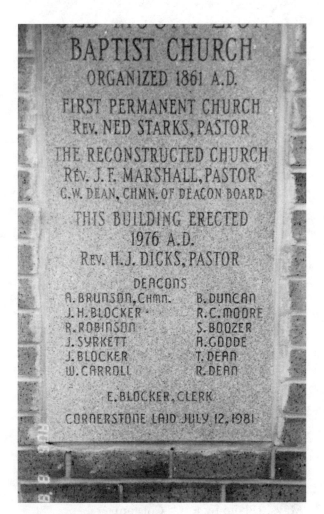

5. Cornerstone at Old Mount Zion.
(Photo by F. C. Colston)

6. Sign erected on a stretch of former Highway 178 in Epworth, South Carolina, honors Dr. Mays. (Photo by F. C. Colston)

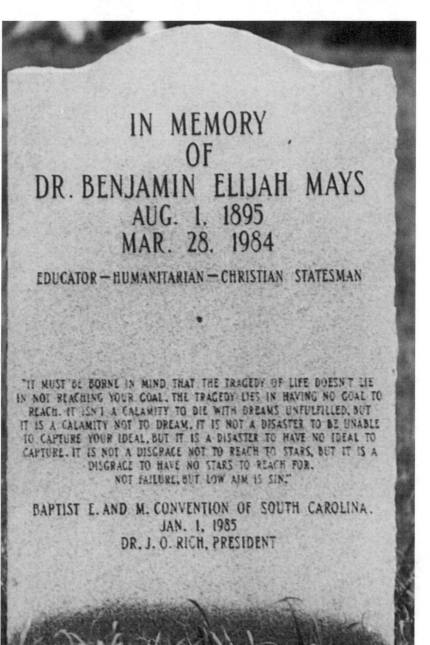

IN MEMORY
OF
DR. BENJAMIN ELIJAH MAYS
AUG. 1. 1895
MAR. 28. 1984

EDUCATOR — HUMANITARIAN — CHRISTIAN STATESMAN

"IT MUST BE BORNE IN MIND THAT THE TRAGEDY OF LIFE DOESN'T LIE
IN NOT REACHING YOUR GOAL. THE TRAGEDY LIES IN HAVING NO GOAL TO
REACH. IT ISN'T A CALAMITY TO DIE WITH DREAMS UNFULFILLED, BUT
IT IS A CALAMITY NOT TO DREAM. IT IS NOT A DISASTER TO BE UNABLE
TO CAPTURE YOUR IDEAL, BUT IT IS A DISASTER TO HAVE NO IDEAL TO
CAPTURE. IT IS NOT A DISGRACE NOT TO REACH TO STARS, BUT IT IS A
DISGRACE TO HAVE NO STARS TO REACH FOR.
NOT FAILURE, BUT LOW AIM IS SIN."

BAPTIST E. AND M. CONVENTION OF SOUTH CAROLINA.
JAN. 1. 1985
DR. J. O. RICH, PRESIDENT

7. Monument in front of Old Mount Zion erected in memory of Dr. Mays. (Photo by F. C. Colston)

MAYS CROSSROADS
NEAR HERE AUG. 1, 1894
DR. BENJAMIN E. MAYS. Ph. D.
WAS BORN
EIGHTH CHILD OF PARENTS
WHO HAD BEEN SLAVES
'ONE OF THE STATE'S MOST
DISTINGUISHED NATIVE SONS
ONE OF THE GREAT FORCES FOR
CIVIL RIGHTS NOT ONLY IN THIS
COUNTRY BUT AROUND THE WORLD
DEAN, SCHOOL OF RELIGION
HOWARD UNIVERSITY
1934 —— 40
PRESIDENT, MOREHOUSE COLLEGE
1940 —— 67
PRESIDENT EMERITUS 1967 —
PRESIDENT
ATLANTA BOARD OF EDUCATION
1969 —— 81
MINISTER AUTHOR ORATOR
DR. MARTIN LUTHER KING, Jr
SAID OF DR. MAYS: HE WAS MY
SPIRITUAL MENTOR AND INTELLEC-
TUAL FATHER.
DEDICATED 1981
BY ACTION OF S. C. GENERAL
ASSEMBLY

8. Monument at Mays Crossroads honors the great educator and native son. (Photo by F. C. Colston)

9. Hezekiah Mays, Jr. ("H.H."), brother of
Benjamin E. Mays. (Courtesy Moorland-
Spingarn Research Center)

10. Dr. Benjamin E. Mays, University of Chicago
(Ph.D.). (Courtesy Moorland-Spingarn Research
Center)

11. Dr. and Mrs. Benjamin E. Mays twenty-fifth wedding anniversary, October 14, 1951. (Courtesy Moorland-Spingarn Research Center)

12. Commencement procession, front row, Dr. Benjamin E. Mays and Dr. Martin Luther King, Jr., 1959. (Courtesy Moorland-Spingarn Research Center)

13. Dr. Albert Manley, President of Spelman College, Dr. Martin Luther King, Jr., Dr. Mays, Nelson Rockefeller, and Ivan Allen, III, Atlanta, Georgia, 1965. (Courtesy Moorland-Spingarn Research Center)

14. Dr. Benjamin E. Mays, commencement speaker, Emory University, Atlanta, Georgia, June 8, 1970. (Courtesy Moorland-Spingarn Research Center)

15. Dr. Benjamin E. Mays accepts the presidency of the
Atlanta Board of Education, 1970. (Courtesy Moorland-
Spingarn Research Center)

16. Below, Dr. Mays delivers the eulogy at the funeral of Dr. Mordecai Wyatt Johnson, Howard University, 1974. (Courtesy Moorland-Spingarn Research Center)

17. Dr. Mays delivers comments in the Rose Garden as President Carter and an unidentified lady listen, 1980. (Courtesy White House Staff Photographer's Collection, Jimmy Carter Presidential Library, Atlanta, Georgia)

18. Multipurpose building named Benjamin E. Mays Center, Bates College, Lewiston, Maine, 1994. (Courtesy Black Cow Photo, Inc., Portland, Maine)

19. Members of Dr. Mays's family at the dedication of the Benjamin E. Mays Center, 1994. (Courtesy Black Cow Photo, Inc.)

20. Dr. Donald W. Harward, President of Bates College, welcomes the visitors at the dedication ceremony, Bates College, October 29, 1994. (Courtesy Black Cow Photo, Inc.)

21. The Bates College Choir sings at the dedication ceremony. (Courtesy Black Cow Photo, Inc.)

22. Robert G. Wade, Sr., Bates, '23, former collegemate of Dr. Mays reminiscences. (Courtesy Black Cow Photo, Inc.)

23. Dr. Charles V. Willie, Morehouse College, '49, Harvard University Professor of Urban Education, speaks at the Bates College Symposium honoring Dr. Mays, October 29, 1994. (Photo by F. C. Colston)

24. Hathorn Hall, oldest building on the Bates College campus, completed in 1857. (Photo by F. C. Colston)

25. The old Coram Library where Mays spent many hours during his student days at Bates. (Photo by F. C. Colston)

26. Bates College Chapel, 1994. (Photo by F. C. Colston)

27. Harkness Hall, Clark Atlanta University, where Dr. Mays delivered the eulogy for Dr. Martin Luther King, Jr., on a platform erected on the steps of the building on April 9, 1968. (Photo by F. C. Colston)

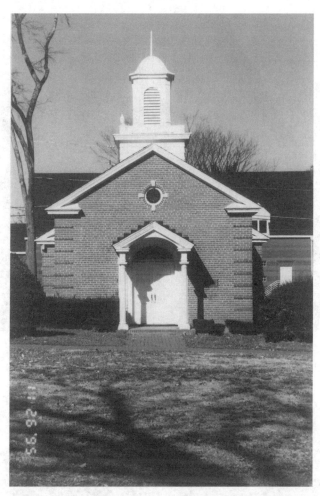

28. Danforth Chapel, Morehouse College erected during the Mays presidency. (Photo by F. C. Colston)

29. Statue of Dr. Martin Luther King, Jr., in front of the International Chapel named in his honor on the campus of Morehouse College. (Photo by F. C. Colston)

30. Dr. Benjamin E. Mays National Memorial on the Morehouse College Quadrangle in front of historic Graves Hall, dedicated May 21, 1995. (Photo by F. C. Colston)

31. Mrs. Coretta Scott King speaks at the dedication of the Dr. Benjamin E. Mays National Memorial (Photo by F. C. Colston)

32. Dr. Samuel D. Cook, President of Dillard University and classmate of Dr. Martin Luther King, Jr., delivers remarks at the ceremony. (Photo by F. C. Colston)

33. Mrs. Bernice Perkins, niece of Dr. Mays, recollects about "Uncle Bennie." (Photo by F. C. Colston)

Chapter 3

Commencement Addresses

The Paradox of Life*

Bringing his oratorical skills to the University of Minnesota in Minneapolis, Dr. Mays spoke at their Spring commencement on March 19, 1959, in Northrop Memorial Auditorium to an audience of graduates, administrators, faculty, parents, relatives, and friends. The crowd was estimated at approximately 4,800, and 560 students received degrees, according to the *Minnesota Daily*, the student newspaper.

At the time of this address, Dr. Mays had been a college president for almost nineteen years. He was the kind of speaker a graduating class would like to have to deliver their commencement address: Dr. Mays was timely, well informed, and aware of the significance of the inspirational needs of students about to leave the cloistered halls of academia to pursue their chosen professional careers. He also knew the attention span of the graduates seated in the audience who were anxious to get their degrees; embrace their classmates, proud relatives, and friends; and leave. For these reasons and more, Dr. Mays was in great demand as a commencement speaker.

In his scholarly and eloquent style, Dr. Mays developed his address around the thesis of the three categories of people who walk the earth.

* * *

* Mays Collection, Moorland-Spingarn Research Center, Howard University

The peoples of history and those of contemporary life may be roughly divided into three distinct classes: those who take the low road, those who take the high road, and those who take the middle road—the low, the high way, the middle way.

I get my insight from a biblical passage—"Two robbers were crucified with him at the time, on his right hand, and the other on his left." The first class is represented by the robbers. Who were they? They were the people who walked the low road. They were not amateurs. They were not unskilled. They were not petty thieves. They were experts, professionals in their chosen fields. They knew their jobs.

What did they do? They took it upon themselves to infest the highways and the seas; they seized decent, law abiding, respected, and respectable citizens, beat them up, robbed them, and frequently left them half dead. This is what they did. They walked the low road.

The Roman government did not like robbers. For repeated robbery, the penalty was death. The government used various methods to liquidate the robbers. They crucified them, hanged them by the neck until dead, threw them from the Tarpeian Rock, threw them to the wild beasts in the arena, burned them alive, and put them in sacks with serpents and drowned them. This is what the Roman government did to the people who walked the low road.

Who are they? In the modern parlance, they are the murderers, the gangsters, the kidnappers, the cutthroats, the dope peddlers, the John Dillingers, the Al Capones, the Leopolds, the Loebs, the members of the Ku Klux Klan and the White Citizens' Council.

The second class is represented by Jesus. In contrast to the robbers who walked the low road, Jesus walked the high road. Who was He? Jesus was a good man. Men may argue about his divinity, split hairs over his virgin birth, deny the authenticity of the miracles, and doubt the historicity of his resurrection. But no man denies the assertion that Jesus was a good man.

What did Jesus do? In contrast to the robbers who went around doing evil, He went around doing good. The record declares that he opened blind eyes, gave hearing to the deaf, speaking to the dumb, and walking to the lame. He gave ordinary men, fisherman and tax collectors, a sense of dignity and worth. He took men steeped in the inferiority-complex—exploited men, cringing, kowtowing men—and said to them in essence "stand erect, throw your shoulders back stick your chin out, and walk the earth with dignity and pride." He taught that the life of every person is of intrinsic worth and value.

But this is the paradox. The people did not like Jesus any better than they did the robbers. They took this good man and killed him. So, both the good and the bad disturb the quiet, the calm, and the traditions and uproot the mores. Society does not like them. This is the paradox of life.

It often happens that the exceptionally good and the exceptionally bad, the prophet and the robber, the sinner and the saint, suffer the same fate at the hands of the same people. The Roman government killed Jesus, and the Roman government killed the robbers. The Athenian government that killed Socrates, at the same time, condemned to death Alcibiades, although Alcibiades died later at the hands of unknown parties. The same government that put Gandhi and Nehru in jail killed Jumbulinganada, a notorious criminal in South India.

The same government that sent Eugene Debbs to federal prison had John Dillinger shot down on the streets of Chicago. The same city government that put murderers and thieves behind prison bars also put behind bars Martin Luther King, Jr. This is the paradox of life. The exceptionally good and the exceptionally bad often suffer the same fate at the hands of the same government.

The third class is represented by the traditionally good people—the people who walk the middle road. They are the people who defend the status quo. And the thing that disturbs me most is the fact that Jesus was not killed by gangsters and murderers. The respectable people killed Jesus. And this is so paradoxical. I could take it much better if a man like Hitler or Stalin or Tojo had killed Jesus. But the decent people did it. The Roman officials, the judges of the Sanhedrin Court, the learned scribes, and the aristocratic Sadducees—all these had a hand in killing Jesus. They were the leading people, comparable to our senators, governors, judges, ministers and college and university professors. The constituted authorities killed Jesus. This too is a paradox.

This third class is represented by those who fought the development of science and surgery. They are the people who fought Darwin, who made Galileo recant at age seventy, who put Roger Bacon in jail at the age of sixty-six because he advocated the experimental method in science; they are the people who burned Bruno and Joan of Arc alive, who opposed the development of medicine and fought against the education of women.

They are the people of our time who argue with the eloquence of a Demosthenes, the fluency of a Cicero, the logic of a Socrates, and the choice words of a Shakespeare that the time is not ripe to make changes.

Now from this all too brief analysis, let me make three brief observations: The first observation is that the future of human progress is always with those who walk the high road of truth, justice, fair play, and brotherhood. It is sometimes with those who defend but never with those who walk the low road. I am not saying that the status quo should never be defended, but I do contend that when mankind is seized, so to speak, by the neck, and given a great thrust forward, it is usually when some brave, heroic soul dares to break with custom and tradition, dares to think and act in the light of what he conceives to be a higher truth, and who dares to give his allegiance to the highest and best that he knows.

The future of science was not with the men who made Galileo recant, not with those who put Roger Bacon in jail, and not with those who fought the doctrine of evolution. But the future of science was with Galileo, with Darwin, and with Bacon. The future of medicine was not with those who for centuries opposed surgery, and the future of preventive medicine was not with those who fought the idea of vaccination against smallpox. The future of women was not in the hands of the feudal lords who at one time had the right of a bride's body for three days after marriage. Rather, women's future was in the hands of a prophet like Jesus and a crusader like Susan B. Anthony. The future of mankind is always with those who walk the high road.

The second observation is that only those who walk the high road are truly free. If it is true that only the disciplined mind is free, certainly the man who walks the middle way and he who walks the low way can hardly be free.

Those who walk the low road are slaves to the things that are low, mean, and base. They are creatures of passion, low aims, and vicious habits. By and large, those who defend the middle way, the status quo, are usually slaves to their environment, to tradition, to the mores, and to what they fear their friends may think if they live contrary to the current patterns of behavior. No man is free who is afraid to speak the truth as he sees it; no man is free who is afraid to stand for what he believes to be right, and who fears his political, social, or economic future will be jeopardized if he stands and acts on the principles of truth, justice, and democracy. The politician whose aim is to get elected, the businessman whose chief aim is to make excessive profit, the man who must know in advance what will happen to his economic security before he takes a position in this age of turmoil and indecision, can never be free. Only the disciplined mind is free: disciplined and free to pursue truth and proclaim it, when to do so is unpopular; disciplined and free to live without prejudice, when to do so is dangerous; disciplined and free to walk the high road, when to do so may lead to social ostracism, death, or imprisonment. As Henry Van Dyke so beautifully says: "It is better to follow even the shadow of the best than to remain content with the worst. And those who would see wonderful things, must often be ready to travel alone." Such a man is free.

I come to my third and final observation. We often hear it said that those who take the high road are ahead of their time. We say they should wait for the time to get ripe. The essence of genius is proper timing. But I advance the thesis tonight that no man is ever ahead of his time; every man is within his star.

I ask you: was Jesus ahead of his time? How long would Jesus have had to wait for the Roman officials and the religious leaders of his day to accept his message so he might have lived to be three scores and ten rather than die at thirty-three? How long? Was Paul ahead of his time? How long would Paul have had to wait before his Gentile world have had unrestricted access to Christianity? Was Martin Luther ahead of his time? How long would Martin Luther had to wait for the church to clear out the corruption against which he proclaimed? Was Lincoln ahead of his time? How long would Lincoln have had to wait for the union to save itself and for a race to be emancipated? How long would Mahatma Gandhi have had to wait for Britain to free India voluntarily and for the upper caste men to give up untouchability? How long would the thirteen colonies have had to wait for Britain to take the initiative to give us freedom? How long would Martin Luther King, Jr., have had to wait for the capital of the Confederacy to abolish segregation on the buses of Montgomery?

Now if those men had a hundred lives to live, they would have had time to wait. But man has but one life to live. He must respond to the higher call in his lifetime, or he will never respond. To shirk one's responsibility by passing it on to the next generation is the act of a coward.

Abraham leaving his country in obedience to God's call; Moses leading his people out of bondage; Copernicus battling for scientific truth against terrific odds; Garrison and Harriett Beecher Stowe thundering against the institution of slavery; Ridley and Latimer promulgating the doctrine of the Reformation, burned at the stake for it; Jesse Lazear exposing himself to the bites of mosquitoes, in order to find a cause of yellow fever, dying as a result of it; Lincoln dying of an assassin's bullet; Woodrow Wilson crusading for a League of Nations; the nine Justices of the Supreme Court declaring segregation in the public schools unconstitutional—none of these were ahead of their time. They are to progress what the dawn is to the sunrise and what the sunrise is to noon. No man is ahead of his time.

You are graduating tonight from a great university. Most of you will follow in the footsteps of your elders—you will defend the status quo—walk the middle way. You, too, will seek economic security, social prestige, and political power. You, too, may sacrifice principle to gain these. But I hope some of you will walk the high road and lift the torch of freedom, justice, and democracy, which this world so sorely needs. For no man can maintain the integrity of his soul by giving his allegiance to a lesser good. I close with these words from John Oxenham: "To every man there openeth a way, and ways, and a way; and the high soul climbs the higher way, and the low soul gropes the low; and in between, on the misty flats, the rest drift to and fro. But to every man there openeth a high way, and a low, and every man decideth the way his soul shall go."

The Challenge to Overcome Major Disabilities of 341 Years in a Quarter of a Century*

The year 1960 marked the beginning of massive college student involvement in the civil rights movement. On February 1, 1960, three freshmen from North Carolina A & T University in Greensboro sat-in at the lunch counter at Woolworth, requesting service. They were denied service, later arrested, and the sit-in movement commenced at public accommodations that previously denied service to blacks under the separate but equal doctrine. Subsequently, demonstrations were held in college communities throughout the South, aimed at desegregating public facilities in cities such as Atlanta, Nashville, Knoxville, Tallahassee, and several others, using the technique of nonviolent direct action.

Dr. Mays addressed parents, relatives, friends, and graduates at Florida A & M University in Tallahassee, Florida, on Saturday, May 28, 1960, 6:00 p.m. at the graduation ceremony held in Lee Hall Auditorium. Approximately 1,700 were in attendance, and 266 students received degrees.

Dr. Mays divided the sojourn of blacks in America into three periods: the era of slavery from 1619 to 1865; the second era from 1865 to May 17, 1954; and the third era he called the era of desegregation beginning in 1954. These periods symbolized the 341 years of disability. He used his extensive knowledge of black history to analyze the developments in these time periods.

In remarks designed to inspire and challenge the graduating class, he affirmed, "These disabilities we are now challenged to overcome in twenty-five years." He informed the class that because they were young; they would live twenty-five years, and he probably would not. This statement is drawn from a cliché he sometimes referred to: young men may die, but old men must. Dr. Mays was almost sixty-five years old at the time of this address, yet all those in attendance knew that his inspiring example and presence would endure long after his passing.

* * *

* Mays Collection, Moorland-Spingarn Research Center, Howard University

I am using tonight a rather strange subject. I hope you will like it. If you do not agree with my proposal, you must give reasons for your disagreement, in which case I will have stimulated you to think in order to justify your opposition. If you agree, I have convinced you. So, head or tail, I win. The subject is, "The Challenge to Overcome the Major Disabilities of 341 Years in a Quarter of a Century."

The Negro's sojourn in the United States may be roughly divided into three eras: the era of slavery from 1619 to 1865; the second era from 1865 to May 17, 1954; and the third era which may be called the era of desegregation or, as it is wrongly called, integration, beginning in 1954.

The slave era was the era of sub-humanity, the era of depersonalization, when the Negro was not human but property owned and sold like cattle, like mules and horses, cows, hogs, cats and dogs, sheep and goats. He had no standing in law. The bodies of the slaves belonged to the masters, and if they so desired, they possessed the bodies of the female slaves, and there is considerable evidence to show that many of the masters did desire and did possess the bodies of the female slaves.

Slavery, like all great evils, had to be justified. Conscience had to be silenced if the system was to be perpetuated. And all experience proves that there is no sin, however colossal, that the human mind cannot justify, thus making it easy for one to sleep at night without a disturbed conscience. Four arguments were advanced to justify and to perpetuate this crime against God and humanity. The slave, they argued, is fundamentally, biologically, and inherently inferior. It was even argued that the slave had no soul and that he was incapable of being educated. If a person can accept the fact that the object he holds in subjection is inferior by nature, he has no pangs of conscience when he kicks it around.

Perhaps the strongest argument in support of slavery was the argument that slavery is God's will. God sent the Negro into the world for the expressed purpose to hew wood, to draw water, to till the soil, to pick cotton, and to cultivate tobacco. And one must never interfere with the designs of God. It was argued thirdly that civilization depended upon slave labor and that abolition of slavery would mean the collapse of civilization.

There was a fourth argument to support the slave system. It was the most insidious of them all. "It is good for the slave that he be a slave." This fourth argument reminds me of an old African proverb: "Full belly child said to empty belly child, be of good cheer." How strange! It often happens that the one man at the top argues that it is good for the man at the bottom to be at the bottom. Slavery was our lot for 246 years.

Finally, the slaves themselves began to rebel; the system was unprofitable to the North; and the abolitionists began to denounce the system as inhuman and as a sin against God. Four years of bloody war split the nation in twain; Lincoln issued his Emancipation Proclamation; the Civil War ended; and four million Negroes came out singing—"Thank God, free at last. Before I would be a slave, I would be buried in my grave and go home to my Lord and be saved."

But Lincoln's proclamation and the eventual emancipation were not adequate. The slave had to be humanized, made a citizen, guaranteed the equal protection of the law, and given the ballot; hence, the enactment of the 13th, 14th, and 15th amendments.

The second era was the era of segregation. The real problem came with emancipation. As a slave, the Negro's status was definite and fixed. As a free man, he became a problem and was unwanted. Four solutions were sought to get rid of the newly emancipated people: first, colonize them—give them a separate state; secondly, send them back to Africa; thirdly, leave them alone and they will die out because they will not be able to compete in a civilized society; and fourthly, segregate them. Up to May 17, 1954, segregation was the only program that the United States government and the governments of the South had advanced to solve the so-called Negro problem.

The privileges exercised by the Negro during the few brief years of reconstruction were short-lived. So, the segregated era may be roughly designated as the period embracing the years from 1865 to May 17, 1954.

Even before emancipation, segregation had begun, and it was practiced in God's church. Between 1864 and 1910, segregation had entrenched itself by law in every area of southern life. The Negro was segregated by law in the South and by custom in the North.

Though not usually considered so, segregation by law was another form of slavery, in many ways just as devastating. Segregation by law, imposed by the strong upon the weak, was the main objective. The first aim of segregation by law is to brand the segregated as inferior, pin a badge on him or print a sign on his back marked "inferior" so that the whole wide world would know that here is an object unfit to associate with other human beings. The second object of segregation is to instill in the mind of the segregated the idea that he is inferior so that he will walk and talk like an inferior and cringe and kowtow like an inferior. The third object of segregation was and is to set the segregated apart so that he will be denied the ballot, given inferior goods and services, assigned inferior jobs, provided inferior education, and given inferior accommodations. It was not until May 17, 1954, that the back of this deadly sin, segregation, was broken. And it was not until we began to sue in federal courts that we began to move toward equality in education. So the period from 1619 to 1954 is 335 years. We speak of 341 years of disability because segregation is still as ever-present as evil.

Let us now briefly examine these 341 years of disability—246 years of slavery and 95 years of segregation—and see what they have done to the heart, mind, soul, will, and body of the Negro people. Let us not deceive ourselves; let us not be naive: these 341 years of disability have left their visible marks and scars upon the Negro. What have they done to you and me?

These 341 years of disability made millions of Negroes believe that they were inferior—so much that millions of Negroes since 1865 accepted without protest their inferior status, behaved like an inferior. How could it be otherwise? Economically suppressed, politically disfranchised, educationally illiterate, physically afraid, and deliberately set apart so that everything in the environment said to the Negro, "You do not belong. You are nobody." Tell this to a people for three and a half centuries, and you have a situation in which millions of men and women will never be able to stand erect and will never be able to walk the earth with dignity and pride.

These 341 years of disability destroyed the ambition of millions, crushed the potential genius of thousands, and cut the nerves of aspirations of hundreds of thousands. Every Negro boy and girl knew before he was six that the ceiling, and not the sky, was the limit for him and that the best things in politics, economics, and education were not meant for the Negro. Potential scientists, statesmen, engineers, authors, artists, and philosophers were still born.

This created an intellectual ghetto in the Negro race. The few who aspired to be "somebody" never gazed beyond the accomplishments of the few successful Negroes they saw about them. I was considered an "uppity" boy when it was learned in my community that my ambition extended far beyond that of being a teacher in a four-month school at $25 a month. In this ghetto, competition was racial and still is to some extent. Negro professionals sought to be the most outstanding Negro teacher, the best Negro preacher, the finest Negro farmer, the leading Negro professional to compete beyond the race. In fact, it was considered dangerous to compete with white men lest you be branded as trying to be white. Negroes were expected to stay in their subordinate place.

Furthermore, these years of disability made Negroes ashamed of their race. Many Negroes wanted to be anything except a Negro—a Mexican, a Chinese, an American Indian, a poor white man—anything except a Negro. For a long time, Negroes were proud of their ignorance of Negro history and wanted to hear nothing of their African ancestry.

These years of disability naturally made Negroes disbelieve in themselves. Even the most competent Negro needed the endorsement and approval of white people before Negroes would accept his competence. Negroes had little faith in Negro doctors, dentists, businessmen, and lawyers. That which was white was best. Authority resided in a white skin.

These 341 years of disability have made us politically impotent. For a long time, we were, and in some places still are, voteless. We have little voice in the governments that rule us. There is not one Negro in a single legislature in the deep South and virtually none on city councils. Out of 437 Congressmen in the House of Representatives, only four are Negroes. Normally there should be 47 Negroes in the House of Representatives, but there is not one Negro Senator out of a total of 100. No Negro has ever been a full member of the Cabinet. No Negro has ever sat as one of the nine justices of the Supreme Court. We have produced no governors.

It is true that we have come a long way in our economic quest. And yet despite the gains, we are at the bottom of the economic ladder. The average income of the Negro family is half or less than that of the average white family. Most of the Negro workers are common laborers and semiskilled workers.

Most of all, these years of disability have thrown us behind in education. By and large, we do not do well on national tests. A few of us do exceptionally well on these tests, but most of us fall behind the national average. We are 10 percent of the population, but we have less than 4 percent of the collegiate enrollment. Only a fraction of one percent of all the Ph.D.s in the United States are Negroes. Our percentage of Negro doctors, engineers, lawyers, chemists and physicists is miserably low. We cannot deny the fact that we have more than our share of disease,

crime and delinquency. These are but a few of the disabilities resulting
from 341 years of slavery and segregation.

Members of the graduating class, it is these disabilities we are challenged to overcome in twenty-five years. I challenge you because you
are young. . . .

Do I hear you say, "Fantastic?" It is fantastic, but not impossible. I
hear another say, "An empty dream." It does not have to be an empty
dream. "Foolishness," say someone else. It is foolishness only to the
lazy, the cowards and the unimaginative. To men of faith and courage,
we can overcome these disabilities in twenty-five years.

But how can it be done? First of all, we must accept the fact without
bitterness and without ill will that we are behind. Admit that we have
come a long way under adverse circumstances and also that we have
further to go than we have come. We cannot brag too much about the
number of Negro Ph.D.s and Phi Beta Kappas. The number is negligible. A few Negroes have accumulated a million dollars, but to find
them is like looking for a needle in a haystack. There are hundreds of
fine homes owned by Negroes, and yet in 1950, 60 percent of all Negroes lived in substandard houses.

We have done well in education, and yet there are hardly enough
able Negro scholars to staff all the divisions of the University of Chicago. We have made fine progress in medicine, but there are too few
Charles Drews. There are hardly enough Negro specialists to staff from
top to bottom Presbyterian Hospital in Medical Center, New York. We
have done mighty well in banking, but there are not enough Negroes
skilled in money and banking to take over the Chase National Bank. We
are very successful in insurance, but not enough to run from top to
bottom the Metropolitan Life Insurance Company. To overcome these
disabilities in twenty-five years, we must recognize the fact that we are
behind and get on with the job. This truth must be drilled into our hearts
and mind: "The group that starts behind in the great race of life must
forever remain behind or run faster than the race in front."

These facts must be made clear to Negroes everywhere. They must
be known in the classrooms, expounded in the churches, printed in the
press, impressed upon youth in the home, made the theme of fraternities
and sororities, and stamped indelibly upon the minds of parents and
teachers. Our pace is too slow. We can run faster than we are running if
we develop the will and the determination to do so. Our academic pace
from the first grade through college is entirely too slow; too little pursuit

of excellence. Students read and study too little, and teachers demand too little. We write too few books, too few articles, and do not do enough research.

Our teachers must be motivated to teach Negro students with a sense of mission, as if God the Father called them into the world for the expressed purpose to teach. For some time yet, the vast majority of Negro students will be taught by Negro teachers. We must each do as the prophets prophesied: as Amos, who said, "When the eternal God speaks, who can but prophesy; as Jeremiah, who explained, "The spirit of the Lord is upon me for he has anointed me to preach the Gospel to the poor; as Paul, who declared, "I am ruined if I preach not the Gospel." We must teach, preach, do business, build bridges, practice medicine and plead for justice as the poets write poetry. It was John Bunyan who said: "I had to set aside the writing of sermons and other serious tracts in order to write *Pilgrim's Progress*. It was Horace who explained: "I could not sleep at night because of the pressure of unwritten poetry." Whatever we do, if we are to overcome the disabilities of 341 years in a quarter of a century, we must do it as if God called us into the world to do it. We cannot allow any sand to burn under our feet.

If it takes the sacrificing of social privileges in order to become master teachers, in the name of the Lord God almighty, let us sacrifice social privileges. Most of the Negro students are not necessarily dumb. They are handicapped by the disabilities of three and a half centuries. If it takes more patience in order to open their minds, for God's sake let us develop patience. If it takes extra love and affection in order to get the students to see the light, let us love them and give them the affection they need.

We can say to students now what we have never been able to say to them before. We can motivate them by making it clear to them that the future for the competent never looked so bright as it does today, as competence broke the color bar in every other area of American life. There are too few chemists, physicists, mathematicians, engineers, and too few top flight scholars for colleges and universities, and too few dedicated ministers. The time is near and possible at hand when no industry will refuse to hire a first-class physicist or chemist because his skin is black. The government in the future can ill afford to refuse to place a first-class psychologist because he happens to be a Negro. We could not say that to Negro students twenty-five years ago. We can tell them that the sky—and not the ceiling—is beginning to be the limit.

Now that segregation is a decrepit old man, discredited everywhere, fighting a losing battle for his life, the Negro can now look unto the hills from whence cometh his help.

I do not mean to give you the impression that the battle for equality has been won—far from it. But we can win it in twenty-five years, if we continue the battle for first-class citizenship. If we stop the program to desegregate America, segregation will take a new hold, and it will fasten its tendencies upon us for another fifty years. The state legislatures placed these disabilities upon us, but the federal government must remove them. The state governments will not. The battle for respect which we who are older have waged for decades and which Negro students are carrying on now with a new technique must be continued. As you leave these hallowed walls, some kind of leadership will be thrust upon you. Never rest until every qualified Negro in your community is a registered voter. We will be respected in proportion as we exercise the ballot and participate in government. A voteless people is a helpless people.

What we use to motivate students we must use to motivate ourselves. The day of racial competition is over. We can no longer aspire to be a leading Negro surgeon. Today the competition is worldwide. Every surgeon competes with surgeons everywhere. Every scientist is in competition with scientists the world over. Every artist competes in the world market. Every businessman competes with businessmen in the world market.

If we are to overcome the disabilities of 341 years in one-quarter of a century, we must close ranks and look with contempt upon no man. We are no better than our fellows. Let us identify ourselves with all mankind—the high and the low, the great and the small, the learned and the unlearned, the rich and the poor, white and black, yellow and brown. No man of himself is better than his fellow.

If any man is more favorably circumstanced than another, it's an accident—it's by the grace of God. No child can choose his parents. They may be rich, they may be poor. He didn't choose them. No man can choose his mind. If lucky to have a brilliant mind, let him thank God but never boast about it. He might have been a moron. One cannot choose his race. If born white, given privileges and opportunities by virtue of whiteness, let him not boast about it. He might have been born black. One cannot choose his nation. If born in rich America with a silver spoon in his mouth, let him thank God but never boast about it. But for the grace of God he might have been one of the starving millions of India.

Every man is a part of humanity. The fate of one is the fate of all: birth, life, and death. Do not look down upon this illiterate Negro living in Tallahassee and New York. Eugene Debbs was so right when he said: "As long as there is a poorer class, I am in it. As long as there is a man in jail, I am not free." John Donne was equally right when he said: "No man is an Island," etc.

The white graduate may neglect the spiritual and the moral, but the Negro student cannot and must not. In seeking to overcome the disabilities of 341 years in twenty-five years, we fight not for ourselves, for it matters little what happens to Negroes. But it matters much what happens to the Christian Gospel and to democracy. Either democracy and Christianity will function in America, or it will perish from the earth. In this great fight of ours, we fight not for ourselves alone, but for the United States.

Finally, if we are to overcome the disabilities of 341 years in a quarter of a century, let us create in ourselves a divine discontent, a divine restlessness, an eternal dissatisfaction with mediocrity. Let us declare war on the average. Let us seek status not in our cars, not in our houses, but seek it as leaders of thought, as experts who extend the bounds of knowledge in research, seek it as authors of books and articles, as outstanding chemists, teachers, ministers, and builders. Let us declare war on mediocre, ordinary performance.

The satisfied life is the dying life. The satisfied teacher will never improve his teaching. The man who is satisfied with slum living will never move out of the slums. The minister who brags about his sermons and is satisfied with them will never preach better. The artist who is satisfied with his art will never paint a better picture. The physician who is satisfied with his skill will never be a greater surgeon.

Houses and land, stocks and bonds, silver and gold, will keep you living, but only your ideals will keep you alive: ideals of justice, love, good will, brotherhood, and ideals in the pursuit of excellence. I close with two poems which I hope will challenge you to do your part to help us overcome the disabilities of 341 years in a quarter of a century.

To every man there openeth a way,
And ways, and a way.
And the high soul climbs the higher way,
and the low soul gropes the low,
And in between, on the misty flats,
the rest drift to and fro.

But to every man there openeth
A high way, and a low.
And every man decideth the way
his soul shall go.

John Oxenham

God, though his life is but a wraith,
Although we know not what we use,
Although we grope with little faith,
Give me the heart to fight—and lose.
Ever insurgent let me be,
Make me more daring than devout;
From sleek contentment keep me free,
And fill me with a buoyant doubt.
Open my eyes to visions girt
With beauty, and with wonder lit—
But always let me see the dirt,
And all that spawn and die in it.
Open my ears to music; let
Me thrill with Spring's first flutes and drums—
But never let me dare forget
The bitter ballads of the slums.
From compromise and things half done,
Keep me with stern and stubborn pride;
And when at last, the fight is won,
God, keep me still unsatisfied.

Louis Untermeyer

A Crisis and a Challenge*

Just three days before Martin Luther King, Jr., led the March on Washington, and delivered the immortal "I Have a Dream" speech, on August 28, 1963, Dr. Mays presented this oration at Texas Southern University, a predominantly black publicly supported institution in Houston, Texas. Dr. Mays also participated in that historic civil rights demonstration. In Houston, on August 25, 1963, he spoke to an audience of administrators, faculty, staff, students, alumni, community leaders, and friends of the speaker. The occasion marked the sixteenth annual commencement exercises. Bachelor's and master's degrees were awarded to 229 students. His speech challenged, inspired, and motivated his listeners.

Dr. Mays urged the graduates to place a high premium on professional excellence in order to make recent civil rights gains more meaningful and permanent. He further advised them that despite long years of crippling circumstances, blacks are expected to meet the same standards of performance required of other Americans. Mays affirmed that this predicament created both a challenge and a potential crisis.

* * *

In speaking to you this afternoon on a simple subject, "A Crisis and a Challenge," I do not pretend to say anything new nor astonish you with great ideas. Really, I am talking to you about the obvious. Even so, it often happens that the obvious truths need to be repeated again and again in the hope that urgent matters might be attended to more quickly and necessary changes wrought with greater speed.

No group of teachers in the United States, and, I suspect, in the world, has a responsibility as great as that of us whose primary job it is to teach, to inspire, and to motivate Negro youths—whose handicaps and disabilities reach back for 346 years. No people in history have been so deeply, so maliciously, and so deliberately maligned as Negro Americans. I could prove these assertions that degrade and dehumanize Negro Americans by quoting the words of eminent men of the nineteenth and twentieth centuries. But why take your time when you are as knowledgeable as I am on these points?

---

* Mays Collection, Moorland-Spingarn Research Center, Howard University

There is something unique and deceptive about the human mind. There seems to be something innate in man which makes him want to live at peace with himself. When he sinks too low in the scale of human decency or commits deeds which his conscience tells him are wrong and finds himself at war with himself, he seeks peace of mind by attempting to find a rational basis for his wicked behavior. Thus, slavery and caste have had to be justified.

When our nation was born, we fought a war on the Declaration:

> We hold these truths to be self evident, that all men are created equal, that they are endowed by their Creator with certain inalienable rights, and among these are life, liberty and the pursuit of happiness.

This country held slaves, and it was 87 years after 1776 before Lincoln issued the Emancipation Proclamation. And during the slave era of 246 years, the Gospel of Christ was eloquently expounded. Men preached the fatherhood of God and the brotherhood of man. They declared that the life of each and every child was sacred in God's sight, and that God cares so minutely for each person that the strands of hair on our heads are all numbered, and that it was better for a millstone to be placed around a man's neck and he be drowned in the depths of the sea than for him to injure one of God's little ones.

Clinging to the Declaration of Independence and the revolutionary Gospel of the fatherhood of God and the brotherhood of man, slavery had to be given a rational basis, though a false one. You know the arguments. The Negro is subhuman. He has no soul. He is incapable of mastering the upper branches of knowledge. God ordained slavery so that the Africans could be brought to America to be Christianized. The major arguments were:

1. The Negro is an inherently, biological inferior race. His mental inferiority is a permanent condition. God made him that way. He was born to be a slave—hewer of wood and drawer of water.
2. Civilization depends on slavery. Abolish it and civilization would collapse.
3. It is good for the Negro that he be a slave.
4. How strange it is that one who sits at the top can argue that it is good for the man at the bottom that he be at the bottom.

The more the abolitionists pressed for the slaves on moral grounds, the more eloquent the argument of Negro inferiority was expounded by pseudo-scientists, ministers, statesmen, politicians, authors, editors, and orators.

Eventually, the Civil War ended physical slavery. Although the emancipation of slaves on moral grounds was not the objective of the Civil War, their freedom was inevitable once the war began. The good effects of physical emancipation were soon swept away by caste. The Hayes-Tilden Compromise and the withdrawal of federal troops in the late 1870's made segregation another form of slavery. As slavery, caste, too, was justified on the grounds of Negro inferiority. If the Negro is an inferior person, the declaration of rights enunciated by Jefferson did not apply to him. And the slave holder could live with his conscience and go on preaching the fatherhood of God and the brotherhood of man, go on clinging to the Declaration of Independence and go on repeating: I swear allegiance to the flag of the United States of America and to the Republic for which it stands, one nation, indivisible, with liberty and justice for all.

So it is clear that slavery and segregation were justified and made palatable on the ground that Negroes are inherently inferior. It should be noted here that in order to justify slavery and segregation, the interpretation of the Declaration of Independence had to be falsified. When the Declaration of Independence says that we are endowed by our Creator with certain inalienable rights, that among these are life, liberty, and the pursuit of happiness, it is not speaking of biological equality. Jefferson and others are saying that every man, whether he is a fifth grade student, a high school graduate, an A.B., A.M., or Ph.D., has certain inalienable rights that are God-given—among them are life, liberty, and the pursuit of happiness. But evil-minded men applied this, as Myrdal points out, to biology. If the Negro is an inherently inferior person, the Declaration of Independence was not meant for him, just as it was not meant for the horses and mules, hogs and dogs. In this way they could exclude the Negro from the confines of the Declaration of Independence and mistreat him without the pangs of conscience. They could hold slaves, practice caste, and be loyal churchmen at the same time.

This view of the Negro was expressed by the leading scientists of the 19th century and the first quarter of the 20th century. It is only within the last thirty-five or forty years that anthropologists and other scientists have unearthed new data and gained new insights which today enable them to repudiate the doctrine of inherently inferior or superior races. Thanks to Negro scholars, with the exception of one Negro writer, Negroes were the prophetic voices declaring what science now attests—that differences in racial achievements are environmental.

But the damage has been done. This conception of Negro inferiority was eloquently dramatized in books, magazines, newspapers, movies, and on the platform. It reflected itself against the Negro by providing him with inferior education and poor-paying jobs, inferior public accommodations and the denial of the use of the ballot. It reflected itself in lynching, police brutality, and in inequality before the law.

Living in such an environment, irreparable damage was done to the spirit, soul, and mind of Negroes. Some apparently accepted the myth of inferiority and governed themselves accordingly. Virtually all Negroes had to aim low. There was little incentive for them to strive for excellence because a low ceiling, and not the sky, was the limit for them. Under these circumstances, it is miraculous that so many Negroes have achieved distinction in American life.

Our task as educators is great because something spectacular has happened. As the nations of Asia and Africa are determined to throw off the yoke of segregation and discrimination, the Negro's objective is to walk the earth with dignity. He is overcoming fear. He is willing in large numbers to suffer, go to jail and even die to gain freedom at home for which his comrades fought, bled and died that others might have freedom in foreign lands.

The forces of history have combined: the Gospel of Christ and the Declaration of Independence; the American Dream, liberty, equality and justice; a war to make the world safe for democracy, a war to bring the four freedoms to all mankind; another war to put down aggression; federal decrees to end segregation and discrimination; Negro students and adults sitting-in, wading-in, kneeling-in, boycotting, picketing, and the pressure of world opinion upon a nation that has a double standard of citizenship—all these forces have combined to produce the social revolution through which we are passing. These forces contribute to the destruction of segregation and an end to the penning up of Negroes, opportunities undreamed of twenty-five years ago.

We thank God for the social revolution, and we pray that it may continue until the American dream is equally applicable to every American. But we would be naive indeed if we did not see that these forces and automation have created a crisis in education for Negroes. We contend, and rightfully so, that there shall be a single standard for citizenship. But a single standard for citizenship means a single standard for performance. As the walls of segregation crumble and discrimination diminishes, we are expected, despite 346 years of crippling circumscription, to meet the same standards of excellence required of other Americans. And yet most of the boys and girls you teach come from homes that are educationally, economically, and culturally deprived. Our students are given the same tests and are expected to do as well as students having a more favorable stance.

The low scores our students make on the various tests and the small number that qualify for national science, Danforth, Woodrow Wilson, and National Merit fellowships—and the few who pass the entrance examinations for government and foreign service—all these are highly publicized. We are told again that, "We will hire Negro engineers, chemists, physicists, but where are they? We want more Negroes in the foreign service, but few are qualified." No consideration is given to the fact that the doors of hope were closed for three and one-half centuries, and now almost overnight, Negroes are expected to be able to meet the competition of the modern world. To expect this on a large scale is to expect the miraculous. And yet no one can deny that this situation creates both a crisis and a challenge.

I say to you again that no group of teachers in the U.S.A. has a responsibility as great as ours, we who are responsible for the training of Negro youth. In saying this, I assume three things: I assume that for a long time the majority of Negro students in public schools will be taught by Negro teachers. I also assume that you and I will have more concern for helping Negro students to overcome the handicaps of the past than any other group of teachers in the world.

If this isn't so, it ought to be so. I assume further that if you and I do not do this job of preparing Negro students to meet the competition of the modern world, it will not be done. In years past, boards of education in the South had little or no concern for providing education for Negroes. And since the boards didn't care, Negro teachers and principals didn't care very much. Even now, it is mainly the responsibility of teachers and principals, and not the boards of education, to see to it that an excellent job is done in the classrooms. Some boards of education are still not interested in preparing Negroes to meet the competition of the modern world.

If as a result of the de facto segregation, segregation will be with us for a long time, we must not assume that we can have first-rate education only if there is desegregation. The task is ours to provide quality education whether we teach all Negroes, all whites, or a mixture.

We are against segregation and discrimination based on race. But if circumstances which we cannot now control give us schools whose enrollments are all Negro, I will not believe that such schools must be second-rate. The prerequisites for a good school are a competent, devoted faculty, adequate equipment and buildings, and students eager to learn and easily motivated. Given these facilities, whether the faculty and students are integrated or non-integrated, the school can be first-rate. If this is not so, we are stuck with inferior education for a long time.

The major choice is the teacher. It is my belief that thousands of students are crippled for life because too many teachers are poorly prepared. The first job confronting any teacher is to know his subject matter so well that he or she will be at home and poised at all times. Even if the author of the book you teach visited the classroom, you would be cool, calm, and collected. The competent teacher is not disturbed when the principal or the superintendent enters the room. If the teacher is really competent, the chances are great that he knows the subject matter better than the superintendent. There is no need to get high blood pressure or stop teaching when the boss comes around. Only the incompetent teacher is jittery. Only the incompetent teacher must cringe and kowtow. Most of our students come from homes where there is economic education and cultural deprivation. It requires love, devotion and patience to deal with them. You may be tempted to be complacent, keep order, draw your breath and your salaries. But there are many diamonds in the rough. Our job is to find them, to love them, and to motivate them. Moses was born a slave. Jesus did not belong to the first family of the Jews. Spinoza came out of a Jewish ghetto. Horace was the son of a former slave. Ramsey McDonald was born in a two-room cabin in Scotland; Lincoln in a one-room cabin in Kentucky. Frederick Douglass and Harriet Tubman, Phyllis Wheatley and Booker T. Washington, were born slaves. Mary McLeod Bethune came from the rice fields of South Carolina.

The teachers we need are those who teach beyond the pay—teachers who teach not merely to make a living but teachers who teach to make a life, teachers who teach not merely because they are hired and are needed but teachers who teach because they must. I believe that the poet writes poetry because he is compelled to; that the painter paints because he has to; that some men do research because there is an inner compulsion; that some men preach because they must preach; that the artist sings because of an inner urge; that the dedicated surgeon operates because he has no choice. This is what Paul meant, etc., Jesus, etc., Amos, Jeremiah, Hampden, Bunyan, and Horace.

Given this kind of teacher, thoroughly competent and called to do his or her task, the motivation of students will be easy. The first spark of motivation is a competent teacher. No poorly prepared, incompetent teacher of mathematics can inspire a student to do his best in mathematics. The teacher who has no interest in the cultural life of the community cannot motivate students to become interested in cultural things. As Jesus admonished his hearers to go the second mile, do more than required, the Negro teacher must go the second mile to open the hearts and minds of the mentally starved Negro student. This is what I meant when I said we must teach beyond the pay check. If a teacher isn't worth more than he is being paid, he isn't worth what he is being paid. The worth of a competent, dedicated teacher cannot be evaluated in terms of money.

Negro students must be motivated to stay in school. We are 10 percent of the population but only 3.5 percent of the collegiate enrollment. The Negro's chance of finishing high school is about one-half that of whites. As automation rolls on, the man without skills in English, mathematics, and science will be on relief.

If too many students drop out and too few strive for excellence because the ceiling of the house has been the limit of his striving, we can honestly tell our students now that the ceiling is being raised and that the sky is beginning to be the limit. We can tell the Negro student today that if he really prepares himself, race as a prerequisite for a job is a diminishing factor. We can tell him that when he finishes college, professional or graduate school, as a top chemist, physicist, biologist, psychologist, social scientist, and teacher—industry, education, government, and business will use his talents. Race will not be a declining factor when a competent man is needed. We must tell our students that it is not enough to be able to sleep anywhere, eat anywhere, swim anywhere, sit anywhere, and even pray anywhere. These things we must possess. But we must also be prepared to hold a job anywhere, be able to teach anywhere and serve our country anywhere. While we strive for first-class citizenship through the courts and through demonstrations, we must also strive for academic excellence.

We can tell our fifth grader that the chances are great that by the time he is thirty or thirty-five, Negroes will be federal judges in Texas, members of the House of Representatives in Texas, professors at the University of Texas, and executives in industry in Texas. You can tell him that by the time he is fifty, every man now holding a significant position will be either retired or dead and that he will be needed to do a significant job. We can now recite with greater confidence the little poem:

> Fleecy looks and black complexion cannot
> forfeit nature's claim. Skin may differ, but
> affection dwells in black and white the same.

We can recite with more confidence:

> Were I so tall as to reach the pole or grasp the
> ocean at a span, I must be measured by my soul,
> the mind is the standard of the man.

Despite 346 years of difficulties, with an indomitable will to meet the challenge created by the crisis, we can join Tennyson in "Ulysses," and say:

> Come, my friends,
> 'Tis not too late to seek a newer world.
> Push off, and sitting well in order smite
> the sounding furrows, for my purpose holds
> To sail beyond the sunset, and the baths
> Of all the western stars, until I die.
> It may be that the gulfs will wash us down;
> It may be that we shall touch the Happy Isles,
> And see the Great Achilles, whom we knew.
> Though much is taken, much abides; and though
> We are not now that strength which in old days
> Moved earth and heaven, that which we are, we are—
> One equal temper of heroic hearts,
> Made weak by time and fate, but strong in will
> To strive, to seek, to find, and not to yield.

Our task as educators is a gigantic and Herculean task, but it is also exciting and thrilling. What a privilege to accept the challenge created by the crisis: this is our task.

Twenty-Seven Years of Success
and Failure at Morehouse*

Morehouse College's Centennial Commencement marked Mays's last address as president of the institution he headed for twenty-seven years. He was retiring at age 72 after having been persuaded by the faculty, alumni, and trustees to stay on for two additional years beyond the mandatory retirement age to preside over the celebration of the founding of the institution. This is a vivid demonstration of the extent to which he was admired as the most outstanding president in the history of the college. In an eloquent and timely fashion, Mays delivered the commencement address to the graduating class on May 30, 1967, in Samuel H. Archer Hall before a capacity crowd. One hundred and nine students were in the graduating class, and the audience consisted of administrators, faculty, students, parents, relatives, friends, and many admirers of the college president, including the author. The venerable retiring president received a prolonged standing ovation at the conclusion of his remarks.

When he became the sixth president in 1940, he had vowed to the student body that he would not cheat on the job. He had promised to give his all in heart, mind, and body to Morehouse. He affirmed to his audience that he had kept his promise.

Dr. Mays took the opportunity to criticize the Atlanta community for not adequately contributing financially to Morehouse and other institutions in the Atlanta University Center. He felt that the Center had been responsible for providing the essential black leadership for city government in the metropolitan Atlanta community for several years; however, the community did not support these institutions in their fund-raising efforts.

He challenged the college alumni to contribute more to their alma mater because he believed the future of the college would rest on more generous alumni support.

* * *

* *Morehouse College Alumnus,* XXXV (Summer 1967): 29-32, Morehouse Collection, Robert W. Woodruff Library Archives, Clark Atlanta University

Since 1967 is Morehouse's one hundredth year, you will understand why I introduce this address with a bit of history, lest we forget the thought patterns about which Morehouse was molded. When Morehouse was founded in 1867, virtually all of science, religion, and statesmanship were speaking with a unanimous voice, declaring that the newly emancipated people were little less than human.

George Washington, Patrick Henry, and many other fathers of the Constitution owned slaves. A majority of the members of the United States Supreme Court at the time of the Dred Scott decision were slaveholders. Many college presidents and professors defended the institution. A Yale professor said: "If Jesus Christ were now on earth, he would under certain circumstances become a slaveholder." Governor McGuffie of South Carolina said in 1835: "No human institution is more manifestly consistent with the will of God than domestic slavery and no one of his ordinances is written in more legible characters than that which consigns the African race to this condition." In 1860, the pastor of the First Presbyterian Church in New Orleans preached a sermon entitled: "Slavery, A Divine Trust—The Duty of the South to Preserve and Perpetuate the Institution As It Now Exists." Eleven years before Morehouse was founded, a Richmond minister said: "The institution of slavery is full of mercy. . . . In their bondage here on earth they (the slaves) have been much better provided for, and great multitudes of them have been made the freemen of the Lord Jesus Christ and left this world rejoicing in the hope of God."

Abraham Lincoln had his misgivings about Negroes. Speaking in Peoria, Illinois, in 1854, he said he would send the slaves back to Africa, but they would perish in ten days. Speaking of social and political equality, Lincoln said, "We cannot make them equal."

The Anthropological Society of America, writing with special reference to the Negro in 1868, said: "The greatest achievement of anthropological science, we conceive, will be the speedy convincing of all the civilized nations of the utter uselessness of all these old and excessive attempts to civilize uncivilized races of men." Nott and Gliddon, in their book, *Types of Mankind*, wrote in 1865, two years before Morehouse was founded: "In the broad field and long duration of Negro life, not a single civilization, spontaneous or borrowed, has existed to adorn its gloomy past." Louis Agassiz, professor of zoology and geology at Harvard, wrote about a century ago: "A peculiar confrontation characterized the brain of the adult Negro. Its development never gets beyond that observable in the Caucasians in boyhood." Thomas Jefferson, the great statesman, said: "Never yet could I find that a black uttered a thought at the level of plain narration; never saw even an elementary trait of painting or sculpture." John C. Calhoun declared he would be willing to give the Negro citizenship when he had mastered the Greek verb. Samuel George Morton, the most eminent craniologist in the United States in the 19th century, concluded: "The capacity of the Negro cranium was less than that of the Anglo-Saxon by twelve inches, and that therefore, the Negro was incapable of intellectual equality with the Anglo-Saxon."

Henry Grady, speaking to the Texas Fair at Dallas, October 25, 1887, said this: "The races and tribes of the earth are of divine origin. . . . What God hath separated let no man join together." Speaking further, this great Georgian said: "Standing in the presence of this multitude, sober with the responsibility of the message delivered to the young men of the South, I declare this truth above all others, to be worn unsullied and sacred in your hearts, to be surrendered to no force, sold for no price, compromised in no necessity, but cherished and defended as the covenant of your prosperity, and the pledge of peace to your children, that the white race must dominate forever in the South, because it is the white race that is superior to that race by which its supremacy is threatened."

Writing in 1910 in his book, *Social and Mental Traits of the Race*, Howard Odum helped to perpetuate the image of Negro inferiority. This is what he wrote: "The Negro has little less conscience or love of home, no logical attachment of the better sort. . . . He has no pride of ancestry and he is not influenced by the lives of great men. The Negro has few ideals and perhaps no lasting adherence to an aspiration toward real worth. He has little conception of the meaning of virtue, truth, manhood, integrity. He is shiftless, untidy and indolent." Fortunately, Dr. Odum lived long enough to change his mind. All this goes to prove how fallible, how finite, and how wrong the most brilliant mind can be when it plays the role of God and speaks ex-cathedra about the future of man.

This was the matrix out of which Morehouse was born. This was the prevailing notion up to and throughout the first quarter of the twentieth century. Though Morehouse did wonders to prove the falsehood of these prejudiced minds prior to 1940, I speak to the subject: "Twenty-Seven Years of Success and Failure at Morehouse."

In September 1940, in my first speech to the Morehouse faculty and student body, I made a vow. I pledged that I would not cheat on the job. I promised that I would give to Morehouse all that I had—mind, heart, body—and have kept that pledge. I have not cheated on the job. No dishonesty is so reprehensible as the dishonesty where one cheats on the job when great responsibility has been placed on his shoulders.

I have no regrets in retiring from the presidency of Morehouse at this juncture in history. I regret, however, that what has been accomplished in these twenty-seven years trails so far behind my dreams for the college and so far behind what I aspired for Morehouse to be that I feel a sense of failure. I wish I could tell you today that the future of Morehouse was guaranteed in the stars.

From this point on, I use the pronoun "we." Friends, alumni, trustees, faculty, and students—all share in the success of the college. Likewise, we all share in the college's failure. If an alumnus could have given to support the college and did not, he must accept blame for not doing his share. If I were derelict in my duty, I too, must be cited as one responsible for not doing what I ought have done.

Unfortunately, in 1940, circumstances had converged so that Morehouse was without a doubt the weakest link among the affiliated institutions in the Atlanta University System. This weakness manifested itself in a highly inadequate physical plant and a faculty that was slowly being depleted in size, a very meager endowment, and low morale at the college. Morehouse had less of everything except manpower, and soon the ravages of the Second World War began to reduce its manpower to a negligible size. A distinguished trustee was so pessimistic about the small college enrollment during the Second World War that he suggested that Morehouse should consider closing for the duration.

We believed when we came, and we believe as we leave, that affiliation is the strength of all and that the weakness of one is the weakness of all. While we seek to cooperate fully, each institution must strive to be strong enough to add strength to the entire center. So our first task in 1940 was to make Morehouse an equal partner in the Atlanta University System so it could give as much as it would receive. Whatever was needed to be done to restore the integrity of the college had to be done, and it was done. Soon Morehouse morale began to rise, and the Morehouse spirit began to hum.

We set out to improve the academic quality of the student body. This accounts for the fact that we have only gradually increased the enrollment since 1941, rather than increase it too rapidly. We have increased the enrollment from 358 to 962, an increase of 169 percent. The number of our graduates who go on to graduate and professional school has risen spectacularly. In the 1964-65 school year, 56 percent of our graduates continued their studies in graduate and professional schools; in the 1965-66 year, 51.5 percent. It is significant to note that of the 118 Morehouse graduates who have earned the Ph.D. degree, 52, or 44 percent of them, graduated from Morehouse since 1943, representing 34 universities. Although the majority of our graduates entering medical schools go to Meharry and Howard, increasing numbers are being admitted to medical schools like the University of Chicago, Emory, Boston, and the University of Texas. Morehouse must forever strive to provide its students with a quality education.

Perhaps the greatest success the college has achieved in twenty-seven years is the high academic quality of the teachers who comprise the faculty. This was our choice despite pressures from many sources to direct our meager funds to other useful and interesting but non-academic pursuits. Not to provide the students with the ablest faculty available is criminal and irresponsible. In 1940, we had the equivalent of two full-time teachers who had earned the Ph.D. degree, or 8.7 percent of the staff. In 1966-67, we have 65 full-time teachers and 34, or 52.3 percent of them, hold doctorates. The number of doctorates on the faculty is 17 times greater than it was the academic year 1940-41. Excepting one or two, the rest hold master's degrees, and many have studied from one to four years beyond. Three hold the B.D. degree.

In academic training, this places Morehouse above all predominantly undergraduate Negro colleges. Comparing the 1964 Morehouse faculty with data on certain faculties taken from American universities and colleges by the American Council on Education in 1964, the Morehouse percentage of doctorates exceeded the percentage of doctorates at Albion, Allegheny, Bates, Colby, Cornell in Iowa, Kalamazoo and Lawrence College; and equaled the percentage at Bowdoin and Earlham. Replies from seventeen predominantly white colleges in the Southeast on this point, colleges of comparable size to Morehouse, show that in faculty training Morehouse was stronger than nine and weaker than eight. In faculty training, Morehouse stands ahead of hundreds of American colleges. It has taken twenty-seven years of constant planning to build and maintain a faculty of this strength.

Do not misunderstand me: I am not naive enough to believe that a teacher is a better teacher because he holds an A.M., a B.D., or a Ph.D. degree. I am not arguing that a teacher is more honest or loves his students more dearly because he has an advanced degree. I am arguing, however, that less training does not make one a better teacher nor a more honest man. There is no virtue in an academically weak faculty. Since this is true, we have striven in twenty-seven years to bring to Morehouse the ablest faculty we could command.

Healthy morale, an outstanding student body, an able faculty must be accompanied by a good physical plant. Although the physical plant needs to be enlarged in housing, worship, and academic facilities, since 1940 the physical plant has been improved by increasing the number of buildings from eight to twenty-five and floor space from 101,612 square feet to 304,836 square feet. The floor space is more than three times what it was twenty-seven years ago, and yet five new buildings are needed now. Our laboratory equipment in physics, chemistry, biology, mathematics, psychology, and health and physical education is first-rate and adds to the healthy morale of our faculty and student body. Again, this was our choice despite pressures from other sources to direct our meager funds to other useful and interesting but non-academic pursuits. The land acres have been increased from 10,691 to 379,444, $40,000 per acre.

We have just spoken of the strong academic faculty that Morehouse has been able to build and maintain. This has been true in part because we have been able to get terminal grants from foundations—grants that must be used up within a specific period of years—and because we have been able to increase the endowment, although the ratio of increase has been entirely too slow. The book value of the endowment is $4,500,000, and the market value is approximately $6,000,000. The book value is an increase from $1,114,000 to $4,500,000, which is four times greater than it was in 1940. We had hoped to increase it to eight times greater, but we were unable to do it despite excessive effort on our part. Although some $15 million for all purposes has been raised in these years, a president of a great university can get $15 million by making two or three visits to a great foundation.

We have made progress in the current budget. Whereas the current budget was only $134,318 in 1940-41, during the present academic year, 1966-67, counting money from all sources, special projects, and operating budget, $1,803,782 came to the College from March 1966, through

March 1967—an increase of 1,200 percent in twenty-seven years. Though salaries are lower than they should be, we are happy to report that the lowest salary is six and two-thirds times greater than it was in 1940-41 and the highest salary is six times more than it was in 1940-41. I know, however, that the cost of living has also increased.

Realizing that it would hardly be possible for Morehouse College to build a first-rate School of Religion in addition to a first-rate College, we played a large role in bringing into being the Interdenominational Theological Center. We initiated conversations with Morris Brown College and Gammon Theological Seminary in 1940; and years later, the Morehouse School of Religion, the Phillips School of Theology of Lane College (Jackson, Tennessee), Turner Theological Seminary of Morris Brown College, and the leadership of Gammon Theological Center were created in 1959. The four institutions working together succeeded in getting in 1958 an appropriation of $1,750,000 from the Sealantic Fund and $250,000 from the General Education Board, which guaranteed the reality of ITC.

What a paradox! Occupying since 1889 a campus that was a great battleground during the Civil War, in the siege of Atlanta, for one hundred years Morehouse has tried to develop a free man in a racially segregated society. The Morehouse philosophy was and is that a man does not have to accept the view that because he is a Negro certain things were not meant for him. He can be free in a highly segregated society. Long before demonstrations and Supreme Court decisions abolished segregation, the Morehouse students were taught to accept no segregated situation except that which was absolutely necessary; and that though their bodies were segregated, their minds could be free. Students who broke faith with this principle and went to segregated theaters, restaurants, and churches went there without administrative sanction.

If the Morehouse graduates, on the whole, have done better than the graduates of most predominantly Negro colleges, it is due in part to the philosophy drilled into them that the Morehouse man can succeed in the world despite crippling circumstances under which he has to live. Morehouse was built on the faith of Negroes and a few white leaders like Joseph T. Robert, Morehouse's first President, a South Carolinian who went North rather than rear his children in a land of slaves.

The college has done well in recent decades, but not well enough. We were naive when we came in 1940. We believed that if you could produce a quality faculty, show that the alumni were making their mark in the world, and that the college's able students did well in graduate and professional schools, it would make fund-raising relatively easy. It isn't necessarily so. We believed that in ten years we could create a scholarly atmosphere at the college so that the majority of the students would pursue excellence and that the purposeless could not survive. We did not fully succeed. We believed in 1940 that if we moved the college forward and made it better year by year, with some cultivation, we could raise the percentage of alumni givers by 50 percent. It wasn't true. That dream has not been fulfilled. If we can maintain the impetus of the Centennial, the dream will come true.

We believed that Morehouse, a Georgia institution for one hundred years and an Atlanta institution for eighty-eight years, would be able to get someone to head a campaign for at least a million dollars in recognition of one hundred years of valuable service to the city, state and nation. We were sadly mistaken. The Negro colleges of Atlanta are not considered part and parcel of the life of the community. My guess is that in a hundred years the six institutions of the Atlanta University Center have not received a million and a half dollars from the Atlanta community. It has accepted no responsibility for the financial health and development of these colleges, despite the fact that we spend millions here each year and provide leadership for the South and for the nation. We believed when we came that each and every person saddled with a responsibility here at Morehouse would do his work so well that constant follow-up would be unnecessary. It wasn't so.

The Morehouse administration, and especially the Morehouse faculty, are able, very able. But it is my considered judgment that we are too educationally conservative, inclined to be afraid to experiment, to blaze new paths. I sometimes think we are allergic to change. We tend to be more tied to tradition and the past. Our danger lies in complacency, a disease that plagues all too many colleges. The Atlanta community is one of the best social laboratories in the nation. Significant community research should be going on all the time. I know we are busy, but as a rule, people do what they want to do. In community research and in projects designed to assist the unfortunate in the Atlanta community, we could do more.

Communication is a difficult art. I think we failed to communicate to faculty, students, trustees, and alumni what our dreams and aspirations are for Morehouse. And as lovely and loyal and devoted as you have been and are, the presidency of a college is a lonely job because communication is so difficult; and yet, there have been many happy moments and joyous returns. In all these areas, we have felt frustration and a sense of failure.

Now, what about the years ahead for Morehouse? One fact is clear: Morehouse cannot live on its past reputation. Without a doubt, the years ahead will be tough years, but perhaps no tougher than the first one hundred years. All of our years have been precarious years, but like England, we have muddled through. The first one hundred years were years of segregation supported by law and religion. During the first one hundred years, Morehouse competed mainly with Negro colleges, similarly segregated. No one questioned their survival for, after all, Negroes had to have schools. The power structure in politics, in economics, and education, whether the school was private or public, never intended to make schools for Negroes first-rate. The racial attitude in America, whether in slavery or in education, has consistently been that what was meant for Negroes has to be inferior to that which is designed for whites. It was expected and deliberately planned that segregated schools for Negroes would be inferior. For almost a hundred years, no one even questioned the philosophy. A great leader in the Commission on Interracial Cooperation once said in my hearing that in order to advance the Negro child one step, the white child must be advanced two steps.

Desegregation, won through court decisions, congressional legislation, and demonstrations, has not changed the basic philosophy of inequality. So to use a good Methodist phrase, Negro colleges have been by design kept on short grass! For the health of Morehouse and other colleges similarly circumstanced, the philosophy must be accepted by philanthropic America and governments that a good college, whether it is predominantly Negro or predominantly white, deserves equal consideration in bidding for the tax and philanthropic dollar. If this philosophy cannot be developed, there will exist under the guise of desegregation and liberalism a form of discrimination as rancid and foul as anything that existed under legal and de facto segregation.

Discrimination in the future will not be administered by poor whites and the people who believe in segregation, by the "liberals" who believe in a desegregated society. If this battle can be won, Morehouse will have an equal chance to develop like any other good college in America. If discrimination against Negroes is directed now against the predominantly Negro institutions rather than against the individual, the future will be difficult indeed. The Negro's battle for justice and equality in the future will not be against the subtlety of our "liberal friends" who will wine and dine with us in the swankiest hotels, work with us, and still discriminate against us when it comes to money and power. The battle must be won because, for a long time, the wealth of this nation will be in the hands of white Americans and not Negroes. The abolition of economic, political, and philanthropic discrimination is the first order of the day, not for the good of Negroes alone but for the nation as a whole. The future of Morehouse will depend upon the ability to "buy" the intellectually talented students, just as many of the predominantly white institutions are able to do with finances given for that purpose. To finance white schools for this purpose and not Negro schools is gross discrimination, not by the admittedly prejudiced but by our "liberal friends." Morehouse's record in the educational world has been made by the able records our graduates make in the best graduate and professional schools. If this record is diminished, we will be reduced to the role of mediocrity.

Finally, the future of Morehouse rests with the alumni. Yale, Columbia, Harvard, Princeton, and Chicago will survive because their graduates will see to it that they do. Morehouse men have not accumulated millions, but if they really cared, they could contribute to the College $100,000 a year and, in time, $500,000. If the Morehouse alumni will do this, they will cause corporations and foundations and friends to contribute millions of dollars to the College. This is my final plea to the Morehouse alumni. If you really care, the future of Morehouse is secure. If you do not care, its future is precarious.

I cannot close this address without publicly paying tribute to Charles Merrill, chairman of the Morehouse Board of Trustees. If the Morehouse salaries are fairly competitive, give large credit to Charles Merrill. If we have sent able students to the best professional and graduate schools, give credit to Charles Merrill through the Early Admissions Program. If our faculty is widely traveled, salute Charles Merrill. If sixty-odd Morehouse students have studied and traveled in Europe, let us give thanks to Charles Merrill. If Morehouse is on the verge of being accepted as worthy of membership in Phi Beta Kappa, let us take our hats off to Charles Merrill. It had to be an act of God that Charles Merrill came into our lives.

Now my dear seniors, let me say to you that what I said to the class of 1964. Will you please rise?

The curtain has fallen forever on the activities of your years at Morehouse. What you should have done and neglected to do cannot now be done. Not even an omnipotent God can blot out the deeds of history. It has been beautifully said:

> The Moving Finger writes; and having writ,
> Moves on; nor all your Piety nor wit
> Shall lure it back to cancel half a Line,
> Nor all your Tears wash out a Word of it.

Since the events of history are irrevocable, I can only advise you to utilize the past, whatever it is, to good advantage and look to the future with courage and confidence. Twenty-five years from today, it is more likely that my days will be long since passed, and you will be about forty-seven years old. I hope you will return in 1992 to celebrate your twenty-fifth anniversary. I trust you will remain economically secure in houses and land, stocks and bonds, cars and bank accounts; intellectually secure in the constant pursuit of knowledge, and affectionally secure with fine wives and handsome children.

Wherever I may be twenty-five years from today—on earth, beneath the earth, or above it—you will make my spirit glad if you are known in life by the quality of your work and the integrity of your character, rather than by the quality of your possessions.

If your work is government, I hope you do your work so well that you will be diligently sought after and widely acclaimed by government. If your work be that of a chemist, a physicist, a mathematician in industry, I hope you will perform so excellently that when promotions are in order, your record will be so impressive that those in power will be compelled to examine your credentials. If you make business a career, I hope the people will say in discussing you that you are both competent and honest. If it's politics, may they say that you achieved office through honest means.

If you choose the ministry, I pray that you will be so eloquent in speech, so profound in thought, so honest in performance, and so understanding in the knowledge of the strength and frailties of man that the people will say of you, "He must be a man of God."

If you choose medicine, dentistry, or surgery, I hope you will be so dedicated to the healing art, so skilled in the performance of your duty, and so loyal and devoted to the people you serve that in the reunion at Morehouse in 1992, your classmates will flock around you to talk about your skills in surgery and your knowledge of medicine rather than the size of your bank account or model of your car.

If you choose teaching, may you be so knowledgeable in what you teach, so devoted to your students, so inspiring in your teaching, and so stimulating in your writing, that the students will say of you, "He was born to teach."

My dear young friends, I do not know what happiness is, and I do not think it is important to be happy. But it is important that you find your work and do it as if you were sent in the world at this precise moment in history to do your job. If happiness can be achieved, it will be found in a job well done and in giving and not in receiving.

May the years ahead be motivating, challenging, and inspiring years, and may they be gracious and kind to you and bring success in all the good things you do.

Leben Sie Wohl!

The Universities' Unfinished Work*

The graduating class at Michigan State University in East Lansing was honored to receive Dr. Mays's commencement speech on June 9, 1968. The audience in Spartan Stadium numbered approximately 25-30,000, including administrators, faculty, alumni, parents, relatives, and friends. The address was delivered the same year that the nation mourned the assassination of two great leaders, Martin Luther King, Jr., and Senator Robert Kennedy, a presidential candidate and the brother of the late President John F. Kennedy. At the graduation ceremonies, President John A. Hannah conferred upon Dr. Mays the honorary degree of Doctor of Humane Letters, and Mays would spend the next year on campus as an advisor to the president.

In the address, Dr. Mays declared that universities should train students to conquer the enemies of humankind: war, poverty, and racism.

* * *

We will do many wonderful things with the mind in the years ahead. Longevity will be further extended. The number of people living ninety and one hundred years will increase. Many more diseases will be conquered. Cancer will eventually be cured. We will very soon place a man on the moon. Passenger planes will fly a thousand miles an hour. We will develop more deadly implements of war. The comforts of life will be multiplied many times. Soon we will have more leisure time than we know how to use. We will increase the number of college graduates, and the number of Ph.D.s will be tripled. More brilliant scholars will be born. Shakespeare was partly right when he makes Hamlet say, "What a piece of work is man. How noble in reason; how infinite in faculty! In form and moving how express and admirable; in action how like an angel; in apprehension how like a god!" Modern man has more than fulfilled the expectation of Alexander Pope when he says in his *Essay on Man*:

> Go, wondrous creatures! Mount where science guides; go, measure earth, weigh air, and state the tides; instruct the planets in what orbs to run; correct old time, and regulate the sun.

---

* Michigan State University Archives-Historical Collections

I hope the university will always be what Disraeli says it is, "a center of light, liberty, and learning." In this sense, the university's work will never be finished.

But a university must be more; and as marvelous as man is, he has not yet conquered three of the major enemies of mankind: war, poverty, and racism. It will not be enough for our universities to train their graduates how to make themselves secure in the economic and educational world and forthwith insulate themselves from the basic issues of our time. The day has come for educational institutions to train their students to be seriously concerned about the urgency and the commitment to eliminate war, abolish poverty, and exterminate racism.

Education has done very little toward creating a world in which mankind can live without war. And I am not wise enough to give you a blueprint as to what the role of education in this area should be. I do know, however, that the trained mind has provided the instruments that are capable of destroying the human family. On the contrary, education has not trained the mind to appreciate human values so that man will be able to live without war. When it comes to war, it can be argued with considerable logic that man is not any more civilized today than he was ages ago. Centuries before the dawn of the Christian era, the Persians, the Babylonians, and the Egyptians sought to settle their differences on the battlefield. The Greeks, the Romans, and the Carthaginians resorted to the sword in order to achieve their objectives. We do the same thing. We are much wiser than they, certainly much better educated, but we fought World War I thinking that we were fighting the war that would end wars. Americans fought and died on the battlefield of Europe under the slogans:

> We are fighting to make the world safe for democracy, and we are fighting for self-determination so that each nation will have the right to determine its own destiny.

Woodrow Wilson believed it, too, that World War I was the last war in history—the war to end all wars.

We did not learn anything from the tragic experience. Millions died: millions more were crippled and maimed in both mind and body. Two decades after World War I, we found ourselves in World War II (between 1939 and 1945), engaged in the same folly. We followed the second World War with Korea. And for a decade, we have been bogged down in Vietnam, and only God knows what the end will be. We have more colleges and universities than ever before, establishing more at the rate of one a week. But education is wholly irrelevant when it comes to providing ways to build a war-free world.

We have fought 3,300 wars in 3,000 years. I read recently that in the last 3,500 years, man has been at war somewhere on the earth nine hours out of every ten hours. It can be argued with considerable evidence that education has given us more facts and better trained minds, but it has hardly made us any more sensitive to the perils of war.

Education has not necessarily made a man better. We are spending $2 billion a month in the Vietnam war alone; and some $45 billion annually on past, present, and future wars and for national defense. With this amount of money, we could endow every college and university in the United States with $22,500,000 each, and at five percent interest, each of the two thousand colleges and universities would have an additional income of $1,125,000 a year.

Our universities do not educate to this condition. When it comes to the need to eliminate war, our educational institutions are largely irrelevant. Our purposes for existence seem to be mainly to help students to develop their minds in order that they might be able to get ahead in the world, and not how they might use their minds to establish programs designed to eliminate the conditions that keep mankind forever at war. Some university should list as one of its major objectives a blueprint for universal peace. The question of mankind's survival on the earth is too critical a matter to be left entirely in the hands of politicians and heads of state. Make no mistake: we will abolish war, or war will abolish mankind. The United States must be made to work so that the behavior of big nations will come under its judgment as well as that of other nations.

The second problem confronting mankind, and to which universities should give priority, is the question of poverty—poverty not only in far-off South America, Africa, Asia, and the Middle East, but poverty in the affluent U. S. A. When we speak of half of the people of the earth not getting enough to eat, are malnourished, and have diseased bodies, we are unaware of the amount of hunger and malnutrition that exist in our own country. Within the last ten months, it has been my privilege to be a member of a team to study hunger and malnutrition in the United States. Hunger and malnutrition exist in every section of our country— north, south, east, and west.

The federal government admits that in 1967 there were 8,876,700 families in the United States in poverty; or 29,900,000 persons (15 percent of the population) recognized by the federal government as impoverished. In 1967, it was estimated that there were fifty million children of school age in the United States, and six million of them came from poor families received free lunches, leaving four million poor children without lunch, or they had to buy it. Millions of these kids are hungry at home and have no money with which to buy food at school. These are the poor—black and white, red and brown, Catholic and Protestant.

There is evidence that many children go to school without breakfast, are too hungry to learn, and are in such pain that they must be taken home. In some cases, mothers keep their children from school so that at least they can cry themselves to sleep from hunger in their mothers' arms. Right here in the United States, in some areas, there are pregnant mothers so ill-nourished that a minimum of blood transfusion must be given routinely to each pregnant mother during childbirth as a part of her regular prenatal care. Studies have been made that show that some pregnant mothers do not get sufficient iron, calcium, and calories, so the nutritionally motivated craving for iron and calcium leads them to eat clay and to eat starch for calories to supplement their food. There are thousands of babies being born daily who have protein deficiency during their early years, and it has been established that protein deficiency in early childhood can cause permanent brain damage, causing I.Q. deficits of as many as 18 to 22 points, from which the child will never recover. Thousands of these kids are not inherently dumb. Our society has neglected them. Were they properly fed, they would develop good minds, and some of them would be brilliant. These are people in the United States, and possibly in your city, who go to the city dump digging for food. When the dump trucks come, the people are there going through the garbage to get cheese, butter, meat, doughnuts, or whatever is edible that has been thrown away.

I have recently talked with widows living on $45 per month, mothers with seven children trying to make it on $200 a month. I know a case where a woman, 26, two children, a husband unable to work, are virtually starving. The lady said to an interviewer, "One thing we always got is milk, cuz my Ma keeps a goat. We don't always eat the same all the time either. One day I'll fix macaroni for lunch, the next day spaghetti, or potatoes, so we get a little variety, too. I had steak once about three months ago. A friend of my husband's was serving it and invited us over. Imagine that, my going twenty-six years without tasting steak! I took one little, bitty bite, and said, 'Boy, it sure was worth waiting for!'"

We found another case where a woman has twelve children, ages three and a half to twenty-one. Their income is $25 per week, and $30 more monthly from a son who is working. After this woman pays rent, electricity, and heat, she has $90 a month to get food for thirteen. There are no free lunches, and she cannot get welfare because she cannot tell welfare where her husband is. The food stamp program, even if she had it, would be grossly inadequate.

Our colleges and universities must not, certainly should not, educate ourselves and our students away from the problems of the poor. We should know the condition and circumstances under which the poor people live in the slums and ghettoes of our cities, and, wherever feasible, the universities should become involved so that we will help to build a United States where no family of four will get less than $3,300 a year income, where every able-bodied man will be guaranteed a job with an adequate minimum wage, where good schools exist, and where recreational facilities and schools are adequate. The town comes to the gown, and the gown should go to the town so that there will be no unnecessary gap between those who live on the boulevards and those who live in the slums. The problems of poor people should be the concern of the university, and how to eliminate poverty should be one of its major objectives. We must eliminate poverty not only because it's right so to do, but because there will be security for none of us until we do.

The third and final enemy of mankind which our colleges and universities should work to abolish is racism. It is difficult for us to understand that racism does exist in the United States; however, some of us did not have to be told by the President's Commission on Civil Disorders that it does exist. We know it from years of bitter experience. Ruth Benedict defines racism as follows: "Racism is the dogma that one ethnic group is inferior and another group is destined to heredity superiority. It is the dogma that the hope of civilization depends upon eliminating some races and keeping others pure. It is the dogma that one race has carried progress throughout human history and alone ensures future progress." Anyone, whether black or white, who believes that he is superior to members of another race, and in his behavior treats the other person as an inferior, has earned the right to be called a racist.

Slavery and segregation, which have been with us in this country for a total of 350 years, are proof that there is racism in this country. Virtually all civil rights legislation and all victories in federal courts designed to make our democracy applicable to Negroes came about through some kind of coercion. Negroes are the only people in the United States who have had to spend tens of millions of dollars to get what the Constitution guarantees them and what all Europeans who come to this country get by virtue of being born white. No other ethnic or racial group has had to sit-in and demonstrate in order to have places of public accommodation open to them. No white has had to sue in federal courts in order to get the ballot. No white group has had to coerce Congress to pass a bill to prohibit discrimination in housing. No other group found it necessary to sponsor a March on Washington, 250,000 strong, to make Congress know that we will pay any price to eliminate second-class citizenship in this country. Fourteen years after the May 17, 1954, decision of the United States Supreme Court outlawing segregation in the public schools, many sections of the nation are resisting the court orders; 85 percent of our public schools are still segregated. Martin Luther King, Jr., should never have been assassinated with the approval of thousands because he wanted America to live up to its pronouncements. It is not only good for the United States to exterminate racism, but it is good for the world that we do it because there will be no permanent peace on the earth until we do.

The President's Commission on Civil Disorders has spoken about racism more eloquently than I can. Despite Black Power, or those who argue for separatism, the destiny of white and Negro America is still one destiny. It must be one of education's aims to strive to desegregate and integrate America to the end that this great nation of ours, born in revolution and blood, conceived in liberty, and dedicated to the proposition that all men are created free and equal, will truly become the lighthouse of freedom where none will be denied because his skin is black and none favored because his eyes are blue; where the nation is militarily strong but at peace; economically secure but just; learned but wise; and where the poorest will have a job and bread enough to spare.

Educators should define the kind of world we are trying to build. We should have ways of measuring the progress in goodness and in the developing of right attitudes, just as we measure the progress in intellectual development. After defining the kind of society we want to build, we should develop skills and techniques designed to make our students that kind of citizen. We should begin in the kindergarten to develop people who believe in our Christian principles and a democratic idea. Goodness is as important as literacy. An honest heart is as important as a brilliant mind. The assassination of Senator Robert Kennedy makes it all the more urgent that we build the kind of world which I tried to describe. Senator Kennedy was committed to a program of peace. He wanted poverty and racism exterminated. It is too bad that we live in a world where men like John Fitzgerald Kennedy, Robert F. Kennedy, Martin Luther King, Jr., and Mahatma Gandhi are in as much danger of being killed as murderers and thieves. It is our responsibility, as educated men, to create a world where good men will be free and safe to work to improve society and to make men better.

I predict that most of you will be very successful in your chosen field. Some of you will be famous. Some of you will accumulate great wealth. Some of you will occupy positions of prestige and power. My best wishes go with you. Whatever you do, however, I implore you to become involved in worthy programs designed to make a better world. I hope you will never turn your back on the millions who are poor, but rather do your part to enable them to rise to positions of respectability and power. I hope you will never be satisfied until America is committed to the proposition that equality, freedom, and justice are the God-given rights of every American.

I challenge you, members of the class of 1968, to join in a crusade to eliminate war, abolish poverty, and exterminate racism.

The Challenge of the Seventies*

At the 147th commencement exercises, Dr. Mays spoke to parents, relatives, friends, administrators, and graduates at Centre College in Danville,
Kentucky, on Sunday night, May 31, 1970, at Farris Stadium. Dr. Mays
became the first black American to deliver the commencement address
at the institution. One hundred and twenty-two students received degrees.

In his address, Dr. Mays surveyed the developments of the year
1970. He concluded that the race problem was the most important problem facing the country. He acknowledged that some progress had been
made. But he noted that the younger generation would be dealing with
the problem of making progress in race relations for a long time.

In his inspiring and eloquent address to the graduates, he pronounced
a call for strong men and women in the future who would attempt to
solve the problems facing society such as poverty, racism, drug addiction, population control, and water pollution.

* * *

In the words of Thomas Paine, "These are the times that try men's
souls." There are wars and threats of wars. We spend billions annually
in Vietnam. The President has spread the war into Cambodia. The purpose for which we fight is unclear. And only omniscient God knows
what the end will be and when. We are spending $2 billion a month in
Vietnam, and some $45 billion annually on past, present, and future
wars. With this amount of money we could endow every college and
university in the United States with $22,500,000 each and at five percent
each of the two thousand colleges and universities that would have an
additional income of $1,125,000 a year.

Our youths are confused and frustrated all over the world. Across
this nation, our college students are protesting the war and saying to the
President: "Get out of Southeast Asia NOW!" The uprisings of our students on our campuses are due in part to our involvement in Southeast
Asia. The students are earnest, and their clamor against the war will not
soon subside. The killings of black and white by the National Guard and

---

* Reprinted from *Centrepiece*, Volume 11 (August 1970): 8-10, Centre
College, Danville, Kentucky

police in Ohio, Georgia, and Mississippi will not bring peace, neither at home nor abroad. The Arabs and Israelis will not bring peace, either at home or abroad. The Arabs and Israelis may plunge us into the Third World War any day.

Twisted Values

Our values are thoroughly twisted. Our national political leaders appropriate money more freely for expeditions to the moon than for the physical well-being of the nation. The United States would rather outdo Russia in space than in providing adequate food for millions of poor Americans. There are in this affluent United States some 30 million persons who live below the poverty line. In 1967, the federal government admitted that there were 8,876,700 families or 29,900,000 persons in the United States in poverty. It was estimated that there were then fifty million children of school age in the United States, and six million of them came from poor families, families with annual incomes below $3,300. Only two million received free lunches, leaving four million hungry children without lunch every day, or they had to buy it. Millions of these kids were hungry at home and had no money with which to buy food at school. The situation has not improved in the past three years.

In 1968, in a report with which I was involved entitled "HUNGER: USA," we substantiated the fact that there are many newborn babies who survive the hazards of birth and live through the first month, but die between the second month and their second birthdays from causes which can be traced directly and primarily to malnutrition. Our report pointed our further that protein deprivation between the ages of six months and a year and a half causes permanent and irreversible brain damage to some infants. Nutritional anemia, stemming primarily from protein deficiency and iron deficiency, was found in degrees ranging from 30 to 70 percent among children from poverty backgrounds. But I wager that Congress will appropriate more freely—and we will very soon spend as much or more money annually—for expeditions to land on Mars than we will spend to eliminate poverty.

I am not a prophet of doom, and I disagree with those who say that we have made no progress in black-white relations in the last quarter of a century. I must admit, however, that progress has not been uniform. It is a fact that many doors are open to Negroes—or black people, if you prefer—that were closed to them in 1950, twenty years ago. Most hotels, restaurants, theaters, and recreational facilities are now available to black people, which was not the case decades ago. Black people can be seen working in industries, banks, department stores, in communications; holding high political posts in city, state, and federal government undreamed of in 1950; and the color line has been all but eliminated in professional sports. Colleges and universities which denied black professors and students in the 1950s are open to them in 1970.

One Side of the Picture

It is easy for one who sees only one side of the picture to say that, interracially, things are fine. We are making great strides toward improving black-white relations, but we must admit that the problem of race is the most explosive problem confronting the United States today. A few blacks are much better off in 1970 than they were in 1950. This is not good enough. Economically, the masses of black people are hardly any better off than they were twenty-five years ago. Relatively speaking, the gulf of economic inequality between black and white has widened. Poor housing, unemployment, low paying jobs, poor schools, slums, and ghettoes plague the black man incessantly. Fresh in our minds are the riots in Los Angeles, Cleveland, Detroit, Newark, Washington, and other cities, telling us that our race problem is far from being solved, 105 years after the Civil War. The uprisings and rising demands of black students on white campuses indicate that there is enduring tension between black and white. The killing of six blacks, shot in the back by the National Guard in Augusta, Georgia, and the killing of two blacks at Jackson State College reveal a frightening situation.

The May 17, 1954, decision of the United States Supreme Court outlawing segregation in the public schools led many to believe that segregated schools would soon be a thing of the past. But sixteen years after, segregated schools still exist all over this country. De facto segregation has taken the place of de jure segregation, and we find all-black and all-white schools throughout the nation. Segregated housing patterns make de facto segregation inevitable. Whites and blacks do not seem to be able to live in the same neighborhood. Whites move out when blacks move in.

It is clear that you, the young generation, will be wrestling with the black-white problem in this country just as those of us of my generation and before tried to solve it for many decades. Racism is a cat with nine lives. In addition to war, poverty, and racism, you will also have to deal with the population explosion, water pollution, and the increased use of drugs by the young. What will you do to assume leadership in your respective communities? There is no doubt in my mind that a leadership role will be thrust upon you by virtue of the fact that you now have better training than the vast majority of the young people in the world. I wager that a very high percentage of those who entered first grade with you have long since fallen by the wayside. You are among the favored few.

You Will Succeed

I predict that most of you will do well in life. Barring long economic depression and wars that will destroy our economy, you will succeed in life. Poverty will never knock at your door. Most of you, being white, will never know what it is like to be black and robbed of opportunities, opportunities which you will have for the sole reason that you were born white. I must remind you, however, that "To whom much is given, much is required." So, I ask again, what attitude will you take toward the mammoth problems inadequately described above—problems which my generation is leaving with you—war, poverty, racism, population explosion, pollution, and drug addiction?

You may take a laissez-faire attitude toward these problems and say, "Such problems are inherent in existence, so there is no need to worry to much about them. The poor have always been with us—even Jesus recognized that."

"Men have always fought wars and always will. Racism is as old as the human race. We will let the next generation worry about the population explosion. Science will conquer pollution. So I will take care of myself and my family. Let well enough alone. Enjoy life. Each person is largely responsible for himself."

I hope you will never take the laissez-faire attitude. For whether we like it or not, the destiny of each and every person is the destiny of all men. We will travel the same road from our mothers' wombs to the grave. Eugene Debs was eminently correct when he said something like this: "As long as there is a lower class, I am in it. As long as there is a criminal element, I am of it. As long as there is a man in jail, I am not free." John Donne expresses it well:

> No man is an island, entire of it selfe; every man is a piece of the
> Continent, a part of the maine, if a Clod bee washed away by the Sea,
> Europe is the lesse, as well as if a Promontorie were, as well as if a

Mannor of thy friends or of thine owne were; any man's death diminishes me because I am involved in Mankinde; And therefore never
send to know for whom the bell tolls; It tolls for thee.

By virtue of the fact that we are born, we are obligated to do our bit
to improve life and make our communities better. We cannot afford a
laissez-faire attitude. I believe that every person is sent into the world to
do something worthwhile, something unique, something distinctive, and
if he does not do it, it will never be done. If Columbus had not discovered America, somebody else would have discovered it. But if Shakespeare
had not written *Hamlet, The Merchant of Venice, Julius Caesar, Othello,
Macbeth*, they would have never been written. If the Wright brothers
had not done their work with the airplane, others would have done it.
But if James Weldon Johnson had not written "Lift Every Voice and
Sing," this song would have never been composed. Somebody else might
have built Tuskegee, but only Booker T. Washington could have given
the world *Up From Slavery*. I hope that you will do two things: do
something worthwhile which others can do, but by all means do that
unique, distinctive thing which if you do not do it, it will never be done.

The Plight of the Poor

We might try to avoid involvement again by arguing that the plight of
the poor is their fault; they are lazy, trifling and good-for-nothing. Too
lazy to work and too lazy to use their minds. If they are lacking in mental
ability, blame their parents and God, not me. Anyone who wants to
work can find a job. Do food stamps and surplus foods make the poor
more helpless? If a man is well and has a strong body, he can earn
enough to live on.

This is one way to look at it, but another way to look at it is to
consider the fact that we are largely what we are by luck or the grace of
God. If one man is better off than another, it is largely accidental. No
man has the right to thank God that he is better than another man. Two
things a man cannot choose: his parents and his place of birth. Nor can
he determine which member of his family will be a brilliant mind and
which a dull one. I have seen families where only one child out of six or
seven had an extraordinary mind. I have seen a genius and a moron born
into the same family—same mother and same father. Certainly the genius can take no credit for his brilliant mentality nor look down on his
less fortunate brother, for he might well have been the moron and his

brother the genius. Neither did anything to get himself born; neither chose his parents.

For example, two babies are born on the same day, one of parents who are wealthy and the other of parents who are poverty-stricken and live in the slums. By virtue of the origin of their births, the son of wealthy parents will experience cultural surroundings almost from birth, and his educational advantages will be unlimited. The poor boy may never go beyond the fifth grade. Why should the wealthy boy think he is better and look down on his brother in poverty? Neither chose his parents, and they did not choose their places of birth. The Brahman in India did not choose his Brahmanhood, and the Untouchable did not choose his untouchability. The black boy who has been beaten down by his more fortunate white neighbors did not choose his blackness. In one sense, therefore, we are what are not by any goodness of ours. This knowledge should give every man an attitude of humility which should permeate his struggle to improve life and make men better.

Not only are these times the times that try men's souls, but these are the times when sensitive souls hear the call to respond to the needs of our time. Every generation has felt, no doubt, that it was living in the most crucial time in history. There has never been a time in the history of men when everything was sweetness and light. Every time is a time that tries men's souls, and out of tragedy, turmoil, and crisis, men are called to lead the people forward.

The times were not serene when God called Abraham to seek a strange land and become the father of his people. It wasn't a good time for the Jews when God called Moses to lead them out of bondage, spending forty years in the wilderness in pursuit of freedom. The Jews were in bondage to Rome when Jesus was called to establish the Kingdom of God, and Paul to universalize Christianity. The great Roman Empire had fallen, and the future of Christianity and the world was at stake when Augustine was motivated to write *The City of God*.

The crisis in Roman Catholicism brought forth Martin Luther. Taxation without representation led to the Declaration of Independence and the Revolutionary War, which brought forth the United States of America. Slavery instigated the Civil War and a leadership which saved the Union and emancipated the slaves. Slavery and oppression are responsible for the leadership of such great Americans as Frederick Douglass, Booker T. Washington, and Martin Luther King, Jr. The 1929 Depression created the opportunity for Franklin Delano Roosevelt to institute programs that saved the country from economic ruin.

Truly, these are the times that try our souls, but they are also the times that will call forth strong men and women in the decades ahead to strive to abolish war, eliminate poverty, eradicate racism, blot out drug addiction, control the increase in population, and save us from air and water pollution.

These are some of the problems which present a challenge to the class of 1970. I hope you will accept the challenge.

Three Enemies of Mankind:
A Challenge to the University*

Dr. Mays was serving as president of the Atlanta Board of Education and president-emeritus of Morehouse College when he delivered the commencement address at the Quadrangle on the Emory University campus on June 8, 1970. More than 4,000 parents, relatives, friends, trustees, and faculty witnessed the informative address. Dr. Mays appeared as one of six men who received honorary degrees at the event. And he also became the first black speaker to deliver the commencement address at the university. Degrees were awarded to 1,134 graduates.

Although Dr. Mays painted a very optimistic picture of the future in the areas of health, science, and education, he maintained that a university must do more. He encouraged the graduates to become involved in efforts to make this a better world.

* * *

President Atwood, members of the Board of Trustees, Members of the Faculties, Members of the graduating classes, ladies and gentlemen.

I am indeed grateful that President Atwood has honored me by inviting me to address you on this momentous occasion. However, I am not deceived. I am not naive. I know that nobody came here this early in the morning just to hear me speak. The trustees, the President, and faculties are here in the line of duty. The members of the graduating classes are here to get their diploma. The rest of you are here to see your sons and daughters, sisters and brothers, aunts and uncles, husbands and wives, sweethearts and friends graduate. You really didn't come to hear me— but tradition has decreed that you cannot graduate today without first listening to me or feigning to listen. So, whether you like it or not, you are stuck with me for approximately twenty minutes, beginning now.

We will do many wonderful things with the mind in the seventies and in the decades to come. Longevity will be further extended. The number of people living ninety and one hundred years will increase.

---

* Robert W. Woodruff Library Special Collections, Emory University; reprinted from Doris Levy Gavins, *The Ceremonial Speaking of Benjamin Elijah Mays: Spokesman for Social Change, 1974-1975*

Many more diseases will be conquered. Cancer can be cured. We will soon place a man on Mars. Passenger planes will fly a thousand miles an hour. We will develop more deadly implements of war. The comforts of life will be multiplied many times. Soon we will have more leisure time than we know how to use. We will increase the number of college graduates, and the number of Ph.D.s will be tripled. Shakespeare was partly right when he has Hamlet say: "What a piece of work is man. How noble in reason; how infinite in faculty; in form and moving how express and admirable; in action how like an angel; in apprehension how like a god!" Modern man has more than fulfilled the expectation of Alexander Pope when he says in his *Essay on Man*: "Go, wondrous creature! Mount where science guides; go measure earth, weigh air, and state the tides; instruct the plants in what orbs to run; correct old time, and regulate the sun." I hope the university will always be what Disraeli says it is, "a center of light, liberty, and learning."

But a university must be more; and as marvelous as man is, he has not yet conquered three of the major enemies of mankind: war, poverty, and racism. It will not be enough for our universities to train their graduates how to make themselves secure in the economic, political, and educational worlds and forthwith insulate themselves from the basic issues of our time. That day has come for educational institutions to train their students to be seriously concerned about the urgency and the commitment to eliminate war, abolish poverty, and exterminate racism.

Education has done virtually nothing toward creating a world in which mankind can live without war. The trained mind has provided the instruments that are capable of destroying the human family. On the contrary, education has not trained the mind to appreciate human values so that the man will be able to live in a world without a war. When it comes to war, it can be argued with considerable logic that man is not any more civilized today than he was ages ago. Centuries before the dawn of the Christian era, the Persians, the Babylonians, and the Egyptians sought to settle their differences on that battlefield. We do the same thing. We are much more knowledgeable than they, certainly much better educated, but we do not know how to make universal peace. We thought when we fought World War I that we were fighting the war that would end wars. Americans fought and died on the battlefields of Europe under the slogans:

> We are fighting to make the world safe for democracy; for self-determination so that each nation will have the right to determine its own destiny.

Woodrow Wilson believed that World War I would be the last war in history, the war to end wars, and he made us believe it, too.

We did not learn anything from that tragic experience. Millions died; millions more were crippled and maimed in body and mind.

Yet two decades after World War I, we found ourselves in World War II. We followed the second World War with Korea. And for a decade, we have been bogged down in some way in Vietnam, and now Cambodia, and only God knows what the end will be and when.

We have more colleges and universities than ever before, but education is wholly irrelevant when it comes to providing ways to build a war-free world. We have fought 3,300 wars in 3,000 years. I read recently that in the last 3,500 years, man has been at war somewhere on the earth nine out of every ten hours. It can be argued with considerable evidence that education has given us more facts and better trained minds, but it has hardly made us any more sensitive to the perils of war.

We are spending $2 billion a month in the Vietnam War alone; and some $45 billion annually on past, present, and future wars and for national defense. With this amount of money, we could endow every college and university in the United States with $22,500,000 each and at five percent interest each of the 2,000 colleges and universities would have an additional income of $1,125,000 a year.

Our universities do not educate to this condition. Our purpose for existence seems to be mainly to help students develop their minds to get ahead in the world: not how they might use their minds to establish programs designed to eliminate the conditions that keep mankind forever at war. Some university should list as one of its major objectives a blueprint for universal peace. The question of man's survival on earth is too critical a matter to be left entirely in the hands of the politicians and heads of state. Make no mistakes: we will abolish war, or war will abolish mankind. And the United States cannot forever police the world.

The second problem confronting mankind, to which universities should give priority, is the question of poverty—poverty not only in far-off South America, Africa, Asia, and the Middle East, but poverty in the affluent U.S.A. In 1967, the federal government admitted that there were 8,876,700 families in the United States in poverty; or 29,900,000 persons—15 percent of the population—recognized by the federal government as impoverished. In 1967, it was estimated that there were fifty million children of school age in the United States, and six million of them came from poor families, families with annual incomes below

$3,300. Only two million received free lunch every day. This situation has not improved in the past three years.

Many children go to school without breakfast, are too hungry to learn, and are in such pain that they must be taken home. In some cases, mothers keep their children from school so that at least they can cry themselves to sleep from hunger in their mothers' arms. Right here in the United States, there are pregnant mothers so ill-nourished that blood transfusions are given routinely as a part of their regular prenatal care. Studies have been made that show that some impoverished pregnant women do not get sufficient iron, calcium, and calories, and in some cases the nutritionally motivated craving for iron and calcium leads them to eat clay and to eat starch for calories to supplement their food. There are thousands of babies born daily who have protein deficiency during their early years, and it has been established that protein deficiency in early childhood can cause permanent brain damage, causing I.Q. deficits of as many as 18 to 22 points, from which the child will never recover. There are people in the United States who go to the city dumps digging for food. When the dump trucks come, these people go through the garbage to get cheese, butter, meat, or whatever edible that has been thrown away. These are the poor—black and white, red, brown, Catholic and Protestant.

Our colleges and universities must not, certainly should not, educate ourselves and our students away from the problems of the poor. We should know the conditions and circumstances under which people live in the slums and ghettoes of our cities, and become so involved that we will help to build a United States where no family of four will have to live on an annual income of less than $5,000, where every able-bodied man will be guaranteed a job with an adequate minimum wage, where schools are adequate, and where recreational facilities are available. The problems of the poor should be the concern of the university, and how to eliminate poverty should be one of its major objectives.

The third and final enemy of mankind which our colleges and universities should work to abolish is racism. It is difficult for some of us to understand that racism does exist in the United States. . . .

Anyone, whether black or white, who believes that he is superior to members of another race, and in his behavior treats other persons as an inferior, has earned the right to be called a racist.

Slavery and segregation, which have been with us for a total of 350 years, are proof that there is racism in this country. Virtually all civil rights legislation and all victories in federal courts designed to make our democracy applicable to Negroes came about through some kind of coercion. Negroes are the only people in the United States who have had to spend tens of millions of dollars to get what the Constitution guarantees them and what all Europeans get when they come to this country simply by virtue of being born white. No other ethnic or racial group has had to sit-in and demonstrate in order to get the ballot. No white group has had to coerce Congress to pass a bill to prohibit discrimination in housing. No other group has found it necessary to sponsor a March on Washington, 250,000 strong, to make Congress know that we will pay any price to eliminate second class citizenship in this country. Sixteen years after the May 17, 1954, decision of the United States Supreme Court outlawing segregation in the public schools, many sections of the nation are resisting court orders. Our public schools are still largely segregated.

Despite these conditions, I believe that the destiny of black and white America is still one destiny. It must be one of education's aims to strive to desegregate and integrate America to the end that this great nation of ours, born in revolution and blood, conceived in liberty, and dedicated to the proposition that all men are created free and equal, will truly become the lighthouse of freedom where none will be denied because his skin is black and none favored because his eyes are blue; where the nation will be militarily strong but at peace; economically secure but just; learned but wise, and where the poorest will have a job and bread enough to spare.

Educators should define the kind of world we are trying to build. We should have ways of measuring the progress in goodness and in developing right attitudes, just as we measure the progress in intellectual development. We should begin in kindergarten to develop people who believe in our Christian principles and democratic ideals. For goodness is as important as literacy, and an honest heart is as important as a brilliant mind. It is too bad that we live in a world where men like John Fitzgerald Kennedy, Robert F. Kennedy, Martin Luther King, Jr., and Mahatma Gandhi are in as much danger of being killed as murderers and thieves.

I hear your silent refutations. I read your cynical minds: war, poverty, and racism, you say, are as old as man. We cannot eliminate them. I disagree. But even if you are right, we have no choice but to try. I hold that, win or lose, I might give my allegiance to the highest and the best that I know. For I believe that peace is better than war, so I must give my allegiance to peace. I believe that an adequate standard of living is due every living creature, so I must do my bit to eliminate poverty. White folks and black folks may never get rid of race prejudice, but, win or lose, God knows I must try to help build a society where black and white can live in the same community in peace and with justice, for I believe that brotherhood is better than "Honesty is the best policy." No man can maintain the integrity of his soul by giving allegiance to a lesser good. I agree with Henry Van Dyke that "It is better to follow even the shadow of the best than remain content with the worst."

I predict that most of you will be very successful in your chosen fields. Some of you will become famous. Some of you will accumulate great wealth. Some of you will occupy positions of prestige and power. My best wishes go with you. Whatever you do, however, I implore you to become involved in worthy programs designed to make a better world. I hope you will never turn your back on the millions who are poor, but rather do your part to enable them to rise to positions of respectability and honor. I hope you will never accept the dogma that wars are inevitable. I hope you will never be satisfied until America is committed to the proposition that equality, freedom and justice are the God-given rights of every American.

Again, I hear your misgivings. I hear you say, "I am only one man. What can I do to make things better? I am only one person." May I remind you that great ideas are born for the most part in the mind of one man? The call to leave his country and go to a strange land to become the father of a great people did not come to a number of men; the call went to Abraham. The call to lead the Hebrew people out of bondage did not go to a multitude but to Moses. The call to establish the Kingdom of God on earth went to Jesus, not to a thousand Jews. The call to make Christianity a universal religion went to Paul. The idea to build a great clinic at Rochester, Minnesota, was born in the mind of one of the Mayos. The idea of building Tuskegee Institute, in an effort to help black people and solve the race problem, was born in the mind of Booker T. Washington. George Washington Carver was one man. Harriett Tubman, leading black people to freedom, was one woman. Martin Luther King, Jr., was one strong enough, called to do something worthwhile, something unique, something so distinctive that if he did not do it, it will never be done.

I challenge you, members of the class of 1970, to join in a crusade to eliminate war, abolish poverty, and exterminate racism. God bless you and goodbye.

Education to What End?*

At Albany State College in Georgia on June 6, 1976, Dr. Mays inspired and challenged a capacity crowd of parents, relatives, friends, college administrators and faculty, trustees, and visitors in Stanford Hall with his commencement address. One hundred and seventy-six received undergraduate degrees, and forty-four were awarded master's degrees.

Dr. Mays developed his remarks around the aims of education, which he contended should be to glorify God and to serve humanity. This is consistent with the religious and philosophical ideas he embraced: he often noted that if happiness was to be found, it would be in serving others less fortunate, not in selfishness. And it is also congruent with his emphasis on the fatherhood of God and the brotherhood of man.

* * *

Why the struggle, the toil, the sacrifice to get an education? In answering these questions, I reveal here my philosophy of education.

Generally speaking, education is designed to train the mind to think clearly, logically, and constructively; to train the heart to feel understandingly and sympathetically the aspirations, the sufferings, and the injustices of mankind; and to strengthen the will to act in the interest of the common good. To state the purpose in Christian perspective, the aim of education should be to glorify God and to serve mankind.

Specifically speaking, education should be sought for its own sake. It should be sought for the enrichment of life, for the sheer enjoyment of knowing how to distinguish between truth and error, good and evil, and between that which is first-rate and that which is second-rate. For it is better to be able to count and read than not to be able to count and read. It is far better to be literate than to be illiterate, even if one does nothing with his literacy.

It is good for its own sake to understand why nations and civilizations rise, decay, and fail. It is enjoyable for its own sake to be able to spend an afternoon with the great writers: Dante and Goethe, DuBois and Langston Hughes, E. Franklin Frazier and Charles S. Johnson. It is

* Reprinted from Doris Gavins, *The Ceremonial Speaking of Benjamin Elijah Mays: Spokesman for Social Change*

wonderful to be able to enjoy Jesus in the Sermon on the Mount and Paul and Isaiah, Micah and Martin Luther King, Jr. It is mighty fine to be able to understand philosophy, to be able to argue with Plato in the *Republic*, to debate with Aristotle in science, and to split the hairs with Socrates. It is good to be able to appreciate art: to visit Vatican City and enjoy the works of Michelangelo in the Sistine Chapel and appreciate Tanner's *Daniel in the Lion's Den*. Education is good for its own sake. Although enjoyment for the sake of enjoyment may be a selfish aim, it is nevertheless a worthy goal. I argue and maintain, therefore, that all education is relevant if it improves the man. A knowledge of the works of Shakespeare and Langston Hughes may not help the engineer build a better bridge, but an appreciation of poetry may make the engineer a better man. If so, a knowledge of Shakespeare is relevant. It also may make living more worthwhile: if so, a knowledge of Shakespeare and Hughes is relevant.

There is another selfish reason why education is so precious. An educated man, a trained race, or a literate nation is much better qualified to defend itself against the strong and the unscrupulous than an untrained man, race, or nation. Whether we like it or not, there is a fundamental selfishness or defect in human nature. I call it original sin. We respect strength and not weakness, courage and not cowardice, knowledge and not ignorance, the man who stands on his feet in a manly way and not the one who cringes and kowtows. History shows that strong nations, for the most part, exploit weak nations, that strong races usually take advantage of weak races, and that strong individuals are inclined almost always to push weak individuals around—even blood relatives or a weak brother or sister. As one who believes in the power of religion to transform mankind, I reluctantly make this confession. I have seldom, if ever, known an individual, however Christian in his confession, who would not take advantage of the ignorant, the weak, and the cowardly. Whether nation or individual, the weak, the exploited, and the ignorant will be cheated, the lazy and the idle will be trodden upon, the coward will be kept running, and the jittery will be kept bouncing. The poor do not have an equal chance to bargain with the rich. The ignorant man starts out handicapped when confronted with the man who knows. The coward is licked as soon as he faces the fearless. This is the nature of man—not as I would like for him to be but as it is June 6, 1976. Leadership comes from strength and not weakness, respect comes from knowledge and not ignorance, and nations are advanced on economic power and not in poverty. Selfish though this purpose is, it is the only way one can respect himself and be respected by others; the only way to keep the strong and the unscrupulous off your neck. It has always been true, it is true now, and I predict that it always will be true—that the man farthest down catches the most hell.

If the members of the black race do not know this, we are indeed stupid people. Certainly we ought to know it after 246 years of slavery when we were property and not human, 100 years of segregation and denigration, another form of slavery in which we were denied our dignity as persons, and the present era of pseudo-integration when discrimination runs riots and thousands upon thousands of black teachers have lost their jobs under the hypocritical guise of integration.

I have been telling my people for five decades that a penalty has been placed upon us because we are black. The cards are stacked against us, and the dice are loaded. One way out is to learn a lesson from the Jew—develop our minds so well and become so accomplished in some art, craft, and profession that nobody can dismiss us with a wave of the hand or a shrug of the shoulder. Protest, and at times we must; demonstrate, as sometimes we have to, but I tell Negroes that there is no substitute for skills and a trained mind. If these were all, education would be worth all the toil and all the sacrifices that we endure to get it.

Up to now the purposes of education have been defined in selfish terms and narrowly conceived. If I should stop, here I would be untrue to myself and play false to my beliefs and convictions. Education is not designed merely to lift one above his fellows, to enable one to make a living, to keep the strong off his back, but rather its purpose is to equip man (1) to HELP his fellows, (2) To ELEVATE the masses, the less fortunate. For if one has a better mind than his fellows, more wealth than his fellows, is more favorably circumstanced than his fellows, has a better opportunity to develop than his fellows, he is obligated to use his skills in the interest of the common good. To use his education for the common good is mandatory because trained minds are rare—only a small percentage of the total population of the world are trained minds. And to whom much is given, much is required.

Furthermore, man can fulfill his true destiny in this life only in proportion to his skills that are used in the services of mankind. A surgeon's skill will keep him from being pushed around, but the real purpose of surgery is to relieve human suffering and to extend life—not money alone and not mere social security and prestige. An engineer's knowledge will give him prestige and social standing in the community, but his engineering skills are given to him to build roads and bridges, skyscrapers and cables, provide systems of communication and transportation, and electric power to the end to the end that civilization may be advanced and human life made more enjoyable. A lawyer's skill may give him respect among his neighbors, but the main purpose of law should be to extend the reign of justice, not only among the economically secure but among the lowly and the poverty stricken. Political office does bring power and prestige, but the main purpose of education in government and skills in politics should be to launch programs designed to raise the economic level of the people, to abolish disease, to educate the masses, and to extend freedom to each and every citizen. For after all, we are what we are by God's Grace, by the gift of our fellows or by sheer luck, and maybe all three. No man can choose the country into which he is born. No man can choose the cultural and economic environment into which he is born. No man can choose the quality of his mind. Perhaps it will always be a minority that can boast of sufficient ability to benefit by a college or university education which you are receiving today. If so blessed, the more brilliant mind is a gift of God and not of man. The brilliant mind is not of its own creation, so if we rise above our fellows, let's give the glory to God and the people.

The truly great men in history are those who identified themselves with the common man, such as Jesus of Nazareth, Gandhi and Nehru of India, Saint Francis of Assisi, Lincoln and Booker T. Washington of America, Schweitzer of France, Tubman of Liberia, and Martin Luther King, Jr., of Georgia.

I am convinced that in the parable of the Rich Farmer, Jesus condemns the farmer and calls him a fool not because he tore down his barns and built greater barns, but because as he tore down his barns, diseased bodies cried out for health, starving stomachs cried out for bread, a class-divided society yearned for brotherhood, and the illiterate minds prayed for literacy. All of these things were in evidence as this man failed to share and tore down his barns and built greater barns. Education should aim to sharpen insights so that we see man not as he is, but as he can and ought to be. Education should sensitize us so that one sees not only the potential of a Cicero born with a silver spoon in his mouth, but also the potentials of James Weldon Johnson and Countee Cullen; not only the potential of a Milton, born in favorable circumstances, but also the potential of a Shakespeare, whose father was a bankrupt butcher; not only the potential of George Washington, a rich Virginia planter and white, but also the potential of a Booker T. Washington, a slave and black; not only the potential of Nehru, born a Brahman, but also the potential of a lower-caste man, Mahatma Gandhi; not only the potential of John Kennedy, born with more than he needed, but the potential of Ralph Bunche, born with less than he needed.

Education should make one sensitive to the needs of the world. The world can hardly be secure as long as more than half of the peoples of the earth are starving, more than half have diseased bodies, and more than half can neither read nor write. If it is important to train the mind to fly to the moon and walk on it and now soon to go to Mars, to build atomic and hydrogen bombs capable of destroying the human family, it is equally important, or more, to train our children and students to have sympathy and empathy for all classes of men who dwell on all the face of the earth. If parents can train their children in the ways of prejudice by walking 600 miles to protest busing, if our politicians, north and south, so-called liberals and conservatives, can unite against busing, and if enlightened Boston can be led by a Yankee to oppose busing, the aim of education should be to create a society where black and white, Gentile and Jew, Protestant Catholic can live together, study together, and worship together. . . .

One writer put it this way: "There is but one virtue, to help human beings to free and beautiful life. But one sin, to do them indifferent or cruel hurt. The love of humanity is the whole of morality. This is humanism, this is goodness, this is the social conscience." Shakespeare was extremely impressive when he made Calpurnia say in *Julius Caesar*, "When beggars die, there are no comets seen; the heavens themselves blaze forth the death of Princes." And yet the destiny of the Prince and the Beggar is the same. Whether we like it or not, the ultimate destiny of every man is the same. The destiny of the rich is irrevocably tied in with the destiny of the poor, the learned with that of the unlearned, the great with the small, beggars with princes: we all travel the same road—from our mother's womb to the grave.

The final end of education which I shall mention in this address is to create in the individual a wholesome state of dissatisfaction—what I call divine discontent with ordinary, mediocre performance. To make one dissatisfied with the better, if the best can be achieved. Satisfaction means "enough done." The artist who is satisfied with his past performance will hardly make new discoveries. The man who is satisfied with his poverty will never have enough bread to spare. Harriet Du Autremont has beautifully said:

> No vision and you perish; no ideal, and you're lost;
> your heart must ever cherish some faith, at any cost,
> some hope, some dream to cling to, some rainbow in the sky,
> some melody to sing to, some service that is high.

Education, college or university, is designed to make one restless and dissatisfied with things as they are. Dissatisfied with war, poverty, disease, and illiteracy. Thorwaldsen, the great Danish sculptor, dramatizes the sad plight of the satisfied man. Thorwaldsen had made a great statue of Christ. It was so marvelous that people from far and near came to see it. They congratulated him, and tears began streaming down his face. The more the people congratulated him, the more he cried. Finally, someone asked him, "why the tears? Why do you cry? This is the finest piece of art we have ever seen." Thorwaldsen was heard to exclaim: "My genius is decaying; this is the first piece of art I have ever been completely satisfied with. I shall never create a great work of art again." And Thorwaldsen was right. When satisfaction comes, a man ceases to grow; he stagnates and dies. Nothing is worse than a state of satisfaction. Louis Untermeyer prayed that he would never be satisfied. His poem is impressive—he says:

> God, though this life is but a wraith,
> Although we know not what we use,
> Although we grope with little faith,
> Give me the heart to fight—and lose.
> Ever insurgent let me be,
> Make me more daring than devout;
> From sleek contentment keep me free,
> And fill me with a buoyant doubt.
> Open my eyes to visions girt
> With beauty, and with wonder lit—
> But always let me see the dirt,
> And all that spawn and die in it.
> Open my eyes to music; let
> Me thrill with Spring's first flutes and drums—
> But never let me dare forget
> The bitter ballads of the slums.

From compromise and things half done,
Keep me with stern and stubborn pride;
And when at last the fight is won,
God, keep me still unsatisfied.

It is clear from what I have said up to now that education may not make a man good. It may not make a people wise. It may not make a nation just. Nevertheless, education is an indispensable weapon if the mind is to be developed, the welfare of the people advanced, and if the nation is to survive.

When peace is established among the nations, trained minds will establish it. When poverty is abolished on the earth, trained minds will abolish it. When cancer, heart disease, tuberculosis, malaria, and leprosy are completely eliminated, trained minds will do it. When freedom and independence come to aspiring peoples, trained minds will accomplish it.

When you return in 2001 to celebrate to celebrate your 25th Anniversary, if your profession be medicine, I hope your classmates will seek you out—not to know what your fine house, your yacht, and your car are, but they will want to know about your recent discovery in medicine, how many lives you have saved by your skill in surgery. If it be law, you will be sought after in 2001 to find out how you secured justice for the poor and the unlettered.

Shakespeare is not known by his wealth but by *Othello* and *MacBeth, Hamlet* and *Julius Caesar*. Nobody stops to ask how much wealth Socrates had when he died; Socrates is known by dying as the first martyr for freedom of speech. Nobody cares how much wealth Booker T. Washington had when he died in 1915. Tuskegee gave Washington immortality. Martin Luther King, Jr., will not be known by his wealth but as one of the greatest prophets of the 20th century, bringing hope and liberation to millions of peoples across the world. Carter G. Woodson is known as one possessed with a dream, a Harvard Ph.D., who left his comfortable job at Howard University and founded the Association of Negro Life and History. Charles Drew is known by the Blood Bank. Mordecai Johnson is known by building a great university. Nehru was wealthy and high caste, but history knows him as one who turned his back on wealth and caste, suffered with his people, and became the first Prime Minister of Independent India. Gandhi is known as the 98- pound man who lifted the British empire off its hinges through nonviolent activities.

And it is to this task that the colleges and universities of the world and the men and women who teach in them should dedicate their lives. In no other way can we justify that toil and sacrifices we endure to maintain them.

Finally, as you go forth from this place, I wish success in all the good things that you do. I hope you will always live above the poverty line. But I hope most of all that whatever you touch, you will always leave it better than you found it.

May the years ahead be gracious and kind to you. I pray that the words of dissatisfaction, success and creative living will be always at your back.

Goodbye and may God bless you.

Chapter 4

Sermons

Except a Man Be Born Again, He Cannot See the Kingdom of God*

On April 12, 1949, Dr. Mays delivered this sermon at Christ Church Cathedral in St. Louis, Missouri, as a part of the Lenten Noonday Services for the week, presented under the auspices of the Metropolitan Church Federation.

The *Christ Church Cathedral Bulletin*, dated April 3, 1949, provided a statement to remind the worshipers of the meaning of Lent:

> The season of Lent in the Church Year grew out of the very ancient custom of a fast in preparation for Easter. By the standards of the primitive Church, it is also a time for instruction in the faith and for self-examination, self-discipline, and penitence. It is above all a time for recalling the meaning of our Baptism, and for preparation for the Victory of Easter. The word "Lent" is derived from the Anglo-Saxon "Lenten," i.e., the spring, the time of lengthening the days.

The services were held from 12:05-12:35 p.m. each day, for the last three weeks of Lent.

Dr. Mays used the words God spoke to Nicodemus as the title of his text. He frequently started his sermons with a Biblical quote, and used John 3:3 to illustrate his sermon.

---

* Mays Collection, Moorland-Spingarn Research Center, Howard University

Dr. Mays used sociology, psychology, the scriptures, and personal experiences in his sermon and applied the same to everyday human problems. He firmly believed that religion should provide practical solutions to everyday human needs.

* * *

To some, God does not exist. We call such people atheists. There are others who say, "There may be a God, but I do not know." We call them agnostics. There are others who attach no special significance to the Christian religion. They reject Christianity as a divine revelation. We call them infidels.

But there are many Christian people to whom God is a problem. They want to know who God is, where God is, what God is doing, and if God is all that the Christian religion says that He is, why doesn't He rise up in His righteous might and do something about this wicked world. These questions do not bother me. I have lived into a satisfactory, workable experience of God that stands in good in the midst of the wrecks of matter and the crush of worlds. And if all around my soul gave way, my faith in God would still remain unshaken. I would still be able to say, "I know God is." Nothing can happen in this world to shake my faith in God. I believe in God. So my greatest problem is not God.

And as it may seem, my greatest problem is not the devil—certainly not the devil who spells his name with a capital "D" and who resides in a place beneath called hell. And the devils I know anything about are men and women. My greatest problem, therefore, my greatest worry, my greatest concern is not God. It is not the devil. My greatest concern is man. Man is God's problem child number one.

I am disturbed about man because I have no guarantee that man is going to make it. I have no guarantee that he is going to pull through. I call history to my aid, and the evidence is negative. It is true that man has built great civilizations, but it is true that practically every civilization man has built, he has destroyed that civilization. He built and destroyed Egypt and Babylon, Persia and Assyria, Carthage and Rome. He built modern civilizations: England and France, Germany and Austria, Japan and Italy, the United States and Russia. And between 1939 and 1945, man did his best to destroy modern civilization. And it seems that the United States and Russia may finish the job.

All my life, I have been disturbed about man. I have never been able to understand to my complete satisfaction why it is that one man, one race, one nation doesn't want to see another rise; why one wants to suck the life blood out of another. Despite psychology, sociology, and even theology, I just do not understand.

I am further disturbed about man because of the paradoxical, contradictory, diabolical nature of man. Here he is, born in the image of God; born also it seems, in the image of the devil: potentially good, potentially evil, potentially sinner, potentially saint, potentially God, potentially devil, potentially capable of building a heaven on earth, potentially capable of building a hell on earth, potentially peace loving, potentially a warrior, potentially honest, potentially dishonest. That's man: that's you, that's me. And it is for that reason that Jesus said unto Nicodemus, "Except a man be born again, he cannot see the Kingdom of God."

I am disturbed about man for still another reason. There is no guarantee that when we increase a man's knowledge, we will increase his goodness. For a long time, we have tried to explain man's sins on the basis of his ignorance. We have tried to make ourselves believe that man exploits man, that race takes advantage of race, that nations fight war because they don't know any better. We used to believe that the road to salvation was through knowledge. But we know now that Socrates was wrong when he implied that if man only knew what was right, he would do it. We now know that man can know the truth but deliberately lie; that he can know the good and choose the evil; that he can see the light and walk in darkness; that he can see the high road and deliberately walk the low road. We agree with the apostle Paul when he said in essence, "I find myself doing that which I know I ought not to do and I find myself failing to do that which I know I ought to do." The apostle Paul was simply saying what every honest man knows: knowledge alone is simply not enough. Man needs God. He needs to be born anew.

It must also be admitted that all this knowledge leads to an impasse. It leads to a blind alley. We are today intellectually wiser than at any time in history. We know more about science, history, economics, art, philosophy, religion, than we have ever known, and yet we are just as befuddled and confused today as at any time in history. We knew a decade in advance that the second world war was in the making, and we couldn't stop it. We know now that the seeds of the third world war have been planted, and despite all our learning, we may not be able to stop it. All knowledge leads ultimately to an impasse.

Is there any hope that man can be redeemed, changed so that this brutal, cruel nature of man can be touched by divinity, so that no man will want to take advantage of another, no race will want to keep another down, no nation will want to exploit another? Is there any balm in Gilead? Is there any hope?

There is a balm in Gilead. There is a ray of hope. There is something in man that keeps him forever reaching for that which is high and noble, for that which is just and right. And bad as man may be, he clings to his ideals. He wages a relentless war, spends billions, kills millions, yet dreams of a day when wars will cease, when swords will be beaten into ploughshares and spears into pruning hooks. The strong race takes advantage of the weak, and yet from the race of the strong come prophets of God, pronouncing judgment upon His own people.

Men lie, but they cling to the truth as an ideal. Men cheat and exploit, but they contend and insist that honesty is the best policy. The drunkard wants his son to be sober. Mothers want their daughters to be chaste. There is something in man that will not let him rest satisfied down in the gutter. Man and God were made for each other, and his soul is restless without God.

There is another ray of hope. Man has an uneasy conscience. Define it in terms of psychology or sociology, the results are the same. The strong nation that goes out to ravage and exploit, to trample its big feet over the backs of the weak nations, that nation is on the defensive—its conscience is uneasy. You find that nation apologizing and explaining to the world, trying to justify its position. The race that denies the other races the rights and privileges that it covets for itself can never sit at ease in the midst of its injustice. The individual who deliberately goes out to hurt, to bruise, to scandalize the name of another, will spend restless nights and terrible days trying to justify his position. There is such a thing as conscience, which haunts us by night and chases us by day.

And as long as a nation's conscience is uneasy, as long as the individual's conscience is uneasy, as long as it haunts him by night and chases him by day, that individual is a candidate for the Kingdom of Light. The final hope is in repentance. If a man will repent of his sins; if nations will repent, cease to study war, and trust God; if races will repent and deal justly one with the other, a merciful God will forgive us. And eyes have not seen and ears have not heard what God will do for the world if man will repent and be born anew.

His Goodness Was Not Enough*
Luke 16:19-31

At the Baccalaureate services at Bucknell University in Lewisburg, Pennsylvania, Dr. Mays preached this sermon on Sunday evening, June 13, 1954, in the Davis Gymnasium. The audience included administrators, faculty, parents, relatives, and friends.

Awarded the degree of Doctor of Divinity on the occasion, Dr. Mays was cited by the university for his courage in the face of difficulties, for his distinguished service to black Americans, and for his moral and intellectual achievements.

Dr. Mays based his sermon on the Biblical passage from St. Luke regarding the fate of the rich man, Dives, who ignored the beggar at his door, and he made a strong plea for the development of a social conscience.

Dr. Mays told his audience that Dives went to hell not because he was rich, and not because he was bad, but because he had no social conscience. "Dives had no concern for the beggar lying outside his door," Dr. Mays stated.

* * *

In the New Testament passage just read to you, the rich man is not named. It was not until the 14th century that the rich man was referred to as "dives." "Dives" is a Latin adjective meaning "rich." It is used that way in the Vulgate—the Latin version of the Bible used by the Roman Catholics. Chaucer, the father of English poetry, used it as a proper name in the 14th century and related it to the rich man in this chapter. Since that time, we call him Dives. In this passage, Dives is pictured as going to hell, and Lazarus, the beggar, is consigned to a place in heaven. Perhaps you, like many people of our time, do not believe in hell. And yet I am inclined to believe that if there is no hell somewhere, there ought to be a hell. There ought to be a hell for a man like Nero who burned innocent Christians alive and a heaven for the Apostle Paul. A hell for Hitler and his associates, who killed six million Jews, and a heaven for Albert Schweitzer; a hell for Mussolini, a heaven for Abraham Lincoln; a hell for Jumbulinganada, a notorious criminal of South Af-

---

* Special Collections/University Archives, Bucknell University

rica, a heaven for Mahatma Gandhi. But all this is beside the point. It is not my purpose in this address to split hairs as to whether there is or is not a hell. My purpose is to explain the reasons why a man who, in the traditional sense, was a good man and despite that fact was condemned and consigned to a place of torture and torment.

With apology to orthodoxy, I believe this passage has been grossly misrepresented. I do not believe that Dives is condemned to hell just because he was rich. Some of the finest men of ancient and modern times were and are rich. Abraham, whom God called to be the father of a great people, was a rich man. Some people are rich and accumulate great fortunes because they are thrifty and industrious. Jesus Himself complimented and rewarded the man who had five talents and gained five more, but He criticized and punished the man who had the talent but did not use it. It was not this wealth that sent Dives to a place of torment and torture. I do not even believe that Lazarus went to heaven because he was poor. There are those who are poor because they are lazy, trifling, and good-for-nothing. There is no virtue in poverty per se, and there is no vice in wealth per se. There is nothing here to indicate that Dives was a bad man; no indication that he exploited the poor; nothing to show that he was immoral, a drunkard, or a gambler. It is quite possible that Dives was a decent, respectable, law-abiding citizen. Nor is there anything to prove that Lazarus was a good man. He might have earned his gore through riotous living, and he might have earned his poverty because he was lazy and good-for-nothing.

Let me tell you, if I may, why I believe Dives is consigned to hell. This man goes to hell not because he was rich and not because he was bad, but because of his attitude toward life and his attitude toward people. Dives is pictured as going to hell because he had no social conscience. Here is a man whom God had blessed. He fared sumptuously every day and dressed in purple and fine linen. His barns were filled with plenty, and his presses were bursting open with new wine. In modern everyday parlance, he had houses and lands, stocks and bonds, and bank accounts galore. He had economic security, social standing, and prestige, but he had no concern for the beggar lying outside his door.

At the other extreme of the economic ladder sat Lazarus, a man whom life had beaten and licked—so beaten that he was willing and satisfied to catch the crumbs that fell from the rich man's table. Apparently there is no ill-will, hatred, jealousy, or rancor in his heart against Dives because of his superior status. Lazarus was so weak that he could not push away the dogs that came in to lick his sores. But Dives was not moved. He did not care. He did not even see Lazarus. Dives should not only have given charity, but he should have been interested in building a society where no man needs to beg, where each and every man has bread enough to spare, and where each person has an opportunity to develop a sound mind in a sound body. Dives is symbolic of a type.

This man Lazarus was not asking for much. He was not seeking to invade the privacy of Dives' home. He was not seeking social equality. He was not asking for a Porterhouse steak nor Smithfield ham, nor ham and eggs—not even for hot rolls and coffee—only the crumbs that fell from the rich man's table. But Dives did not care. He had no social conscience.

Whether Dives realized it or not, he was his brother's keeper. He was responsible for what happened to Lazarus. They tell me that more than half of the peoples of the earth never know what it is to get enough to eat and to have a balanced diet. More than half of the peoples of the earth can neither read nor write. I have seen the starving millions of Asia. I have seen their diseased, emaciated bodies. Not many months ago, while walking down the streets of Bombay, Mrs. Mays and I saw a strange figure approaching us, such as we had never seen before. Our Indian friend said that the strange-looking figure was a leper. If we have bread enough and to spare, and if our bodies are strong and healthy, we must be concerned about the plight of other people. Whether we like it or not, our destiny is tied up with their destiny, and their welfare is ours. Jesus, in the 25th Chapter of Matthew, makes it clear that our relationship to God is dependent upon our relationship to man. "Inasmuch as ye did it unto the least of these, ye did it unto me." Dives goes to hell not because he was rich and not because he was bad. Dives was a good man, a decent respectable, law-abiding citizen. He went to hell because he had no social conscience. He did not care.

Dives is condemned for another reason. He evidently drew false distinctions based on class. He saw Lazarus not as a human being, not as a child of God, not as one born in God's image, but Dives saw Lazarus as a diseased beggar not only unfit to associate with him, but unworthy of the crumbs that fell from his napkin. I make bold to assert that if the man at the gate had been a Roman official, say the Emperor, or even Pilate, the Roman prosecutor of Judea, it would have been a different story. If the beggar had been a Roman Senator, a learned scribe or Pharisee, a judge of the Sanhedrin Court, or an aristocratic Sadducee, Dives would not have given him crumbs, but he would have invited the man in, given him the best wine, and prepared the best of food. It hardly dawned upon Dives that God is no respecter of persons, that He calls the great and the small, the rich and the poor, the lettered and the unlettered to do his work. He did not realize that God called Abraham, a rich man, and made him the father of his people; and the same God called Moses, a keeper of the flock, and made him the lawgiver and the great emancipator. God called Lincoln from a Kentucky log cabin and, according to H. G. Wells, made him one of the six great men of history. God called the two Roosevelts, born with silver spoons in their mouths, and made them great. God called Ramsey McDonald from a two-room cabin in Scotland and made him a great premier. He called Churchhill, more favorably circumstanced, and made him a great premier. He called George Washington, a wealthy Virginian, and made him a great American. He called Booker T. Washington, the slave-born, and made him great. He took Milton, an aristocrat, and trained and made him a great poet, but he took Shakespeare, the son of a bankrupt father and mother who could not write their names, and made him greater than Milton. Dives could not understand this. He did not know that God is no respecter of persons. He drew false distinctions based on class.

The test of good religion is not how we treat our peers and those above us, but how we treat those beneath us; not how we treat the man highest up, but how we treat the man farthest down; not how we treat the President of the United States, but how we treat the man in the slums. It is reasonable to suppose that I would be gentle and kind to the millionaire who might someday endow my college, give me money for a building, or endow scholarships. But the real test of my religion would be how I treat the man who has nothing to give—no money, no social prestige, no honors; not how I treat the educated, but how I treat the man who can't write his name. Someone has wisely said, "There is but one virtue, to help human beings to free and beautiful life. But one sin, to do them indifferently or cruel hurt. The love of humanity is the whole of morality. This humanism, this is goodness, this is the social conscience."

This man goes to hell because he thought that which he had accumulated belonged to him, and that he alone was responsible for his wealth. He did not realize that we own nothing, that we bring nothing into this world and we carry nothing out. Everything that Dives made he died and left behind. All that we accumulate we will leave for others—houses and lands, stocks and bonds, bank accounts. The gold we hoard, the oil the nations fight about, we will leave. We may hoard ever so much, but we can use only a certain amount. We can sit in only one chair at a time, ride in only one car at a time, live in only one house at a time, and eat only so much steak at a time. Dives not only made the mistake of believing that what he had belonged to him, but he acted as if he alone accumulated it. He thought that he was self-made, an island apart to himself. He did not realize that for what he was and what he had accumulated, he owed a debt of gratitude to God who made him wealthy. No man can lift himself by his own bootstraps. One may come into this world with a brilliant mind. He may develop it and use it to good advantage, but he is not responsible for his brilliant mind. His mind comes from his ancestors and God. No other American gets the fame and prestige that is experienced by a president of the United States. But no man alone can make himself President. If Mr. Eisenhower goes down in history as a great president, the people and history will make him great. Marion Anderson has a great voice, but without the acclaim of the people, Marion Anderson would not be great. One man through blood, sweat, and genius may become rich, but without the people to use the materials he creates, there would be no accumulated wealth. We owe everything to God and the people. The destiny of each man is tied up with the destiny of another. We are so interlaced and interwoven that what affects one touches all. We are all bound together in one great humanity. This Dives did not understand. . . .

The tragic part of the story is in verse 26: "Besides all that, a great gulf yawns between us and you, to keep back those who want to cross from us to you and also those who want to pass from you to us." That's a way of saying it was too late. Any man who has no social conscience, who draws false distinctions based on class, who believes that he is self-made, that what he has belongs to him and not to the people, establishes a great gulf between himself and the people, and between himself and God.

The time does come in the lives of individuals and in the lives of nations when it is too late to make amends. It happened to Nero, to Judas and Hitler. They all committed suicide. It happened to Mussolini. He was killed by his countrymen, and his body and that of his mistress were hanged for ridicule on the streets of Milan. When a great gulf yawns, separating us from God and the people, it's too late.

Between Dives who had no social conscience, who drew distinctions based on class, who thought that what he had belonged to him and that he owed nothing to beggars and the people—between him and the people and between him and God, a great gulf was fixed—a gulf so fixed and so wide that it was too late for Dives to make amends.

The Church Amidst Ethnic and Racial Tensions*

These remarks were delivered by Dr. Mays at the Second Assembly of the World Council of Churches in Evanston, Illinois, on August 21, 1954. The First Assembly of the World Council of Churches was in Amsterdam in 1948 and marked the beginning of the ecumenical movement. W. A. Visser't served as secretary general of the Second Assembly, took detailed and careful notes of the sessions, and edited an informative book on the proceedings, *The Evanston Report* (1955).

At Evanston in 1954, the Second Assembly examined the unity that the organization had given to the churches over the period of the past six years and determined those areas where disunity was most evident. Visser't also noted in his book: "Tensions clearly evident were such that of the political ideologies between east and west; and those faced between social and ethnic groups."

The audience for the Second Assembly was composed of delegates, visitors, observers, consultants, fraternal delegates, youth staff, non-accredited visitors, and pilgrims from the United States and other parts of the world. Speakers' words were translated into the official languages of the Assembly: English, French, and German.

This session took place in a plenary gathering on Saturday, August 21, 1954, from 10:00-12:00 p.m. in McGaw Hall on the campus of Northwestern University before a crowd of approximately 3,340, with a horde of news reporters standing in the back of the building to witness the very provocative session.

Dr. Mays, a delegate to the National Baptist convention to the World Council of Churches, spoke on the segregation issue as a leading black member of the World Council Commission on Intergroup Relations, which drafted a preliminary report for consideration before the full assembly. During his presentation, Dr. Mays was interrupted ten times with applause, and the audience stood and applauded him for several minutes at the end, according to a news story printed in the *Christian Advocate* on September 16, 1954.

Dr. Mays asserted, "Segregation remains the greatest scandal in the church." He criticized the churches for their slowness in efforts to end segregation.

---

* Reprinted from Mays, *Born to Rebel,* pp. 349-356

* * *

Within the past quarter of a century, Christians have been forced to think about the bearing of their faith upon the problem of racial discrimination and upon the meaning of races in human history. Wars involving all mankind, the rise of atheistic communism, the development of the Nordic theory of racial superiority, the struggles of the colored people everywhere for freedom, and a new emphasis on the meaning of the Gospel in our time have made us embarrassedly aware of the wide gulf that frequently exists between our Gospel and our practice.

The Jerusalem Conference in 1928 prepared an extensive volume on the subject. Subsequent ecumenical conferences have devoted considerable time to the general topic, "The Christian and Race": Oxford and Edinburgh in 1937; Madras in 1938, Amsterdam in 1948. It suffices to say that in all of these ecumenical bodies, segregation in the Church of Christ based on race and color has been strongly condemned.

Your present Commission has critically examined these documents and has benefitted greatly by them. We have tried to build substantially on the work of previous scholars, and we believe we have dug new foundations. Since the Church gets its authority from the Bible, we have searched the Scriptures anew—both the Old and the New Testaments— to see whether there is anything there to justify our modern policy of segregation based on race, color, or ethnic origins.

The members of your Commission, supported by the best Biblical scholars, conclude that anyone who seeks shelter in the Bible for his defense of racial segregation in the Church is living in a glass house, which is neither rock nor bulletproof. In the Old Testament, the lines are definitely and sharply drawn, but they are drawn along religious and not along racial lines.

For example, when Moses exhorted the Jews not to intermarry with the people in the land they were to possess, he did so on neither racial nor ethnic grounds. In Deuteronomy 7:2-4, this fact is made plain:

> . . .When the Lord your God gives them over to you and you defeat them; then you must utterly destroy them; you shall make no covenant with them, and show no mercy to them. You shall not make marriages with them, giving daughters to their sons or taking their daughters for your sons. For they would turn away your sons from following me, to serve other gods; then the anger of the Lord would be kindled against you, and he would destroy you quickly.

The objection to mixing is religious—not related to race, color, or ethnic group. Ancient Israel was held together by religion and not by race, just as the Jews today are held together by religion and culture. In fact, the nations that surrounded Israel belonged to the same racial stock as Israel. The Moabites shared Israel's language, the Edomites were tied to Israel by bonds of blood, and the Canaanites lived in the same country. But as long as they served their own gods, they were not accepted by Israel. On the other hand, the Gibeonites, who accepted Israel's God, ultimately became Israelites.

The drastic action of Ezra, on the return of the Jews to Jerusalem, in decreeing that the Jews had to put away their foreign wives, was not made on racial grounds. It resulted from an honest belief that they had trespassed against God by marrying wives of foreign religions. We search in vain, therefore, if we expect to find in the Old Testament support for our kind of racial or color segregation. The truth is that the Jews did not constitute a pure strain, and throughout its history, Israel made proselytes from other nations and races.

When we turn to the New Testament, it is equally clear that separateness was based on religion and culture, not on the grounds of race or ethnic origin. Your Commission points out once more that from the beginning of his career, Jesus proclaimed a religion that was supra-racial, supra-national, supra-cultural, and supra-class. His doctrine of God as Father embraces the human race and makes us all children of the same God. God is our Father, and we are his children. When we pray "Our Father, which art in Heaven," we acknowledge our kinship in Him. And His concern for all His children is so great that the very hairs on their heads are numbered. Each is precious in His sight. To deny the universalism in the teachings of Christ is to deny the very genius of Christianity.

It is not surprising, therefore, that Hitler wanted nothing to do with Christ and nothing to do with the Christian religion, because they are antipathetic to everything that he stood for. His doctrine of Nordic superiority cannot stand up against the doctrine of the fatherhood of God and the brotherhood of man, nor against the brilliant account of Peter and Cornelius—a Jew and a Gentile standing face to face, confronted with the same Christ and with the same God—nor against the story of the good Samaritan. It was a Samaritan, a member of another race, who responded helpfully and sympathetically to the Jew's needs, thus dramatizing forever the fact that anyone who is in need is your neighbor and that neighborliness cuts across race and class. Jesus challenged the proud Jews to do as well as the despised Samaritan in displaying love and dispensing mercy across racial and cultural lines.

Jesus declared that he found greater faith in a Roman Centurion than he had found in all Israel. On another occasion he declared, ". . . Many will come from the east and west, and will recline with Abraham, and Isaac, and Jacob, in the Kingdom of Heaven; but the sons of the Kingdom will be cast into the outer darkness" (Matt. 8: 11-12). Speaking in the Synagogue at Nazareth, Jesus made his audience angry when he reminded them that Elijah had been sent not to the widows of Israel in the time of famine, but only to the Gentile women of Sarepta, and that Elisha did not cure the Hebrew leper, but only the Gentile Naaman. The position of Jesus on this point is so clear that he who runs can read and understand.

Some Jewish Christians insisted that, in order to benefit by the Gospel of Christ, one had to be born a Jew or become a Jew by accepting the rite of circumcision and being adopted into the Jewish people; but they were not arguing against Gentiles on the basis of race. Any foreigner who accepted circumcision and who was so adopted was readily accepted. Here we must draw a sharp distinction between Jewish segregation and ours. The kind of segregation or exclusiveness practiced by the Jews generally, and by the Jewish Christians differed widely from modern segregation based on caste, color, and race. A non-Jew could become a member of a local Jewish group. He could qualify by meeting the conditions. But in our time, when segregation is based on race or color, there is nothing one can do to qualify. One cannot qualify even when he accepts the same creed, practices the same ritual, prays to the same God, and partakes of the same culture. Segregation based on color or race makes it impossible for the Christian of color to qualify; for one cannot change his color and he cannot change his race. And this restriction is tantamount to penalizing one for being what God made him and tantamount to saying to God, "You make a mistake, God, when you made peoples of different races and colors."

According to Acts, the Spirit descended on the people on the day of Pentecost, fifty days after the resurrection. The disciples and the people got a new sense of power, and they interpreted this to mean that the Holy Spirit was present. At Pentecost, a new community was created. The church was born. Jews and proselytes gathered together, and representatives of some fifteen different nations were assembled. Acts 2:1 makes this point clear, "When the day of Pentecost had come, they were all together in one place." There they were: Parthians, Medes and Elamites; the dwellers in Mesopotamia, Judea, Cappadocia, Pontus, Asia, Phrygia, Pamphylia, Egypt, and the part of Libya about Cyrene; strangers from Rome, Jews and proselytes, Cretans and Arabians. In their own tongues, the proselytes heard of the mighty and glorious deeds of God.

Peter admitted in his encounter with Cornelius that it was unlawful for a Jew to associate with one of another nation. He told the group at Caesarea, "You yourselves know how unlawful it is for a Jew to associate with or visit anyone of another nation; but God has shown me that I should not call any man common or unclean" (Acts 10:28). Continuing, Peter proclaimed the great universal truth: "Truly I perceive that God shows no partiality, but in every nation anyone who fears him and does what is right is acceptable to him" (Acts 10: 34-35).

Paul carried this universal note further than Peter. Paul saw instantly that these differences could not establish the true church and could not further the missionary enterprise. He took the position that a Gentile did not have to become a Jew in order to be a Christian. The Jewish law had been fulfilled in Christ and had been superseded by Him. In Galatians 3:28, Paul declared: "There is neither Jew nor Greek, there is neither slave nor free, there is neither male nor female; for you are all one in Christ Jesus." Again in Romans 10:12, we are told: "For there is no difference between the Jew and the Greek: for the same Lord over all is rich unto all that call upon him."

Paul set aside racial heritage, social status, and sex. In Christ all divisions are unified, and racial and ethnic groups become one. He declared on Mars Hill, "God that made the world and all things therein, seeing that he is Lord of heaven and earth. . . hath made of one blood all nations of men for to dwell on all the face of the earth" (Acts 17: 24, 26). Thus, centuries before science discovered that all men are of one blood, that truth was apprehended by men of faith. My distinguished colleague, B. J. Marais, sought the thinking of the fourteen leading theologians of Europe on this subject, including Emil Brunner and Karl Barth. They all agree that we can find no justification in the Bible for a segregated church based on race or ethnic origin. This universalism in the Gospel is climaxed and attested to by the fact that Christ died for all mankind. So if there are those among us who seek support in the Bible for segregated churches based on color, race, caste, or ethnic origin, they must turn elsewhere for support.

Your Commission has gone further. We have delved into church history: ancient, medieval, and modern. We have sought to find out what the churches have practiced through the centuries in their worship and fellowship. New Testament scholars and church historians all agree that since its inception, the Christian Church has had in its membership people of different nations, races, and even colors. Nowhere in the early church do we find distinctions drawn on the basis of country or race. James (2:1-6) condemns the separation of cultural and social groups in the local church. The fact that the early church drew no distinctions based on race or color, and that Christians were often described as a "new people" or a "third race," drawn from many racial or ethnic groups, is attested by Tertullian, Origen, Ignatius, Hermas, Barnabas, Clement, and others. Their position is sustained by later scholars—Harnack and Ramsay, Cadoux and Moffat, Griffin, and Latourette. We seek in vain for signs of segregation based on race and color in the church of the first centuries of the Christian era.

What was true of the early church was true of the church of the Middle Ages. In both the ancient and the medieval church, the basis of membership was faith in Jesus Christ, our Lord. The basis of membership was faith, not race; Christ, not color; creedal acceptance and not nationality. The creeds of Christendom have always been formulated and enforced in terms of certain beliefs about God, Jesus, man, sin, and salvation, never on theories about race or ethnic groups. In summarizing this fact, Marais says: "In the extensive literature of the history of the Church till after the Reformation, we look in vain for any sign of a crucial basis for admission to the congregation." If color, race, or cultural background was a condition of membership in the local congregation of the early church or the local church of the Middle Ages, our survey does not reveal it.

It seems clear, then, that the color or racial bar in the church is a modern thing. It was not, in fact, until the seventeenth century that the outlines of the modern race problem began to emerge. It is the modern church that again crucifies the body of Christ on the racial cross. Race and color did not count in the early existence of the Protestant Church. It was when modern western imperialism began to explore and exploit the colored peoples of Africa, Asia, and America, that the beginning of segregation and discrimination based on color and race was initiated. It was then that color was associated with "inferiority," and whiteness with "superiority." Our Commission writes: "The broad pattern of major racial group tensions which trouble the world today had its historical origins in the period of European overseas exploration and expansion into America, Asia and Africa. The resulting exploration of one group by another, involving groups differing in race, varied in the three countries. But the same general relation of asserted superiority and inferiority developed between the white world and the colored world. Color became first the symbol, and then the accepted characteristic of the intergroup tensions."

Your Commission concludes, therefore, that the modern church can find no support for this practice of segregation based on race, color, or ethnic origin in the Bible, no basis for it in the ancient and medieval churches, and none for it in the various theologies of the Catholic and Protestant churches.

Your Commission has probed beyond the church and the Bible. We have sought to find out what support modern science gives for segregation and discrimination. We could quote scientist after scientist on the question of whether there is or is not an inherent superiority which one race possesses over the another. Forty or fifty years ago, scientists were divided on the subject. Also, men argued that some groups were biologically superior to others. Hundreds of volumes were written to justify a denial of equal opportunity to some peoples on the ground that they were inferior and that God had made them that way. But now there is no disagreement among the top scientists of the earth. As a recent UNESCO publication points out: "In matters of race, the only characteristics which anthropologists have so far been able to use effectively as a basis for classification are physical (anatomical and physiological). Available scientific knowledge provides no basis for believing that the groups of mankind differ in their innate capacity for intellectual and emotional development. Some biological differences between human beings within a single race may be as great as or greater than the same biological differences between races." In another connection, the United Nations publication speaks for modern science on race: "All of us believed that the biological differences found amongst human racial groups can in no case justify the views of racial inequality which have been based on ignorance and prejudice, and that all of the differences which we know can well be disregarded for all ethical human purposes." At long last, science has caught up with religion, for it was Paul who declared on Mars Hill nineteen centuries ago, that God made of one blood all nations of men.

If the church can find no support in science for ethnic and racial tension, none in the Bible for segregation based on race or color, none in the practices of the ancient and medieval churches, and none in Christian theologies, the questions naturally arise: How can segregation and discrimination in the church be justified? What can the churches do to put themselves in line with the gospel, the practices of the ancient and medieval churches, and in line with the findings of modern science? If the modern churches cannot practice full Christian fellowship in worship and membership, how can they preach the prophetic word to secular organizations that discriminate on grounds of race, color, and caste? To answer these questions, is our task at Evanston. It is to these problems that the Commission on the Church Amidst Ethnic and Racial Tensions will address itself.

There is one aspect of this subject which we often overlook. Usually the question is, what does discrimination or segregation do to the person segregated, to the disadvantaged person? It is conceded that segregation and discrimination hurt the pride of the person discriminated against, that they retard his mental, moral, and physical development, and that they rob society of what the disadvantaged group might contribute to enrich humanity. We agree that imposed separateness breeds ill-will and hatred, that it develops in the segregated a feeling of inferiority to the extent that he never knows what his capabilities are. His mind is never free to develop unrestricted. The ceiling and not the sky is the limit of his striving.

But we seldom realize what discrimination does to the person who practices it. It scars not only the soul of the segregated but the soul of the segregator as well. When we build fences to keep others out, erect barriers to keep others down, deny to them the freedom which we ourselves enjoy and cherish most, we keep ourselves in, hold ourselves down, and the barriers we erect against others become prison bars to our own souls. We cannot grow to the mental and moral stature of free men if we view life with prejudiced eyes, for thereby we shut our minds to truth and reality, which are essential to spiritual, mental, and moral growth. The time we should spend in creative activity we waste on small things which dwarf the mind and stultify the soul. It is both economically and psychologically wasteful. So it is not clear who is damaged more—the person who inflicts the discrimination or the person who suffers it, the man who is held down or the man who holds him down, the segregated or the segregator. Your Commission will wrestle with this problem.

The churches are called upon to recognize the urgency of the present situation. Even if we laid no claim to a belief in democracy, if the whole world were at peace internationally, if atheistic communism had never developed, if fascism had never been born and Nazism were wholly unknown, a non-segregated church and social and economic justice for all men are urgent because we preach a universal gospel that demands that our deeds reflect our theory. To proclaim one thing and act another is sheer hypocrisy. It weakens the influence of the church, not only in its own fellowship but throughout the world. It hampers our efforts to evangelize Africa and Asia. It is not communism, not fascism, not the struggle between East and West, but the gospel itself which demands interracial justice and an unsegregated church. We should move interracially in the church, not from fear of communism but from "our concern for our brother for whom Christ died." It has always been the responsibility of the church and the Gospel to plow new ground, smash traditions, break the mores, and make new creatures. Such was the role of the Hebrew prophets, of Jesus and Paul, of the early church, of Savonarola and Martin Luther, of Livingstone and Albert Schweitzer.

In the Commission, we will wrestle with the ever-present questions, "To what extent is the church to be governed by expedience? Is it wise to live up to the gospel we preach, or is it wiser to conform to the mandates of a secular society? Shall the church obey the laws of the state when they violate the laws of love, or the law of God which commands us to love one another? What should be the attitude of the churches toward laws that are obviously unjust and discriminatory? Obey them? Seek to change them? Violate them?"

Finally, the task before the Commission and the Assembly is to show how the theme of the Assembly, *Christian Hope*, is related to racial and ethnic tensions, not only in the past days but in he present days. The major problem will not be to demonstrate from the Bible and church history that it is only in modern times that race has become a basis for church membership. The task will be to show how the gospel of Christ can be presented and lived so as to make new creatures of men and women in the area of race, and bring hope and abundant life to all men— not only beyond history but in history. We refuse to believe that God is limited in history and that we must wait until the end of history before his mighty works can be performed.

We have known for centuries what the Bible says about race. We have known for a long time that the early church and the church of the

Middle Ages did not segregate on the basis of race and ethnic origin. We know that there is no scientific basis for our treating one group as inferior to another. The gospel on race has been proclaimed for nineteen centuries. One world conference after another has condemned racial separation in the church. Yet segregation remains the great scandal in the church, especially in the United States and South Africa. The local churches permit secular bodies such as the state and federal courts, the United Nations, big league baseball, professional boxing, colleges and universities, the public schools, and theaters to initiate social change in the area of race. But even when secular bodies initiate the change, local churches, Negro and white, follow slowly or not at all. It will be a sad commentary on our life and time if future historians can write that the last bulwark of segregation based on race and color in the United States and South Africa was God's church.

We have plenty of light on the subject, but like Pilate of old we lack the will and moral courage to act on the light we have and the knowledge we possess. Clearly, knowledge is not enough. Paul knew this centuries ago when he said in essence: "I find myself doing that which I know I ought not to do and I find myself failing to do that which I know I ought to do." We quote Tennyson:

Let knowledge grow from more to more,
But more of reverence in us dwell;
That mind and soul, according well,
May make one music as before,
But vaster.

Drinkwater likewise deserves to be used in this context when he profoundly wrote:

Knowledge we ask not—Knowledge Thou hast lent,
But, Lord, the will—there lies our bitter need,
Give us to build above the deep intent
The deed, the deed.

Here at Evanston, the church will want to know how to deal with race within its own membership, the local congregation. The question will be—how can the local church so exemplify the spirit of Christ in Christian fellowship that the world will be compelled to follow its example?

At this Assembly, the people will want to know whether the church has any responsibility as an organized group for the alleviation of racial injustice in social, political, and economic life. What is the church's responsibility as an organized group? What is the responsibility of the individual Christian? What is the church's duty toward assisting the individual to fulfill his Christian task in his daily vocations? Above all, we should ask ourselves the question: Can there be a Pentecost in 1954?

If there can be a Pentecost in 1954, the individual Christian will be responsive to the Gospel, and he will act on his Christian convictions. There is no dichotomy between what we believe and what we do. We do what we believe. If an atheistic communist can act on his belief, a Christian can act on his. If a communist is willing to suffer for his convictions, go to jail, and die for them, surely the followers of Christ's God can suffer for theirs. The true believer, like Peter, Paul, and Jesus, is not a slave to his environment. He can rise above it and transform it. He will testify to the unity in Christ by his daily deeds.

If there is to be a modern Pentecost, the church must do likewise in its worship and membership. It must also encourage its members to exemplify in their vocations this supra-racial unity in Christ. Being thus convicted, all Christians here in Evanston will take appropriate steps in their respective congregations to make it possible for the will of God to operate to the end that all churches will be opened in membership and worship to all who serve and love the Lord. For the church is God's creation, not man's, and it belongs to God. And in God's domain, all men are equal.

Why Jesus Called the Rich Man a Fool*

In this sermon, Dr. Mays reaffirmed his ongoing philosophy of the commonality of man wherein all men are affected by the twists and turns in the journey through life. The rich, the poor, the learned, and the unlearned are interwoven into a common humanity, with God as the Father and Creator.

Dr. Mays preached at the Rockefeller Chapel on the campus of the University of Chicago on March 11, 1962, to about 150 people from the neighborhood, Hyde Park residents, faculty, and students.

Dr. Mays used the Biblical parable of the rich man to analyze this sermon, and related various aspects of the message to the problems and prospects of everyday living. The sermon stressed the need to develop one's own spirituality, as opposed one's preoccupation with the accumulation of material wealth.

* * *

"I will pull down my barns and build greater barns. And there I will restore all my fruits and all my goods. And I will say to my soul, 'Soul, thou hast much goods laid up for many years. Take thine ease. Eat, drink, and be merry.'" Phillips translates it, "Relax, eat, drink, and have a good time." Slang would put it, "You have it made, soul." But God called this man a fool.

Why should this man be called a fool? I do not believe that he was called a fool because he was wealthy. Some of the finest persons I have known were men of great wealth, compassionate, generous, understanding. Nor do I believe that this man was called a fool because he prepared for the future, a rainy day. Do we not want the same? Do we not prepare for old age, for sickness, for disease, for the unexpected? The more prosperous we become, do we not invest more in houses and lands, stocks and bonds, banks and federal savings and loan associations, mutual funds? It seems to me that a man who doesn't prepare for the future is a fool. No man wants to be pushed around when he is old and sick and feeble. And yet God called this man a fool. Permit me, please, to take a few liberties and go beyond the context and tell you why I think God called this man a fool.

---

* University of Chicago Library Archives (audio transcription)

He was called a fool in the first place because he thought that he could find security, comfort, and peace of mind in the mere accumulation of material possessions. "In order to be secure I will pull down my barns and build greater barns."

"I'll say to my soul, 'Be at ease, relax!'" Evidently this man did not know that no amount of wealth can protect a man from the uncertainties of life; that no amount of wealth can protect a man from sickness, disease, and death; that no amount of wealth can make a marriage succeed. The rich and the poor separate. They both get divorced. No amount of wealth can bring peace of mind. The rich and the poor need psychiatric care. They both are institutionalized in mental hospitals. Whether we like it or not, we all die. Let the state and federal governments build shelters, and yet in a nuclear war we all may die. Those who build shelters will die underground; the rest will die on the ground, clean bombs notwithstanding. He who seeks security, peace of mind in the mere accumulation of material possessions, qualifies for foolhood. This man was a fool because he acted as if he and he alone was responsible for his wealth and for his success. How often have you heard it said that "I am a self-made man. I am responsible to nobody. I lifted myself by my own bootstraps."

What an illusion. No man makes himself. We owe our lives to God and to our parents. No man can succeed alone without the people. A businessman depends on the people to buy. If he accumulates great profit, in a large measure the people are responsible for his profit. A student cannot be educated without others. The student must be taught. Someone else writes the books. Someone else builds the buildings. Somebody else gives the endowment. Often somebody else pays the bills. Artists may succeed, but the artist cannot be great without the people, because they must acclaim and they must applaud. No man can succeed alone. No man is self-made. No man can lift himself by his own bootstraps.

This man was a farmer. He had a good crop, but who gave the land? He didn't create it. Who sent the sunshine, the rain, and the air? God sent the sunshine and the rain forward and created them. Who made the seed sprout and the grain to grow? God made the seeds to sprout, and no doubt the people helped him till the soil. In fact, all that we are and all that we will ever be, we owe to God and to the people.

This man was called a fool because he acted as if he and he alone was responsible for his success. Yes, this man was called a fool because he thought that what he had belonged to him and to him alone. Listen to what he says: "I will pull down my barns and build greater barns and I will say to my soul, 'Relax, you are secure for years to come. You have everything that you need or will ever need.'" What an illusion. The truth of the matter is we own nothing. We bring nothing into this world, and we carry nothing out. We come into this world naked, and we go out almost naked—with a suit of clothes, a shirt and a tie, shoes and underwear. We come into this world empty-handed, and we leave empty-handed. Everything we say is ours, we die and leave. We use it, we keep it, we bank it, we hold it, and when we die, somebody else gets it, and often people who never turned their little fingers to make it. We boast, "This is mine, my house, my land, my stocks and bonds" and somebody else will get it by and by. Really, everything we own belongs to God. The iron and the ore, the silver and the gold, the diamonds and the pearls, the rocks and the mountains, the water and the land—all belong to God. We own nothing. We bring nothing into this world, and we carry nothing out.

This man was called a fool because he acted as if the future belonged to him: "I am fixed for years to come." He acted as if he could manipulate the future and could control the future. I am secure. No man can control the future. No nation can control the future. Ultimately the future is in God's hands, not man's hands. This man acted as if he could manipulate and control the future; any man who believes that is a fool. A great Roman writer thought that the future belonged to the Roman Empire, and it could never fall, but it did fall. The great Nero burned Christians alive and acted as if the whole wide world was in his hands. The mighty Nero committed suicide. The great Alexander the Great conquered the world, according to legend, but his kingdom fell apart, and Alexander died in a drunken stupor in Babylon. The great Napoleon died a prisoner of war. Hitler boasted that he would build an empire that would last one thousand years, in the last ten; in fact, he didn't build it. He lost the war. As far as we know, Hitler and his mistress committed suicide. Mussolini boasted that, "I will restore the greatness of Rome," and Mussolini lost the war, and he was killed by his countrymen, and his body was hanged upon the streets of Milan. People would pass by and ridicule. I have heard southern governors boast of the fact that segregation will never be abolished in their state. It is being abolished before their very eyes. We spend billions for war; yea, we spend trillions for war. The future will still be in God's hands and not in the hands of man.

This man was called a fool because he acted as if the future belonged to him. Whether nation or man, he who believes that way is a fool.

This man was called a fool because he had no social conscience. As he tore down his barns to build greater barns, I think I hear with my mind's ears the starving cry for bread. As he tore down his barns to build greater barns, I think I can hear the groans of the sick begging for medicine and for hospitals. As he tore down his barns, I think I can hear the cries of the ignorant wanting school. As he tore down his barns, I think I can hear the orphan children crying for parenthood, for parents, and for a decent home. But this man didn't hear their cries. He didn't care. While all of these things were happening, he tore down his barns and built greater barns, in the midst of human sufferings and need. Some-one has beautifully said, "There is but one virtue, to help human beings to a free and beautiful life, but one sin, to do them indifferent or cruel hurt." The love of humanity is the whole of morality: this is humanism; this is goodness; this is a social conscience. This man was called a fool because he had no social conscience.

Finally, this man was a fool because he did not realize that we are what we are by the grace of God and never by any great goodness of our own. They tell me that more than half of the people of the earth are starving this morning. Why do I have bread enough and to spare and to waste while my brothers across the world, even in America, starve? Who am I that I should be so favored as to have food and shelter and heat while more than half of the people of the earth have diseased bodies. Why am I well? More than half of the people of the earth are illiterate, can neither read nor write in their own vernacular. Why do I have a high school, college and university degree? Who am I that I should be so favored? Thousands are alcoholics. Why am I not one of the alcoholics? Thousands are drug addicts. Who am I? Two babies are being born in Chicago today—one is born in the midst of wealth and splendor and culture, the other one is being born in the slums. One will have every chance to be somebody. The other one may never have a chance. But the fortunate baby that is being born today has no right to look down on his brother born in the slums—but for the grace of God, he, too, might have been born in the slums. Neither one of them did anything to get them-selves born. This man was a fool because he did not realize—for want of a better way to express it—he did not realize that he was what he was by the grace of God.

This man was a fool because he thought he could find security through mere possession of things, because he acted as if he and he alone was responsible for his success, because he acted as if the future belonged to him, because he had no social conscience. He did not realize that he was what he was by the grace of God. He did not realize that he, too, was involved in humanity. Nor did he realize that his destiny was interlaced, interwoven, intertwined with the destiny of every man on the top of the earth. This he did not know.

The Vocation of a Christian— In, but Not of, the World*

On November 8, 1964, Dr. Mays delivered this sermon in the Duke University Chapel in Durham, North Carolina, to approximately 1,000, including students, parents, faculty, visitors, and townspeople.

Dr. Mays explained that the title of his sermon implies that there is a vast difference between the vocation of a Christian and that of a non-Christian. "Every man whether Christian, communist, fascist, nationalist, or humanist must have a God," Mays asserted. Thus, he acknowledged the existence of different gods in the different cultures of the world. He continued, "So it isn't a question as to whether a man believes in God, but rather what kind of God does he believe in."

To support his analysis, Dr. Mays quoted from Paul and Jeremiah, and he utilized the scriptures and human circumstances to point out that the vocation of a Christian is to follow the will of God.

* * *

The subject, "The Vocation of a Christian—In, but Not of, the World," strongly implies that there is a vast difference between the vocation of a Christian and that of a non-Christian, between the vocation of a Christian and that of a communist or a fascist or a Nazi or that of a humanist. It must be said, however, that I am not wise enough to draw a sharp line of distinction between a Christian professing to be a Christian and one not professing, because many professing Christians are not Christians, and many non-professing Christians may be Christians. But if the implication in the subject is true, the difference lies mainly in two specific areas. One's attitude towards God is revealed in Jesus Christ and one's attitude towards man. I make bold to assert that every man, whether Christian, communist, fascist, nationalist, or humanist must have a God. So it isn't a question as to whether a man believes in God but rather a question of what kind of a God does one believe in.

In order to be a fairly well-organized, well-adjusted and fairly well-integrated personality, one must have an object other than himself to which he can give ultimate allegiance and loyalty: an object to which he

---

* Duke University, School of Divinity Archives

can give all, worship and idolize, bow down before and praise. To the communist, this object of devotion and worship may be a classless society or the communist party. To the fascist it, may be the space. To the Nazi in Germany, it was German blood and soil. In essence, it was Adolph Hitler. To the humanist who believes that man is good enough and wise enough to lift himself by his own bootstraps, the object of devotion may be a glorified humanity. To some people it may be money, to others it may be the worship of power. To the alcoholic, the object of his devotion may be the bottle. But every man needs to give his allegiance to something beyond and bigger than himself.

This is the reason why Jesus said to the young man, "Thou shalt love the Lord thy God with all thy heart, with all thy soul, with all thou might, and with all thy strength. This is the first and great commandment and the second is like unto it—Thou shalt love thy neighbor as thyself." On these two commandments hang all the law and the prophets. And whatever that thing is that we worship and idolize, that's our God. . . . It's too small. It's not big enough. The God of the Christian is the God of Abraham and Isaac, Amos and Hosea, Jeremiah and Isaiah, Jesus and Paul. In other words, the God of the true Christian is supra-nation, supra-class, supra-caste, and supra-clan, supra-race. This is what Paul meant when he said, "There is neither Jew nor Greek, there is neither slave nor free, there neither male nor female, for you are all one in Jesus Christ." This is what Peter meant when he said, "Truly I perceive that God chose no partiality but in every nation anyone who fears Him and does what is right is acceptable to Him." This is also what Paul meant when he exclaimed, "God hath made of one blood all nations of men for to dwell on all the face of the earth."

The Christian in his vocation differs also from the non-Christian in his conception of man. A Christian believes in contrary distinction to a communist that man is somebody, that he is unique, that he has status, not because it was conferred upon him by the state, not because it was given to him by a particular ethnic group; but man is unique, man is somebody because God gave uniqueness to him. As proof of this, Genesis tells us that when God reached man in the creative process, He did for man what He did not do for any other creature that He made. God breathed into man's nostrils the breath of God, and man became a living soul. God did not do this for the beast of the field; He did not do this for the fowl of the air; He did not do it for the fish of the sea, but only for man. Founding fathers recognized this when they wrote, "We hold these truths to be self-evident, that all men are created equal, that they are endowed by their creator with certain inalienable rights, that among these are life, liberty, and the pursuit of happiness." The Christian in his vocation recognizes the uniqueness of man.

The Christian believes more. The Christian believes that the life of every person is significant, is of intrinsic worth and value, is a pearl of great price, even the life of the homeless. The individual person is so significant that to do injury to the least bird is to do injury to God. This point is eloquently and dramatically set forth in the judgment seat of the Sermon on the Mount. There, one's entrance into the Kingdom is based on one thing: how did you treat the man farthest down? He said to them on the right-hand side, "You may come in, for I was hungry and ye gave me bread, thirsty and ye gave me drink, naked and ye put clothes on my back, in prison and ye came to see me, sick and ye ministered to my needs." "No, no," they replied, "You have never been sick. You would speak the word and diseases would cease, you have never been hungry, you could speak the word and stones would turn to bread." The reply was eloquent and eternal, "Inasmuch as ye have done it unto one of the least of these my brethren, ye have done it unto me." The Christian believes that a person is so valuable in God's sight and God cares so much for man that the strands of hair on his head are all numbered. Man is so precious that God sent his Son into the world to bring salvation to man.

The Christian believes this point, that no distinction can be drawn between men. If the life of a rich man is sacred and precious, the life of a sharecropper in Mississippi is also precious. If the life of a learned man is important, the life of the most illiterate man is equally important. If the life of the Queen of England is of intrinsic worth and value, then it must follow as the night to day that the life of a coal miner in Wales is of equal worth and value. And if the President of the United States and his life is precious, then the life of a mill hand in one of the Carolinas is also valuable. Either it is all or none.

So it is this emphasis on the value of the person that sets the Judeo-Christian religion off from most of the world religions. It is this emphasis that makes democracy, as I see it, superior to fascism or communism. This view of man and this view of God gives spirituality to the vocation of the Christian that is not inherent in the vocation of the non-Christian, communist, or fascist. The Christian in his vocation has a mandate from God, not from man, but from God to deal justly, sympathetically, helpfully, and lovingly with his fellows. He is called upon not only to make a living but to make a life; not only to make a living for himself and his family to be physically and economically secure, but he is called upon to make a life by using his talents and skills to the end that no man may go without adequate food and shelter, none without adequate education, none without an opportunity to develop strong bodies, and none without an opportunity to develop to the fullest a talent given to him by God.

To the Christian, his vocation must be beneficial to himself and beneficial to mankind. To the Christian, his vocation is more than a profession, more than skills. It is a calling. He does his job not so much because he wants to do it, but he does it because he must do it. There is a kind of inner urge that drives him on. Whether physician or lawyer, teacher or minister, architect or businessman, engineer or artist, he does his job like the prophet prophesies and as the poet writes poetry. There is an inner urge. There is a compulsion. There is a must. Whether physician or lawyer, teacher or minister, architect or businessman, he is like unto Paul. For it was Paul who said, "I'm ruined if I preach not the Gospel." Jesus said, "When the eternal God speaks who can but prophesy?" It was Jeremiah who said, "I feel that there is a fire shut up in my bones."

The Christian does his job like John Bunyan, who said, "I have to set aside the writing of sermons and other serious tracts in order to write *Pilgrim's Progress*," or like Horace, who said, "I could not sleep at night because of the pressure of unwritten poetry," or like Herndon, who said, "I must play *Hamlet* in order to keep a contract with my soul."

The Christian man in his vocation—whatever that vocation may be— the Christian man in his vocation may gain great wealth; he may achieve great things; he may occupy positions of prestige and power, but his greatest joy, his greatest satisfaction, comes not in owning and keeping but in giving and sharing. The physician who has saved hundreds of lives through his skill in surgery must find great satisfaction. The teacher who has inspired thousands of students to aspire for higher things must find joy. The rich man who has used his wealth to benefit mankind must find peace in his soul. He who will find a cure for cancer could die a happy man or a happy woman.

Finally, the Christian in his vocation is in the world but not wholly of it. He conforms, but he is not a slave to conformity. The Christian in his vocation, whatever it is, is sensitive to and responsive to God's call. He knows that he must be in the world but not wholly of it, that the time may come when in response to God's call, whatever his vocation may be, he must rise above customs, tradition, mores, and respond to the call of God. He is conscious also of the fact that this call usually comes not to the multitude but to the individual, and he is open and responsive to the call because he knows that it might come to him. You see, God did not call a thousand men to leave their country and become the father of a great people; He called Abraham. God did not call a hundred men to lead the children of Israel out of Egypt; He called Moses. He did not call all the Jews to be the Son of God, but He called Jesus. He did not call a hundred men to break the bond and universalize the Christian religion; He called Paul. When the Roman Empire was tottering and had fallen, He did not call a thousand men to give a Christian interpretation of history; He called St. Augustine. When the church needed cleansing, He didn't call a thousand people, but Martin Luther and some others. When time came to free Zion from the domination of religion, Galileo, Roger Bacon, Copernicus, Darwin, and others were called. When there was the need to crusade for the freedom of women, it was Susan B. Anthony. When it was necessary for one to lift up his voice against untouchability in India, He called Mahatma Gandhi. When it was necessary to call someone to demonstrate the doctrine of nonviolence and crusading for civil rights, it was Martin Luther King, Jr.

The Christian man, whether in business or in medicine or in teaching, knows that he is in the world but not wholly of it. No man can live in the world without conforming to it, but the world moves forward on the work of those who are in the world but not wholly of it. The Christian must live in the world, in two worlds, but always in a state of tension between the world that is and the world that ought to be.

Dear God, we pray Thy benediction upon all mankind everywhere, upon the secure and the insecure, upon the sick and the well, upon those in prison and those in slavery, upon the saint and upon the sinner. For we all need Thee, and we all stand in the need of prayer. Go with us throughout the further activities of the years. Further us with Thy continuing help. Now may the strong arms of the eternal God, the love of Jesus Christ, the fellowship of the Holy Spirit guide, sustain, and keep this people now and forevermore.

In What Shall We Glory?*

Dr. Mays focused this sermon on the Old Testament scriptures from the Book of Jeremiah 9: 23-24. The prophet Jeremiah told his people, "Thus saith the Lord, 'Let not the wise man glorify in his wisdom, neither let the mighty man glorify in his might, let not the rich man glorify in his riches. . . . " His sermon, delivered in the Rockefeller Chapel at the University of Chicago, reached a Sunday morning audience of approximately 150 persons on December 5, 1971.

Dr. Mays affirmed a common feature of his religious teachings: that the love of God and the love of man are inseparable. Dr. Mays continued, "The words spoken to Jeremiah require loving kindness, judgment, and righteousness in the earth for these are the things in which he delights."

* * *

It is altogether proper and fitting for me to base my remarks on the words of Jeremiah, who more than twenty-six centuries ago admonished his people, "Thus saith the Lord, 'Let not the wise man glorify in his wisdom, neither let the mighty man glory in his might, let not the rich man glorify in his riches: But let him that glorieth glorify in this, that he understandeth and knoweth me, that I am the Lord which exercise loving-kindness, judgment, and righteousness in the earth: for in these things I delight, saith the Lord." The American translation states it this way, "Thus said the Lord, 'Let not the wise man boast of his wisdom nor the strong man boast of his strength nor the rich man boast of his riches, but if he must boast, let him boast of this, that he understands and knoweth me, how I am the Lord, He who practices kindness, justice, and righteousness on the earth. For in these things I delight.'"

There are approximately three billion people on earth, and each of the three billion differs from the other. Some of them have brilliant minds. Some of them have excellent minds. Some of them have very good minds, and some of them have good minds. Some are mentally retarded, idiots, imbeciles, and morons. It is very human for people who have good minds to boast of their ability to learn, and it is also very human for many of them to feel that because they have good minds that

---

* University of Chicago Library Archives (audio transcription)

they are better than other people. Though speaking to a specific situation many centuries ago, glorifying Israel's religion, the words of Jeremiah speaking for the Lord warns us not to boast or glorify in our wisdom. Though taking liberties in interpreting the passage, let me venture to give three answers.

These things we call wisdom, intelligence, knowledge or brilliance are all relative terms. The wisest man is knowledgeable in only a few things, and a knowledgeable man may lack wisdom, for even his wisdom is highly restricted. The human mind is finite, and even the most brilliant mind can know but so much. The expert electrician, for example, knows more electricity than the philosopher. The expert builder knows more about building than the chemist. The plumber knows more about fixing the water facilities than the President of the United States. The competent auto mechanic knows more about repairing cars than the Chief Justice of the United States. No man is superior in everything. The great painters and the great artists of history gain fame on their art but might have little ability to govern a nation. And I refuse to label one inferior to the other if each one is skilled in his craft or art and if what he does is beneficial to mankind. The human mind is finite and since it does not have the capacity to become omniscient, there is no good reason, therefore, to glorify in our knowledge or wisdom. Furthermore, we are not responsible for the quality of our minds. It is pretty clear that one's mental ability depends in part upon heredity. We cannot choose our parents, and we cannot choose the places of our birth. It is pretty clear that those born in good environments have a better chance to develop their minds than those born in poor circumstances. One cannot choose his parents. If this were possible, we would all perhaps choose parents with exceptional minds, and I do not think any one of us would elect to be born in poverty, say in the slums or ghettos of our great cities. We should not boast or glorify in our wisdom because we cannot choose our parents and we cannot choose the places of birth. And whether we were born rich or poor, wise or foolish, it is largely by accident, and we had little choice in the matter. So Jeremiah warns us not to boast and not to glorify in our wisdom.

Jeremiah warns us further not to glorify in our wealth. What is true of wisdom is true of wealth. The ability to achieve mentally and accumulate wealth often go hand in hand. The man with a good mind is likely to achieve more wealth than the man with a gold mine. Many of the rich people of the earth inherit their wealth from their ancestors, immediate or remote, and sometimes wealth is achieved through political establishment. Any newborn baby who is born in a home of a multimillionaire is born in wealth. The same is true of a baby born of educated or cultured parents. He is born in a good environment. But a newly born rich child had nothing to do with accumulation of the wealth and did absolutely nothing to choose his parents. We should not glorify or boast of our wealth because regardless of how much we accumulate, we cannot take it with us. We will die and leave it, and often through marriage and otherwise, our wealth will pass into the hands of those who never turned their fingers to accumulate it. Then, too, we can use only so much of the wealth that we accumulate. We can live in only one house at a time, sleep in only one bed at a time, sit in only one chair at a time, and eat only so much steak and hamburger at a time.

Jeremiah, speaking for the Lord, tells us not to glorify in our physical might. Here again, the finiteness of man comes to play. The strongest football player cannot compete with an elephant or a bull in physical strength and power. The strongest man may be smitten with cancer, high blood pressure, and heart disease. An automobile crash or a plane crash will kill a Samson as quickly as a newborn infant. The boat sinks on the high seas, and the strong and the weak go down together. The strongest man will die at a certain age.

I believe there is a third reason that we are admonished not to boast of the finite things but rather to look to one that is mightier than we are. Man is inclined to put his trust in power, military might, wealth, and superiority of one race or another, and even in political parties. A nation's wealth, military supremacy, and race are often the gods that many of us serve. In fact, that to which we give our ultimate allegiance and loyalty is our God. I think Jeremiah is trying to say to us that man, however brilliant he may be, the nation, however strong it may become, is not worthy of our ultimate loyalty and allegiance. The wisest man is ignorant; the strongest man is weak; the most powerful nation in history has risen to great heights only to fall and never again to rise. It is said that Alexander the Great was worshiped by some. He conquered much, but his kingdom fell apart, and Alexander died in a drunken stupor in Babylon. Napoleon was feared and idolized, but his war plans miscounted, and he died a broken man at St. Helena. Both Mussolini and Hitler lost the war. Mussolini and his mistress were killed, and Hitler and his mistress committed suicide. In neglecting loving kindness, judgment, and righteousness, no nation can long endure while at the same time worshiping military might and military power. Though too late, Napoleon is reputed to have said, "The more I study the world, the more I am convinced of the inability of force to create anything durable. Alexander, Caesar, Charlemagne, and even I myself founded empires but on what did they depend? They depended upon force. But Jesus Christ founded his empire upon love, and until this day, millions will die for Him."

It is for these reasons that God, speaking through Jeremiah, admonishes us in 1971 not to boast of our wisdom, not to boast of our wealth, and not to boast of our strength. This reduces itself to a very simple philosophy, and that is: no man is wise enough; no man is good enough; no man is rich enough; and no man is strong enough to look down with condescension upon another man. If one man is wiser than another, richer than another, stronger than another, and better than another, it is largely accidental, or it is a result of fate, or he enjoys his more favorable position because of the grace of God. I am not unaware of the fact that what a man does with what he has is largely within his power, but in no case has a man the right to play the Pharisee and thank God that he is better than another man. The genius of religion does not like abstract creeds, rituals, and dogmas; rather, the genius of religion is found when we respond to the needs of men whenever found among rich and poor, learned and illiterate, black and white, yellow and brown. "For as much as ye did it to one of the least of these my brethren ye did it unto me." One of the tests of a civilized nation might well be, how does that nation provide for the man farthest down, the young, the aged, and the poor?

The process of a Judeo-Christian faith makes the love of God and the love of a man inseparable. We often hear people say that the Bible is out of date; it has no relevance for our time; we can forget it; its focus on certain social, political, and economic conditions are not applicable to our time. I, for one, dissent. These words of the Lord spoken through Jeremiah are just as relevant today as they were twenty-six centuries ago. Jeremiah is declaring that the Lord requires loving kindness, judgment, and righteousness in the earth, because these are the things in which he delights. So loving kindness, justice, and righteousness have always been relevant and always will be relevant, not only in our individual lives, but let us see if they are relevant in our political, economic, national and international lives.

I hold that they are. I am sure that the people in power in government would argue that it is relevant to spend billions of dollars in our effort to get to the moon and to Mars. Washington would argue that it is relevant that we pay a few farmers $50 thousand or a quarter of a million dollars a year for not planting, while at the same time people are laid off their jobs. We argue that it is relevant to spend $70 billion a year in the maintenance of our military establishment with bases scattered around the world. We argue it is relevant that a handful of people control the wealth of the nation, that it is relevant to compete with Russia in arms and in space. Some argue that it is relevant to bus to maintain segregation. If these things are relevant, God knows it is relevant to feed the hungry, to clothe the naked, to house the unhoused, to care for the sick and the afflicted, to care for the aging, to provide jobs for those who are able to work, to bring and to sponsor programs designed to raise forty million human beings to positions of respectability and pride and in doing so, do it without robbing them of their humanity. If it is relevant to set a timetable to get to the moon and spend millions of dollars to get there—and soon to set a time table to land a man on Mars and spend more millions to get there—it is relevant to set a time table, say that in 10 years we are going to abolish the ghettos in this country; we are going to provide adequate care for the aged and the aging. We are going to eliminate discrimination based on religion and race in every area of American life; we are going to reduce unemployment, and we are going to see to it that no able-bodied man goes without a decent job. If it is relevant to race Russia in preparation for war and compete with Russia in reaching the moon and Mars, it would be more relevant to compete with Russia in a program designed to abolish war and eliminate poverty on the earth. That these things are not done is not wholly a matter of funds. It is rather a matter of national will and national commitment. It is not even a lack of knowledge. It is lack of will. . . . Anything is relevant that improves a lot of the people and enhances the individual at the center and not buildings, not military might, and not mechanical development and power. It is relevant now and even relevant twenty-seven centuries ago when Micah raised the question, "With what shall I come before the Lord and bow myself before the Lord Most High? Shall I come before the Lord with burnt offerings, with calves, a year old, will the Lord be pleased with thousands of rams, with myriads and streams of oil? Shall I give my firstborn for my transgression, the fruit of my body for the sin of my soul? You have been told, man, which is good and what the Lord requires of you, only to do justice and to love kindness and to walk humbly with Thy God."

I close as I began, in the words of Jeremiah, "Thus saith the Lord, 'Let not the wise man glory in his wisdom neither let the mighty man glorify in his might, let not the rich man glorify in his riches but let him that glorieth glory in this, that he understands and knoweth me, that I am Lord which exercises loving kindness, judgment, and righteousness in the earth. For in these things I delight, saith the Lord."

Why Should We Forgive?*

Dr. Mays was in great demand to deliver sermons during the Lenten season because of his reputation for delivering pragmatic, logical, and understandable presentations, such as this one delivered at the Old Stone Presbyterian Church on Public Square in Cleveland, Ohio, on March 21, 1973.

Dr. Mays reminded his audience that during the Lenten season, when we celebrate the resurrection of God, we are in a forgiving mood. Accordingly, he advised his listeners to celebrate Easter by practicing forgiveness.

I had the opportunity to hear a version of this sermon a year later on May 19, 1974, when he spoke at Shiloh Baptist Church in Atlanta, during the Sunday morning service.

The church was filled to capacity, and the sermon delivered in the eloquent style characteristic of the great orator. It was one of the best sermons I have ever heard. Later that Sunday afternoon, I saw Dr. Mays at the joint Baccalaureate services for Morehouse and Spelman Colleges at the Omni Arena, sitting across the aisle from me. When the services were over, I walked across the aisle, shook his hand, and told him, "I enjoyed your sermon this morning." Still seated, he smiled and nodded his head in approval. He always seemed glad when someone told him they enjoyed an address he had given, especially a former student. I subsequently regretted that I had not asked for a copy of the sermon since it was so stimulating and enjoyable, but when I started to do research on the gentleman-scholar after his death, fate smiled on me. I found a copy in his collection of papers. It had been mimeographed. Later in his career, his speeches were in such demand that he was often asked for written copies after he gave a speech, so he started the practice of carrying some mimeographed copies of his speeches for distribution to those who requested them.

* * *

As we go through Lent and approach Easter to celebrate the resurrection of our Lord, we should be in the forgiving mood. We should try

---

* Mays Collection, Moorland-Spingarn Research Center, Howard University

to cleanse our hearts and minds by forgiving those who wronged us or those we think have wronged us. What is forgiveness? One good definition of forgiveness is this: forgiveness means to set aside revenge. The man who really forgives another man seeks no opportunity to strike back at him. The forgiven man is restored again into the good fellowship of the one who forgives.

The mother seldom, if ever, withholds her love from her children, regardless of how badly they behave toward her. The father forgave the prodigal son even after he demanded his share of goods, went into a far country, and spent his money in riotous living. When the son returned, there was no rebuke; instead, he ran to meet his son, fell on his neck, kissed him, and killed the fattest calf in honor of his return. This is forgiveness par excellence.

Saul was jealous of David for no reason other than the fact that David was too popular with the people. The people shouted, "Saul has killed his thousands, but David has killed ten thousand." This angered Saul, and he set out to find David and kill him. The natural impulse would have been to plan to get Saul before Saul could get him. Not so. Twice David had an opportunity to destroy Saul, but twice he refused. That's forgiveness.

The supreme example of forgiveness is exemplified in Jesus himself. While He was dying on the cross, He asked God to forgive those who were responsible for His crucifixion because they were ignorant people and did not know what they were doing. I shall give five reasons why we should forgive those who trespass against us.

In the first place, one should forgive because every man and every woman wants others to forgive them. In all my years, I have never met a person who didn't want to be forgiven for the wrongs or the sins he had committed. No person really wants justice when he has done a great wrong to the neighbor or committed a wrong deed against society. In such cases, he wants mercy and forgiveness, not justice. It is hardly too much to say that the murderer wants to be forgiven by the family and relatives of the man whose life he has taken. He wants enough forgiveness to be saved from the electric chair. And if he serves his time in jail for the dastardly deed he has committed and returns to society, he wants the people in the community to receive him again into their fellowship, associate with him and help him get a job. It is my belief that a man sick in bed, knowing that death is knocking at his door, wants his neighbors' forgiveness if he has mistreated them. I believe further that before dying, a man wants to be forgiven by God, even if he doubts the authenticity of God's existence. I have known persons to seek forgiveness of others even when they are well and had no notion of death. Very few people, if any, want to be held accountable for the evil things they have done to people or for the evil thoughts they entertain of others.

Every man wants mercy and forgiveness. And if justice is a heavy penalty, we want it tempered with mercy. So if a man wants to be forgiven by others, good sportsmanship requires that he too forgive.

In the second place, we should forgive not only because we want forgiveness, but because we need forgiveness. I do not take much stock in those who claim that they are holy, sanctified, and sinless. I am now beyond three scores and ten, and as I look back over the years, I find in the people I have known everything but perfection, even in the best of them, and that goes for me. I have discovered some defects, some shortcomings, some meanness, selfishness, jealousy, or narrowness in virtually all the people I have known close up. It is one of the shocking things that everybody may discover sooner or later—and that is that his idol is not the epitome of righteousness. And the person who claims such is self-righteous, which is a great sin. Jesus reminds us that only the Father is good.

After men are dead a certain length of time, historians have a way of telling the world just what they were like. The private lives of many men whom we call great in America and the world leave much to be desired. This goes for Biblical characters. The life of David is not wholly complimentary. The great Saint Augustine's life before conversion was not exemplary. Paul before his conversion was hard on the Christians. Every man has missed the mark sufficiently to require that God forgive him and have mercy upon him. Even after conversion, we can all pray, "Lord have mercy on a sinner like me."

I am not saying that all people are the same. I know that some people are better than others and are saints in comparison with others. I am only saying that none is perfect enough not to need forgiveness. I know people, so do you, who wouldn't gamble under any condition, but the same people are heavy drinkers. There are those who boast of their goodness. They do not curse, swear, or steal outright, but they exploit in their business and are loose in their moral behavior. There are extortioners who use their offices to get what they do not deserve. There are others who are meticulously honest in their business but are not true to their marital vows.

I believe the Pharisee told God the truth when he told God that he was not like other people. He paid tithes on all that he possessed, fasted twice in one week, and he was not an extortioner. Evidently, he was a good man. But he was so self-righteous that he thought more of the publican's prayer than he did of the Pharisee's. There is nothing to indicate that Dives had committed any one of the seven deadly sins, but he did not escape hell. So, every man needs the forgiveness of God. I make bold to assert that there are unregenerated spots in every man, and that each and every day we need God's forgiveness and God's grace.

We should forgive for a third reason. God requires that we forgive. In the Lord's prayer, it is assumed that we are going to forgive. We pray, "Forgive us for our trespasses as we forgive those who trespass against us." This is a qualified forgiveness and not an unconditional one.

We are also told that if we do not forgive men for their trespasses, neither will God forgive us for our trespasses. The implication is that we should not expect God to forgive us unless we are willing to forgive those who have sinned against us. This kind of teaching is not easy to accept, and most assuredly, it is not popular. We want God to forgive us even though we may never forgive ourselves. And while I tell you this, I am fully aware of God's grace, sending his rain on the just and the unjust and bestowing upon us that which we don't deserve, which is grace. Man is an odd and selfish creature.

We want God to do for us what we are not willing to do for our fellows. We forget that man's relationship to God is interwoven, interlaced, and intertwined with his relationship to his fellows. Forgiveness, therefore, is a part of this relationship, and man, by God's design, cannot extricate himself from his fellow man. And this requires that we are to forgive those that we know carry ill will against us in their hearts. It means forgiving those that we know are our enemies and have planned to prevent us from becoming what God intended for us to be.

We are admonished to forgive not because we are cowards, but because God requires it: "Love your enemies, bless them that curse you, do good to them that hate you and pray for those who despitefully use you and persecute you." In this way, we earn the right to be called children of the Father.

There is a fourth reason why we should forgive. Forgiveness has a therapeutic value. Television allows hatred to fester in the heart against one another that may lead to dire physical consequences. I have seen hatred of one person against another in operation. The mere mention of a name aroused great emotions, so much so that reason could not function. The man whom he hated had no virtues, and fear of the law is the only reason why the victim hated was not murdered. I know of a case where a person wanted the other person liquidated; but afraid to do so herself, she told me she was asking God to do the job for her by inflicting upon the other woman some incurable disease.

She wanted God to do what she was afraid to do herself. She was indeed earnest when she said to me God usually answered her prayers. Strangely enough, the woman who did the praying died first. The other woman lived many years after the death of the hating woman. A person in a great institution disliked the president so badly that this person said to me repeatedly that he wished the president were dead. He died years before the president. There may be no connection between the deaths of these two people and their hatred of the other persons. But there might be. When we learn more about the causes of high blood pressure and heart disease, it may be discovered that it is possible for one to hate himself to death.

One who hates deeply, harbors prejudice insanely, and holds ill will against another person, race or group can never be happy, nor can the man who is envious of his neighbor's success. Such persons cannot have peace of mind. Forgiveness, therefore, has therapeutic value.

There is a fifth reason why we should forgive. I believe it has redemptive value. Only forgiveness can break the vicious circle of revenge, an eye for an eye, a tooth for a tooth; you rob me, I rob you; you lie on me, I return the compliment. Forgiveness has redemptive value. One is more likely to be won over to a better way of life by your forgiving him than by taking revenge against him. Families are held together through the redeeming power of forgiveness—not by husband and wife, parents and children feuding all the time, seeking an opportunity to get revenge. Forgiving is always in operation in the husband-wife relationship.

Even outside the family, forgiveness is redemptive. The story is told of Abraham Lincoln and Edwin McMuster Stanton. Stanton was a democrat and was reputed to have said mean, unkind things about Lincoln during his campaign for the presidency. During the early days of the Civil War, Stanton was one of Lincoln's most severe critics. Nevertheless, when Lincoln needed a Secretary of War, he appointed Stanton against the advice of his friends and close advisors. He appointed Stanton Secretary knowing his attitude toward him. Lincoln admitted that Stanton was his enemy. But he also said, "Of all of the men I know, Stanton is the best to be Secretary of War." So he appointed Stanton Secretary of War.

Later, Lincoln lay dead of an assassin's bullet. It was reported that Stanton, standing over Lincoln's grave with tears in his eyes, was heard to exclaim, "There lies the greatest ruler of men the world has ever known." More men in personal relations have been won by kindness and forgiveness than revenge and retaliation.

The question arises, "What is the limit to forgiveness?" The plain truth is, there is no limit, as revealed in the passage read to you. In this passage, Jesus is explaining what to do when someone has trespassed against you. He seeks reconciliation between the two of them. If this doesn't work, witnesses are summoned, and if this confrontation in the presence of witnesses doesn't heal the breach, you should tell it to the church. The discussion goes on, and Peter keeps on thinking. Finally, Peter comes up with the question: "Lord, how often shall my brother sin against me and I forgive him? Till seven times?" Jesus says, "No, Peter, not seven times but seventy times seven." It is clear that this is illustrative. Jesus does not really means 490 times. It would be a tedious job trying to record the number of trespasses up to 490. Jesus is really saying: no, Peter, not a thousand times, not a million.

He is telling us in this Easter season: forgiveness is not a matter of arithmetic. We must not recant, jotting down the number of times we have been wronged. Rather, Christ is saying that every time a brother sins against us, we are to forgive him ad infinitum.

Weakness, you say? Not really. It is strength or cowardice, you say? Not at all. It is courage. For the weak, you say? People who are not strong enough to get revenge? Such as the Indians and black people in the United States? Not really. It took a strong man, Mahatma Gandhi, to win freedom from the British Empire through nonviolence, love and forgiveness. It took strength, courage, and will for Martin Luther King, Jr., to face jail, the dogs, the guns, and death in his struggle to lead black people on the road to freedom through nonviolence and love.

Let us forgive because we want to be forgiven. God requires that we forgive, forgiveness is therapeutic, and forgiveness is redemptive.

Chapter 5

Eulogies

Eulogy of Dr. Martin Luther King, Jr.*

D r. Martin Luther King, Jr.'s funeral, held on April 9, 1968, involved three parts. A service was held at Ebenezer Baptist on Auburn Avenue in Atlanta where King was born, baptized, and served a stint as co-pastor with his father, Reverend Martin Luther King, Sr.; Dr. Martin Luther King, Jr.'s close friend, Rev. Ralph David Abernathy, presided over the numerous tributes to the slain civil rights leader at the church service. A funeral cortege followed with some members of the King family, thousands of friends, mourners, attending celebrities, civil rights colleagues, and just plain folks. They all marched in the hot 80-degree weather behind the mule-drawn wagon carrying King's body, which symbolized his commitment to the poor and his previous civil rights marches. The procession moved three and one-half miles from Ebenezer to Morehouse College. On a special platform erected on the steps of Harkness Hall for the ceremony, King's "mentor and spiritual father," Dr. Mays, delivered the eulogy for his deceased friend and former student.

Dr. Mays delivered one of the most eloquent and captivating orations of his distinguished public speaking career on this sad and solemn day before a crowd estimated at 150,000, with an international audience watching via a communications satellite. The CBS news commentator

_____

* Reprinted from Mays, *Born to Rebel*, pp. 357-360

referred to the oratory of Dr. Mays as delivered in the old classical style.

Morehouse College was never the same after that fateful day in April 1968. For King and Mays had become the most significant publicists in the history of the small liberal arts college.

Dr. Mays received more than 250 letters and telegrams after the eulogy, along with numerous telephone calls complimenting his eulogy of King; several requested copies of his remarks; some even requested other writings and speeches by the great orator.

* * *

To be honored by being requested to give the eulogy at the funeral of Dr. Martin Luther King, Jr., is like being asked to eulogize a deceased son—so close and so precious was he to me. Our friendship goes back to his student days at Morehouse College. It is not an easy task; nevertheless, I accept it with a sad heart and with full knowledge of my inadequacy to do justice to this man. It was my desire that if I predeceased Dr. King, he would pay tribute to me on my final day. It was his wish that if he predeceased me, I would deliver the homily at his funeral. Fate has decreed that I eulogize him. I wish it might have been otherwise, for, after all, I am three score years and ten, and Martin Luther is dead at thirty-nine.

Although there are some who rejoice in his death, there are millions across the length and breadth of this world who are smitten with grief that this friend of mankind—all mankind—has been cut down in the flower of his youth. So multitudes here and in foreign lands, queens, kings, heads of government, the clergy of the world, and the common man everywhere are praying that God will be with the family, the American people, and the President of the United States in this tragic hour. We hope that this universal concern will bring comfort to the family—for grief is like a heavy load—when shared it is easier to bear. We come today to help the family carry the heavy load.

We are assembled here from every section of this great nation and from other parts of the world to give thanks to God that he gave to America, at this moment in history, Martin Luther King, Jr. Truly, God is no respecter of persons. How strange! God called the grandson of a slave on his father's side, and the grandson of a man born during the Civil War on his mother's side, and said to him: "Martin Luther, speak to America about war and peace, about social justice and racial discrimination; about its obligation to the poor, and about nonviolence as a way of perfecting social change in a world of brutality and war."

Here was a man who believed with all his might that the pursuit of violence at any time is ethically and morally wrong; that God and the moral weight of the universe are against it; that violence is self-defeating; and that only love and forgiveness can break the vicious circle of revenge. He believed that nonviolence would prove effective in the abolition of injustice in politics, in economics, in education, and in race relations. He was convinced also that people could not be moved to abolish voluntarily the inhumanity of man to man by mere persuasion and pleading, but they could be moved to do so by dramatizing the evil through massive nonviolent victories won in the federal courts. He believed that the nonviolent approach to solving social problems would ultimately prove to be redemptive.

Out of this conviction, history records the marches of Montgomery, Birmingham, Selma, Chicago, and other cities. He gave people an ethical and moral way to engage in activities to perfect social change without bloodshed and violence, and when violence did erupt, it was that which is potential in any protest which aims to uproot deeply entrenched wrongs. No reasonable person would deny that the activities and the personality of Martin Luther King, Jr., contributed largely to the success of the student sit-in movements in abolishing segregation in downtown establishments, and that his activities contributed mightily to the passage of the civil rights legislation of 1964 and 1965.

Martin Luther King, Jr., believed in a united America. He believed that the walls of separation brought on by legal and de facto segregation and discrimination based on race and color could be eradicated. As he said in his Washington Monument address: "I have a dream."

He had faith in his country. He died striving to desegregate and integrate America to the end that this great nation of ours, born in revolution and blood, conceived in liberty, and dedicated to the proposition that all men are created free and equal, will truly become the lighthouse of freedom: where none will be denied because his skin is black and none favored because his eyes are blue; where our nation will be militarily strong but perpetually at peace, economically secure but just, learned but wise; where the poorest—the garbage collectors—will have bread enough and to spare; where no one will be poorly housed, each educated up to his capacity; and where the richest will understand the meaning of empathy. This was his dream and the end toward which he strove. As he and his followers so often sang: "We shall overcome someday; black and white together."

Let it be thoroughly understood that our deceased brother did not embrace nonviolence out of fear or cowardice. Moral courage was one of his noblest virtues. As Mahatma Gandhi challenged the British Empire without a sword and won, Martin Luther King, Jr., challenged the interracial wrongs of the country without a gun. And he had the faith to believe that he would win the battle for social justice. It took more courage for King to practice nonviolence than it took the assassin to fire the fatal shot. The assassin is a coward; he committed his dastardly deed and fled. When Martin Luther disobeyed an unjust law, he accepted the consequences of his actions. He never ran away, and he never begged for mercy. He returned to the Birmingham jail to serve his time.

Perhaps he was more courageous than soldiers who fight and die on the battlefield. There is an element of compulsion in their dying. But when Martin Luther faced death again and again, and finally embraced it, there was no pressure. He was acting on an inner compulsion that drove him on. He was more courageous than those who advocate violence as a way out, for they carry weapons of destruction for defense. But Martin Luther faced the dogs, the police, jail, heavy criticism, and finally death, and he never carried a gun, not even a knife, to defend himself. He had only his faith in a just God to rely on and the belief that "thrice is he armed that hath his quarrel just." This is the faith that Browning writes about when he said: "One who never turned his back, but marched breast forward, Never doubted clouds would break, Never dreamed, though right were worsted, wrong would triumph, Held we fall to rise, are baffled to fight better, Sleep to wake."

Coupled with moral courage was Martin Luther King, Jr.'s capacity to love people. Though deeply committed to a program of freedom for Negroes, he had love and concern for all kinds of people. He drew no distinction between the high and the low, none between the rich and the poor. He believed especially that he was sent to champion the cause of the man farthest down. He would probably say that if death had to come, he was sure there was no greater cause to die for than fighting to get a just wage for garbage collectors. He was supra-class and supra-culture. He belonged to the world and to mankind. Now he belongs to posterity.

But there is a dichotomy in all this, this man loved by some and hated by others. If any man knew the meaning of suffering, King knew.

House bombed, living day by day for thirteen years under constant threat of death, maliciously accused of being a communist, falsely accused of being insincere and seeking the limelight for his own glory, stabbed by a member of his own race, slugged in a hotel lobby, jailed thirty times, occasionally deeply hurt because friends betrayed him—and yet this man had no bitterness in his heart, no rancor in his soul, no revenge in his mind, and he went up and down the length and breadth of this world preaching nonviolence and the redemptive power of love. He believed with all his heart, mind, and soul that the way to peace and brotherhood is through nonviolence, love, and suffering. He was severely criticized for his opposition to the war in Vietnam. It must be said, however, that one could hardly expect a prophet of Dr. King's commitments to advocate nonviolence at home and violence in Vietnam. Nonviolence to King was a total commitment, not only in solving the problems of race in the United States but the problems of the world.

Surely this man was called of God to do this work. If Amos and Micah were prophets in the eighth century, B.C., Martin Luther King, Jr., was a prophet in the twentieth century. If Isaiah was called of God to prophesy in his day, Martin Luther King, Jr., was called to prophesy in his day. If Hosea was sent to preach love and forgiveness centuries ago, Martin Luther was sent to expound the doctrine of nonviolence and forgiveness in the third quarter of the twentieth century. If Jesus was called to preach the Gospel to the poor, Martin Luther King, Jr., fits that designation. If a prophet is one who does not seek popular causes to espouse, but rather the causes he thinks are right, Martin Luther qualifies on that score.

No! He was not ahead of his time. No man is ahead of his time. Each man is within his star, each in his time. Each man must respond to the call of God in his lifetime and not in somebody else's time. Jesus had to respond to the call of God in the first century, A.D., and not in the twentieth century. He had but one life to live. He couldn't wait. How long do you think Jesus would have to wait for the constituted authorities to accept him? Twenty-five years? A hundred years? A thousand? He died at thirty-three. He couldn't wait. Paul, Galileo, Copernicus, Martin Luther—the Protestant reformer—Gandhi and Nehru couldn't wait for another time. They had to act in their lifetimes. No man is ahead of his time. Abraham, leaving the country in obedience to God's call; Moses, leading a rebellious people to the Promised Land; Jesus, dying on the cross; Galileo, on his knees recanting; Lincoln, dying of an assassin's bullet; Woodrow Wilson, crusading for a League of Nations; Martin Luther King, Jr., dying fighting for justice for garbage collectors—none of these men were ahead of their time. With them, the time was always ripe to do that which was right and which needed to be done.

Too bad, you say, that Martin Luther King, Jr., died so young. I feel that way too. But, as I have said many times before, it isn't how long one lives, but how well. It's what one accomplishes for mankind that matters. Jesus died at thirty-three; Joan of Arc at nineteen; Byron and Burns at thirty-six; Keats at twenty-six; Marlowe at twenty-nine; Shelley at thirty; Dunbar before thirty- five; John Fitzgerald Kennedy at forty-six; William Rainey Harper at forty-nine; and Martin Luther King, Jr., at thirty-nine.

We will pray that the assassin will be apprehended and brought to justice. But make no mistake, the American people are in part responsible for Martin Luther King, Jr.'s death. The assassin heard enough condemnation of King and of Negroes to feel that he had public support. He knew that millions hated King.

The Memphis officials must bear some of the guilt for Martin Luther's assassination. The strike could have been settled several weeks ago. The lowest paid men in our society should not have to strike for a more just wage. A century after emancipation, and after the enactment of the 13th, 14th, and 15th Amendments, it should have not been necessary for Martin Luther King, Jr., to stage marches in Montgomery, Birmingham, and Selma, and to go to jail thirty times trying to achieve for his people those rights which people of a lighter hue get by virtue of their being born white. We, too, are guilty of murder. It is time for the American people to repent and make democracy equally applicable to all Americans. What can we do? We, not the assassin, represent America at its best. We have the power—not the prejudiced, not the assassin—to make things right.

If we love Martin Luther King, Jr., and respect him, as this crowd surely testifies, let us see to it that he did not die in vain; let us see to it that we do not dishonor his name by trying to solve our problems through rioting in the streets. Violence was foreign to his nature. He warned that continued riots could produce a fascist state. But let us see to it that the conditions that cause riots are promptly removed, as the President of the United States is trying to get us to do. Let black and white alike search their hearts; and if there be prejudice in our hearts against any race or group, let us exterminate it and let us pray, as Martin Luther King, Jr., would pray if he could: "Father, forgive them for they know not what they do." If we do this, Martin Luther King, Jr., will have died a redemptive death from which all mankind will benefit.

I close by saying to you what Martin Luther King, Jr., believed: if physical death was the price he had to pay to rid America of prejudice and injustice, nothing could be more redemptive. And to paraphrase the words of the immortal John Fitzgerald Kennedy, Martin Luther King, Jr.'s unfinished work on earth must truly be our own.

Eulogy of Dr. Whitney Young, Jr.*

Dr. Whitney Young, Jr., Executive Director of the National Urban League, died March 11, 1971, in Lagos, Nigeria, at age 49. Young, a very popular civil rights leader, suffered a heart attack while swimming at Lighthouse Beach with former U. S. Attorney General Ramsey Clark and his wife. An autopsy report from Nigeria ruled that Dr. Young died of a subarachnoid hemorrhage. The report put to rest the notion of a conspiracy—the belief held by many in the black community given the previous assassination of Dr. Martin Luther King, Jr., and other civil rights leaders who were murdered under suspicious circumstances. Dr. Young was in Lagos attending a meeting of a discussion group of the African-American Association sponsored by the Ford Foundation. The Reverend Jesse Jackson also attended the conference.

Born in Lincoln Ridge, Kentucky, in 1921, Dr. Young graduated from Kentucky State College in Frankfort in 1941. He did graduate study at the Massachusetts Institute of Technology, and he received his Ph.D. from the University of Minnesota.

Dr. Whitney Young, Jr., became Executive Director of the National Urban League on October 1, 1961. At the time of his appointment, he served as Dean of the Atlanta University School of Social Work, a position he had held since 1954. He also served as an industrial relations secretary to the St. Paul Urban League from 1948 to 1950, and Executive Director of the Omaha Urban League from 1950 to 1954.

The National Urban League took charge of the detailed arrangements for the funeral of Dr. Young, flying his body aboard an Air Force plane to New York City, where services were held on March 16.

More than 4,500 persons were seated in the six main meeting halls and chapels of the historic Riverside Church on Tuesday morning, March 16, at 10:00 a.m. for the one-hour service. More than 1,500 people were unable to get into the church. It was considered the largest crowd to assemble in the church's 40-year history, reported *The New York Times*, on March 17, 1971.

The audience was composed of attending celebrities, civil rights leaders and workers, politicians, government officials, New York City residents, and invited guests.

---

* United Negro College Fund Archives, New York City

According to the official funeral program, the participants included Rev. Ernest T. Campbell, Riverside's preaching minister who presented the Invocation and the Benediction; Dr. Benjamin E. Mays, former President of Morehouse College, presented the Eulogy: "The Past"; Dr. Howard Thurman, former Dean of Marsh Chapel, Boston University, presented the Eulogy: "The Present"; Dr. Peter H. Sampson, pastor of the Community Church in White Plains, New York, Mr. Young's church, presented the Eulogy: "The Future."

After the funeral ended, the body of Dr. Whitney Young Jr., was flown to Lexington, Kentucky, and driven to Lincoln Ridge, Kentucky, where his remains were interred. President Richard M. Nixon delivered the graveside eulogy for Dr. Whitney Young.

Dr. Mays, a mentor to Dr. Whitney Young, considered the activities of Young in helping the poor as congruent with his own philosophy of a common humanity and the need for those more economically able to help those farthest down the economic ladder.

* * *

Every man who has sympathy and empathy for the man farthest down, who believes that every stomach should be adequately fed, everybody clothed, each family decently housed, and every mind amply trained; whose philosophy is that no man should be denied because his skin is black and none favored because his eyes are blue, and who believes it is possible for peoples of different races and cultures to live together in harmony and mutual respect must choose the profession in which he will work, the battleground on which he will fight, and the method he will use.

Whitney Young had the mind, the integrity, and the will to succeed in many professions: law, medicine, engineering, and religion. But he chose social work, believing that there he could serve his country and black people whose needs were the greatest.

His method of attack was direct community involvement of educators, industrialists, the middle class, government, and the poor in an effort to abolish poverty and provide better housing for the poor, jobs for the unemployed, decent wages for the underpaid, and better education for the illiterate.

There was no generation gap between Whitney Young and myself. We shared a common philosophy and spoke a common language on what the United States needs to do to make it possible for every American to achieve a life of dignity and respect. I came to know Whitney Young well in 1954, when he became Dean of the Atlanta University School of Social Work. His office was only a few hundred yards from mine. Though both of us were extremely busy, we frequently exchanged views on what should be done to improve the lot of the black man in this country and what we should do to bring whites and blacks closer together in an effort to heal the wound resulting from three and one-half centuries of slavery, segregation, and alienation. Though not obvious on the surface, it soon dawned upon me that Whitney Young was a committed man. And this commitment was to the people, but primarily to the black man who was and is among the most poorly housed and who, for the most part, sits at the bottom of the economic world. When we talked about the offer to head the National Urban League, I sensed that it was not the higher salary which the Urban League offered that attracted him most, but he saw in the Urban League position an opportunity to do something in a big way to provide jobs for thousands upon thousands of people who had no work and to help other thousands to advance on the job and to get business and government more deeply involved in programs designed to lift America's poor to a place of decency and respectability.

In his speeches and writings, there was no pleading and begging. He told the people the truth. He told business and government what the facts were and challenged them in a big way to live up to their responsibilities in improving the life of all people. Whitney Young believed that blacks and whites cannot elude each other and that we must live together and work together. This philosophy was most beautifully phrased by Whitney Young himself when he said not long ago: "If we must polarize in this country, let us not polarize on the basis of race or religion or economic status, but let us polarize on the basis of decent people versus indecent people—between those who are good and those who are bad." I would call his method "effective nonviolence." If one's life is to be judged more by results than rhetoric, Whitney Young's life was most reward-ing. Not as rewarding as Whitney would have it, for a man possessed with dreams and driven on by a sense of mission cannot be satisfied with the results, however commendable they maybe.

If it is true that among the truly great men of history are to be found those who had great compassion for the least of these, and if it is true that immortality is guaranteed for those who respond helpfully, sympathetically, and understandingly to human need, then Whitney Young qualifies. He did so much in just a few years.

Several decades ago, I picked up a dirty page from a newspaper and found these anonymous words which are applicable to Whitney Young. This man allowed no sand to burn under his feet. He did his work as if called into the world to champion the cause of the man farthest down. The title of the poem is "God's Minute," and with it I close.

> I have only a moment
> Only sixty seconds in it
> Forced upon me,
> Can't refuse it,
> Didn't seek it,
> Didn't choose it
> But it's up to me to use it.
> I must suffer if I lose it
> Give account if I abuse it
> Just a tiny little minute
> But eternity is in it.

That was Whitney Young.

Eulogy of Dr. Mordecai Wyatt Johnson*

Dr. Mordecai Wyatt Johnson died of complications due to a cardiovascular illness on September 10, 1976, at age 86. His funeral services were conducted in Andrew Rankin Memorial Chapel on the campus of Howard University, September 14, 1976 at 11:00 a.m.

Dr. Johnson became the first black president of Howard University in 1926 and served in that capacity for thirty-four years until his retirement in 1960. Prior to assuming the presidency of the institution, he had a distinguished career as a Baptist minister, college professor, internationally renowned orator, and uncompromising advocate of the rights of disadvantaged black Americans.

In his tenure as president of Howard University, he delivered hundreds of speeches in America and in foreign countries. I had the opportunity to hear him speak while I was a student at Morehouse College. He exhibited what speech critics call tremendous "presence."

Upon the death of Dr. Mordecai Johnson, *The Hilltop*, the campus newspaper, reported in an editorial, dated September 17, 1976, on the accomplishments and impact of the Johnson presidency: "During his tenure . . . the institution flourished and blossomed into the capstone of black education. The physical plant's value increased from $3 million to more than $34 million, the annual budget from $100,000 to $8 million, and 20 new buildings were erected."

On this very hot and humid September day, funeral services were broadcast via closed circuit television in Cramton Auditorium on campus because of the overflow crowd of local and out-of-town dignitaries, students, faculty, trustees, friends, and acquaintances who wanted to pay their respects to the great educator and orator. The program lasted about an hour and a half.

According to the official funeral program, Dr. Benjamin E. Mays, a friend of Dr. Johnson for more than fifty years, and a former dean of the Howard University School of Religion, President Emeritus of Morehouse College, and then president of the Atlanta School Board, delivered the eulogy. Other remarks included a tribute by Dr. John W. Davis, President Emeritus of West Virginia State University, and a friend of Dr.

---

* Reprinted from *New Directions*, Volume 4, No.1 (January 1977): 24-27, Howard University

Johnson for more than seventy years, dating back to their college days at Atlanta Baptist Institute (later Morehouse), when they were roommates. A recorded tribute was played from Dr. Howard Thurman, Dean Emeritus of Marsh Chapel, Boston University, and a former dean of Rankin Memorial Chapel; Dr. Dorothy B. Ferebee, President of the Women's Institute at American University, spoke. Dr. James E. Cheek, President of Howard University, delivered remarks. The Howard University Choir rendered selections of Dr. Johnson's favorite hymns.

Both Drs. Mays and Johnson embraced the technique and philosophy of nonviolent resistance and its applicability to the civil rights struggle of black Americans. The two men had visited India on separate trips in the 1920s and 1930s to observe first-hand the implementation of nonviolent resistance by Mahatma Gandhi, leader of the struggle of India's independence from Great Britain, achieved in 1948. The men likewise made speeches that espoused the merits of the doctrine and, therefore, had a significant impact in nurturing the use of the doctrine by its most prominent practitioner in twentieth-century American history, Dr. Martin Luther King, Jr.

* * *

The Greeks were right in saying that we funeralize and eulogize for two reasons: to console the bereaved and to exhort the living to an emulation of the virtues of the deceased. It is for these two purposes that we are gathered: to bring condolence to the Johnson family and to exhort the living to an emulation of the virtues of Mordecai Wyatt Johnson—to dwell among us for 86 years, to prick our consciences, and to tell America what the American dream is all about.

If God called Abraham from Chaldea to found a new nation, if he called Hosea to tell us what love is, if he called Amos to tell what justice is, and if he called Michael to tell us what God requires, surely he called Mordecai Wyatt Johnson to expound the gospel to America and to make Howard University a truly great university. To assume the presidency of Howard University in 1926, a puny thing, and leave it a great university, Mordecai had to be called of God for the express purpose of building a black university, integrated in faculty and staff, community and students under the leadership of a black president.

I have known Mordecai for a half a century dating back to 1923 when John Hope gave me my first job after graduating from Bates College. In that year, Mordecai came to Morehouse to speak—then pastor of the First Baptist Church in Charleston, West Virginia. I shall never forget that address. He spoke to us and challenged us so eloquently that we were led to believe that this man was called of God to do his work. I can see Mordecai years later, walking across the Howard campus, walking with a sense of dignity and freedom. Strangers on the campus had to know he was president.

In 1926, fifteen years after graduating from Morehouse College with an A.B. degree in 1911, from Rochester Theological Seminary with a B.D. degree and from earning degrees from the University of Chicago and Harvard University, he had impressed the nation so profoundly and the Trustees of Howard University so deeply that he was called by them to become the first black man to be president of a potentially great university.

It is my considered judgment that no white man in 1926, when virtually everything in this nation, including God's church, was so segregated—every avenue closed to the Negro with locks of steel—no white man could have made Howard a truly great university. I assert this because few white Americans in 1926 believed that black people were the potential equal of white people—that given a fair deal to develop their minds, to sensitize their hearts and they seek freedom, could have done what Mordecai did for Howard from 1926 to 1960. Only a man who believed with all his heart, soul and mind and who had the ability to articulate to Congress and the people what 350 years of slavery, segregation and denigration had done to black people, and who had the courage to expound it, could have built Howard into a truly great university: 1926-1960 was the time; Mordecai Wyatt Johnson was the man; and America, the greatest experiment in democracy God has given to man, was the place on which this battle was to be waged. Surely God was in this deal, and surely Mordecai was called of God to this job.

In 1926, Howard University was a puny thing, hardly known in the nation, except through a few eminent professors like Kelly Miller who drew promising students to Howard. When I saw Howard University for the first time as an undergraduate student, I was a disappointed man. Its fame had been spread abroad by distinguished scholars such as Kelly Miller, but I saw nothing to inspire me and nothing to make my soul glad. The buildings were rather old, and the campus was unimpressive.

Furthermore, Howard University was a political football, kicked around by Southern congressmen who believed that the Negro's place was to be defined forever by the white man—any white man—and that his education was to be inferior to that provided for whites. There was no congressional legislation to make Howard a legal institution, a child of the federal government. In 1926, after Mordecai became president, he took on the federal government, arguing before federal officials that the federal government was obligated to make Howard a federal institution in order to make amends for what the white man had done to Negroes for three hundred and fifty years of slavery, segregation, and denigration. Mordecai won that battle in Congress, and Howard University was made a federal institution supported by the United States government. This was a major triumph; and if Mordecai had done nothing else, his name should be written among the immortal ones like the founding fathers who helped to make our nation great. But this is not all.

It was Ralph Waldo Emerson who said that "an institution is the lengthened shadow of one man." These words are a beautiful description of what Mordecai did for Howard University from 1926 to 1960. Nothing much in 1926, only a fledgling. But in 1960, Mordecai left it a healthy, thriving university, standing on a solid foundation, which Nabrit and Cheek could build upon and carry Howard forward as one of the stellar universities of the nation. Mordecai found a budget of $700,000 in 1926. He left it with a budget of $8,000,000, an increase of more than 1100 percent in 1960. In addition to that, he built 17 new buildings, strong, solid and firm. Besides, the student body increased—and the faculty increased—I make bold to assert that Howard is the best integrated university in the United States. Students are here from five or six different continents. The faculty is made up of white, red, black, yellow and brown, Jews, Catholics, Orientals, Episcopalians, Baptists, Methodists, and Congregationalists are all here. Howard University is supraclass, supra-ethnicity, supra-religion, supra-sex, supra-race, and supracaste. Thus, Howard University is the lengthened shadow of Mordecai Wyatt Johnson.

Mordecai did not cringe and kowtow, though the university is supported by federal money. When L. D. Milton, chairman of the Board during most of the Johnson years, sent out letters to a select group of men requesting the names of men qualified to succeed Mordecai, I was among them. I gave Milton no names, but I described the man who should succeed Mordecai. I said in essence: when the president of Howard speaks, the nation would be compelled to listen. Mordecai was such a man. Academic freedom must be maintained. Mordecai was a fine exponent of academic freedom. Competence and character were the plumb lines of acceptability. As you know, the civil rights movement was born in the law school of Howard University. When black men were arguing against segregation before the Supreme Court, Jim Nabrit says, Mordecai was sitting there giving his moral support to the lawyers.

No man in the 20th century has spoken any more eloquently against racism, segregation, and denigration than Mordecai Johnson. No man in this century spoke more forcefully against German Nazis, Italian Fascism, and Russian Communism than Mordecai Wyatt Johnson, demonstrating that when a man speaks the truth supported by ethical and moral living, girded with deep spirituality, nothing can stop him except illness and death. Mordecai believed as Shakespeare, "Thrice is he armed who has his quarrels just," and that God will sustain that which is right.

As for religion, Mordecai lived his religion. When a distinguished Negro journal wrote a weekly column denouncing Mordecai, he never said a mumbling word. Having known, admired, and loved him, I went to his office one day. I said, "Why don't you say something? Why don't you expose the people who are weekly falsifying your work and filching from your good name? Why don't you refute those lies?" He listened and said: "Dean Mays, in time the people will know that what the paper is saying is false." As I look back over the years and have lived longer, I conclude that Mordecai was right.

He must have believed that, "Truth crushed to earth shall rise again, the eternal years of God are hers; but error wounded, writhes with pain and dies amidst her worshipers." He must have accepted the faith of Robert Browning who said: "One who never turned his back but marched breast forward, never doubted that clouds could break, never dreamed that right through worsted wrong would triumph. Held, we fall to rise, are baffled to fight better, sleep to wake." The words of the psalmist must have been his shield and buckler: "Thou carriest them away as with a flood; they are asleep: In the morning they are like grass which groweth up. In the morning it flourishes, and groweth up; in the evening it is cut down, and withereth." How many times he must have uttered another verse from the Psalms: "Yea, through I walk through the valley of the shadow of death, I will fear no evil; for thou art with me; thy rod and thy staff they comfort me."

Most of those, or all of them, who participated in the slander have gone to their reward, but Mordecai lived to the respectable age of 86. Certainly Mrs. Anna Ethelyn Gardner, the first Mrs. Johnson, sustained him during these rough years; and the second Mrs. Johnson brought fellowship and companionship in Mordecai's declining years.

At the 107th Anniversary of Howard in 1972, I said in substance, the seed sown in 1865 by General Howard and by Johnson, in establishing Howard as a government university, has multiplied many thousand times: from one teacher of four girls in 1867, to a staff of 1,599 in 1974—1,286 are United States citizens and 313 foreign born; definitely integrated, 27 percent white and 73 percent black. Ninety countries are represented in the student body. Students are here from North and South America, Europe, Asia, and Africa—five of the six continents; the Near, Middle, and Far East are represented. They come from the Isle of the Sea. In 1974, the enrollment was approximately 10,000 students. On the Board of Trustees, you have two-thirds black and one-third white.

Beginning with no graduates in 1867, Howard had graduated in 1974, 35,000 men and women who have received diplomas, degrees or certificates; and 14,150 of the 35,000 hold graduate and professional degrees. The campus, land, buildings and equipment are valued at more than $90 million. The drops of water and grains of sand have become an ocean and a great fertile land—not barren. Since 1960, Nabrit and Cheek have furthered the development of the university. I assert again: Howard is the most integrated university in the United States.

Had Mordecai not had the prophetic vision in 1926 to make Howard legally owned by the federal government, this university would have died a long time ago. To Mordecai, this was his most significant act. Let us thank God for Mordecai Wyatt Johnson!

Mordecai was a man who not only talked his religion, but he walked it. Careful analysis of his sermons and speeches reveals one striking thing: all of them reveal a deep-seated concern for the man farthest down. Here he followed in the footsteps of the master. In Matthew 25, where the prerequisite is given for the entrance into the kingdom, we read:

> When the son of man shall come in his glory, and all the holy angels with him, then shall he sit upon the throne of his glory: And before him shall be gathered all nations; and he shall separate them one from another, as a shepherd divideth his sheep from the goats; And he shall set the sheep on his right hand, but the goats on the left. Then shall the King say unto them on his right hand, "Come, ye blessed of my father, inherit the kingdom prepared for you from the foundation of the world: For I was an hungered, and ye gave me meat; I was thirsty, and ye

gave drink: I was a stranger, and ye took me in: Naked, and ye clothed me: I was sick, and ye visited me: I was in prison, and ye came unto me." Then shall the righteous answer unto him, saying, "Lord, when saw we thee an hungered, and fed thee? Or thirsty, and ye gave thee drink? When saw we thee a stranger, and took thee in? Or naked, and clothed thee? Or when saw we thee sick, or in prison, and came unto thee?" And the King shall answer and say unto them. "Verily I say unto you, inasmuch as ye have done it unto one of the least of these my brethren, ye have done it unto me."

If this is the case, Mordecai will have no trouble when catechized by Saint Peter at the pearly gates. I hear Mordecai saying to Peter, "Peter, what have I done to warrant admission to God's kingdom?" Saint Peter replied, "Mordecai, the love of God and the love of man is one love. The two loves are interlaced, intertwined, and interwoven so delicately that when you hurt man, you hurt God. When you make it hard for man to live, you make it hard for God to live. Come in Mordecai, you have earned for your self an immortal crown, a city not made with hands but eternal in the heaven."

Chapter 6

Postscript

My research on the speeches of Dr. Benjamin E. Mays was a challenging and interesting process that involved the use of multiple resources. When my research on Dr. Mays commenced about a year after his death, I became the first researcher to use the Mays Collection housed at the Moorland-Spingarn Research Center at Howard University, Washington, D.C. Dr. Mays made the decision to have his papers housed at the Center because it is professionally staffed and is also the location of important research collections of several other prominent black Americans. A sample of these individuals includes: Benjamin G. Brawley, Mercer Cook, William L. Dawson, Frederick Douglass, Charles R. Drew, W.E.B. DuBois, E. Franklin Frazier, Mordecai W. Johnson, Ernest E. Just, John Mercer Langston, Kwame Nkrumah, Paul Robeson, Booker T. Washington, Carter G. Woodson, and others. Thus, it is a central research center for researching data on black Americans.

The Mays Collection contains approximately 124 boxes of papers and other memorabilia on his life and career. Dr. Mays maintained twenty-nine commercial-size scrapbooks in which he kept news clippings and magazine articles on important dates and occasions in his own career, as well as accounts of the accomplishments of his friends, associates, and former students. Several photo albums with photos from various stages of his life and career are included in these holdings dating back to his days at South Carolina State College as a student and continuing throughout his professional career.

At the time of my first visits to the research center in Spring 1986, I envisioned a comprehensive research approach to the life and career of Dr. Mays. I wanted to collect as much information as I could on as many areas of his life as were available in the collection and in the time I had to visit the area. The speeches were a significant part of my initial plans. I knew very well from experience that he was a great orator and that his speeches were crucial to understanding his philosophy and views on important issues facing American society about which he was honestly concerned: race relations, religion, education, and poverty.

During my visits to the Moorland-Spingarn Research Center in the middle and late 1980s, the Mays Collection had not been catalogued, and there were restrictions placed on researching the papers in the collection. The policy dictated that I could not photocopy Dr. Mays's speeches as I desired in order to make expeditious use of my time on these visits. Instead, I had to hand copy the speeches, and this made for a very slow and tedious process.

It was during these visits that I decided I had to devise another strategy of data collection on the speeches. After a period of reflection and examination of the copies of speeches I had in my possession, I decided to contact colleges, universities, and organizations where my research indicated he had delivered speeches. I started this process in the early 1990s. To my surprise, there were a few institutions where he spoke that no copies of his speeches were kept; neither were there copies of the programs on which he appeared.

I found, on the other hand, that some of the archives at institutions where Dr. Mays delivered speeches were highly organized and very cooperative, as indicated in the acknowledgments of those who aided the research efforts.

In the interim, I produced two research essays for publication, presented a paper, and gave a lecture on the life and career of Dr. Mays. After these projects were completed around 1996, I decided to return to full-time efforts to compile the collection of speeches delivered by Dr. Mays. Since there were gaps in my previous research on the speeches, I decided to start writing letters and making telephone calls again, which produced fruitful results.

In collecting, analyzing, and compiling Dr. Mays's speeches, I aimed to avoid as much repetition as possible. For example, Dr. Mays sometimes delivered the same speech in different parts of the country and during different years, and some speeches were modified versions of earlier orations. Since Dr. Mays was in such great demand as a public speaker, he made adjustments in his speeches according to the occasion and composition of his audiences.

In this second wave of research efforts regarding the speeches, I collected additional information. I wanted to obtain information on the facts regarding the occasion, the size, and composition of his audience, and any assessments of Mays's performances. This information was available and would allow me to write an introduction to each speech.

Again, I contacted the archives at the institutions where he spoke—some for the second, third, or fourth time. This time, I included in my research the archives of churches where he spoke. In most cases, valuable information was provided. In other instances, information was unavailable or very sparse. I wrote hundreds of letters and made numerous telephone calls to those archivists and persons who had important information on Dr. Mays's speeches. Newspaper archives were also called for relevant data.

In the late 1990s I contacted the Moorland-Spingarn Research Center to reestablish my research agenda in order to obtain additional information pertaining to Dr. Mays's speeches. The staff was highly cooperative and professional in their efforts to respond to my many research requests via e-mail, telephone, and letter. In keeping with the technology of the twenty-first century, the Center developed a web page on the holdings in their possessions; however, the Mays Collection has not yet been developed to that stage where the contents can be listed on the web page. The Moorland-Spingarn Center staff's commendable efforts—alluded to earlier—allowed me to finish the project without having to make a fourth trip to Washington. My research efforts were immensely enhanced.

Thus, I was able to put together a collection of the representative speeches of the great orator that is catalogued according to topics, audiences, and occasions. This is considered to be a significant research product that may be utilized to gain a better understanding of the key developments of the twentieth century, including the civil rights era and beyond; this book may also provide a better understanding of the role of black history, religion, education, and oratory in relationship to the development of American life and culture.

***

Dr. Benjamin Elijah Mays did not lead a massive civil rights demonstration nor was he jailed in the struggle for freedom for African-Americans and all Americans, but his sacrifices for the struggle, through public speaking, writing, and mentoring many of the leaders of the civil rights movement of the 1960s and beyond, were significant in the transition from a segregated to a desegregated and multicultural society. In this, his contributions are exceptional and monumental.

It is not possible to measure the impact of his contributions quantitatively because so many have been, and continue to be, influenced by his efforts and deeds that form a continuing chain of thoughts to be handed down from one generation to another. Significantly, Mays's teachings influenced Martin Luther King, Jr.'s model of the Beloved Community, which is based on the notion that God is the father of all, and that all men are brothers interwoven into a common humanity. It can be rationally expected that his teachings will continue to soar to new heights in the twenty-first century. Finally, Dr. Mays possessed a passion for excellence in human endeavors. His legacy will constantly remind us all that one man, one woman, one person can make a difference in improving the quality of life for all Americans regardless of race, creed, religion, color, or ethnicity.

Bibliography

"Benjamin E. Mays: Man of Integrity," WSB-TV, Atlanta, Georgia, March 9, 1981.

Bennett, Lerone, Jr. "Dr. Benjamin E. Mays: The Last of the Great Schoolmasters," *Ebony*, Volume 33 (December 1977): 70-80.

Bradford, Daniel, ed. *Black, White and Gray: Twenty-one Points on the Race Question*. New York: Sheed and Ward, 1964.

Carter, Lawrence E. Jr., ed. *Walking Integrity: Benjamin Elijah Mays, Mentor to Generations*. Atlanta, Georgia: Scholars Press, Emory University, 1996.

Centrepiece, Volume 11 (August 1970): 8-10.

Colston, Freddie C. "Dr. Benjamin E. Mays: His Impact as Spiritual and Intellectual Mentor to Martin Luther King, Jr." *The Black Scholar,* Volume 23 (Winter/Spring 1993): 6-15.

———. "Dr. Benjamin E. Mays: Reflections of an Intellectual Giant of the Twentieth Century," Presented at the Benjamin E. Mays Symposium, Bates College, Lewiston, Maine, October 29, 1994.

Fowlkes, William A. "No Ivory Tower President," *Pittsburgh Courier Magazine Section,* October 21, 1950, Mays Collection, Moorland-Spingarn Research Center, Howard University.

Gavins, Doris Levy. *The Ceremonial Speaking of Benjamin Elijah Mays: Spokesman for Social Change, 1954-1975* (Ph.D. dissertation, Louisiana State University, 1978).

Hunter-Gault, Charlayne. *In My Place*. New York: Farrar Straus Giroux, 1992.

Johnson, Ira Joe, and Pickens, William G., eds. *Benjamin E. Mays and Martha Mitchell: A Unique Legacy in Medicine*. Winter Park, Florida: FOUR-G Press Publishers, Inc., 1996.

Kappa Alpha Psi Fraternity, Inc., *The Journal*, Volume 43, No. 1 (February 1957): 7-12.

Mays, Benjamin E. *Born to Rebel.* New York: Scribner, 1971.

———. *Disturbed About Man.* Richmond, Virginia: John Knox Press, 1969.

———. "In My Life and Times," unpublished essay, September 27, 1966, Mays Collection, Moorland-Spingarn Research Center, Howard University.

———. *Lord, The People Have Driven Me On.* New York: Vantage Press, 1981.

———. *Quotable Quotes.* New York: Vantage Press, 1983.

———. "Why I Went to Bates," *Bates College Bulletin,* Alumnus Issue, Series 63, No. 6 (January 1966):1 & 2.

Morehouse College Alumnus, Volume XIII (March-April 1945): 3-4.

Morehouse College Alumnus, Volume XV (July 1947): 22

Morehouse College Alumnus, Volume XVII (November 1949): 16

Morehouse College Alumnus, Volume XXXV (Summer 1967): 29-32.

New Directions, Volume 1, No. 3 (Spring 1974): 31, 45.

New Directions, Volume 4, No. 1 (January 1977): 24-27.

New South, Volume 5 (September-October 1950): 1-3.

Rovaris, Dereck J., Sr. *Mays and Morehouse: How Benjamin E. Mays Developed Morehouse College.* Silver Spring, Maryland: Beckham House Publishers, Inc., 1990.

Spelman Messenger, Volume 73 (May 1957): 16-24.

Teal, Leonard Ray. "Benjamin E. Mays, Teaching By Example, and Leading Through Will," *Equal Opportunity,* Volume 16 (Spring 1987): 14-22.

The Talladegan, Volume 43 (May 1946): 1-4.

Time, December 11, 1944.

Willie, Charles V., and Edmonds, Ronald R. eds. *Black Colleges in America.* New York: Teachers College, 1978.

Willie, Charles V. "The Education of Benjamin Elijah Mays: An Experience in Effective Teaching," *Teachers College Record,* Volume 84 (Summer 1983): 955-962

Newspapers

Albany Herald (Georgia), 1976.
Atlanta Daily World, 1941, 1942, 1984, 1987, 1992.
Atlanta Journal Constitution, 1941, 1942, 1984, 2001.
Chicago Defender, 1954.
Chicago Sun-Times, 1954.
Cleveland Call and Post, 1973.
Detroit Free Press, 1952.
Detroit News, 1952.
Detroit Times, 1952.
Greenwood Index - Journal (South Carolina), 1970.
Louisiana Weekly, 1980.
Memphis Commercial Appeal, 1955.
New Orleans Times-Picayune, 1980.
New York Times, 1955, 1968, 1971.
Pittsburgh Courier, 1955, 1962, 1963, 1968, 1980.
Raleigh News, 1966.
Union County Standard Journal (Lewisburg, Pennsylvania), 1954.
Washington Post, 1974.

Telephone Interviews

Mr. DeWitt N. Martin, Jr.
President
Butler Street YMCA
Atlanta, Georgia
February 14, 1999

Dr. Samuel Speers
Associate Dean
Rockefeller Memorial Chapel
University of Chicago
February 15, 1999

Mr. William King
University Archivist
Duke University
February 15, 1999

Mr. William Fowlkes
Associate Editor
Atlanta Daily World
February 18, 1999

Ms. Ruth Bledsoe
Library Assistant
Heartman Collection
Texas Southern University
February 24, 1999

Ms. Margaret Jamison
Librarian
Houston Chronicle
Houston, Texas
February 24, 1999

Dr. Dorothy Haith
Former Director of the Library
Albany State University
Albany, Georgia
February 25, 1999

Index

About the Author

Freddie C. Colston has published articles on politics and the black experience in professional journals. He was a student at Morehouse College during the presidency of Dr. Mays where he received his B.A. in political science in 1959. He received an M.A. from Atlanta University in 1966 and a Ph.D. in 1972 from Ohio State University; both graduate degrees are in political science. He has done extensive research on the life and career of Dr. Mays since 1984. The author has taught political science at Fort Valley State University, Southern University, University of Detroit, Dillard University, Tennessee State University, North Carolina Central University, and Georgia Southwestern State University. In addition to his academic appointments, Professor Colston served a stint at the Executive Seminar Center, U. S. Office of Personnel Management, in Oak Ridge, Tennessee, where he resides.